COMMUNICATION DISORDERS

MODERN LINGUISTICS SERIES

Series Editor

Professor Maggie Tallerman
Newcastle University, UK

Each textbook in the **Modern Linguistics** series is designed to provide an introduction to a topic in contemporary linguistics and allied disciplines, presented in a manner that is accessible and attractive to readers with no previous experience of the topic. The texts are designed to engage the active participation of the reader, and include exercises and suggestions for further reading. As well as an understanding of the basic concepts and issues for each topic, readers will gain an up-to-date knowledge of current debates and questions in the field.

Titles published in the series

English Syntax and Argumentation (4th Edition) Bas Aarts
Phonology (2nd Edition) Philip Carr and Jean-Pierre Montreuil
Pragmatics Siobhan Chapman
Linguistics and Second Language Acquisition Vivian Cook
Sociolinguistics: A Reader and Coursebook Nikolas Coupland and Adam Jaworski
Communication Disorders Louise Cummings
Morphology (2nd Edition) Francis Katamba and John Stonham
Semantics (2nd Edition) Kate Kearns
Syntactic Theory (2nd Edition) Geoffrey Poole
Contact Languages: Pidgins and Creoles Mark Sebba

Further titles are in preparation

Modern Linguistics Series
Series Standing Order
ISBN 978–0–333–69344–5 paperback
(outside North America only)

You can receive future titles in this series as they are published by placing a standing order. Please contact your bookseller or, in the case of difficulty, write to us at the address below with your name and address, the title of the series and the ISBN quoted above.

Customer Services Department, Macmillan Distribution Ltd,
Houndmills, Basingstoke, Hampshire, RG21 6XS, UK.

Communication Disorders

Louise Cummings

First published 2014 by
PALGRAVE MACMILLAN

Palgrave Macmillan in the UK is an imprint of Macmillan Publishers Limited,
registered in England, company number 785998, of Houndmills, Basingstoke,
Hampshire RG21 6XS.

Palgrave Macmillan in the US is a division of St Martin's Press LLC,
175 Fifth Avenue, New York, NY 10010.

Palgrave Macmillan is the global academic imprint of the above companies
and has companies and representatives throughout the world.

Palgrave® and Macmillan® are registered trademarks in the United States,
the United Kingdom, Europe and other countries

ISBN 978–0–230–28506–4

This book is printed on paper suitable for recycling and made from fully
managed and sustained forest sources. Logging, pulping and manufacturing
processes are expected to conform to the environmental regulations of the
country of origin.

A catalogue record for this book is available from the British Library.

A catalog record for this book is available from the Library of Congress.

In memory of a dear friend and
devoted speech and language therapist

Laura Millen
29 January 1961 to 9 October 2008

Also by Louise Cummings

Cummings, L. (2005) *Pragmatics: A Multidisciplinary Perspective* (Edinburgh: Edinburgh University Press).

Cummings, L. (2008) *Clinical Linguistics* (Edinburgh: Edinburgh University Press).

Cummings, L. (2009) *Clinical Pragmatics* (Cambridge: Cambridge University Press).

Cummings, L. (2010) *Rethinking the BSE Crisis: A Study of Scientific Reasoning under Uncertainty* (Dordrecht: Springer).

Cummings, L. (ed.) (2010) *The Routledge Pragmatics Encyclopedia* (London and New York: Routledge).

Cummings, L. (ed.) (2014) *Cambridge Handbook of Communications Disorders* (Cambridge: Cambridge University Press).

Cummings, L. (2014) *Communication Disorders Workbook* (Cambridge: Cambridge University Press).

Contents

List of Figures and Tables

Figures

Tables

Preface

The ability to communicate is so fundamental a part of our everyday interactions with others that the complex linguistic, cognitive and physical processes that make communication possible rarely, if ever, enter our consciousness. However, for a significant number of children and adults, communication is anything but a subconscious, effortless process. For individuals with communication disorders, every spoken interaction with family and friends and each exposure to written language creates frustration and dissatisfaction in equal measure. This is a situation that confronts the 2.5 million children and adults in the UK who have communication disorders, according to the Royal College of Speech and Language Therapists. The consequences of these disorders are considerable, ranging from a reduction in quality of life to significant limitations in one's educational and occupational opportunities. The communication disorders that give rise to these grave consequences are the focus of this book.

The field of communication disorders is large and rapidly growing. Research studies in all parts of this field are proceeding apace. New technology is transforming how therapists assess and treat communication disorders. Theoretical developments both within clinical communication science, and the many disciplines that sustain this area, are changing how clinicians conceive of certain communication disorders. One need only consider, for example, the impact that theory of mind research has had on our understanding of pragmatic impairments in the autism spectrum disorders to see that disciplines such as psychology are continuing to make a vital contribution to the study of disordered communication. With so many developments occurring within the study of communication disorders, it is incumbent on students and therapists to keep themselves abreast of the latest work in this area. This book helps clinicians achieve this by examining the most up-to-date empirical research in the field of communication disorders.

But this book offers its reader more than the latest empirical research in communication disorders. It examines in detail areas within the field that have been traditionally overlooked, or treated in a cursory manner, by other survey volumes. The discussion of glossectomy in Chapter 4 and right-hemisphere language disorder in Chapter 5 are cases in point. Other examples include the examination in Chapter 6 of the communication implications of the emotional and behavioural disorders, bipolar disorder and gender dysphoria. There are several features of the text that are designed to facilitate readers as they study each communication disorder. There is an emphasis throughout on the use of data. Often, this takes the form of phonetic transcriptions of disordered speech, but there are also short extracts of narrative and conversation in use. Key points boxes are used to summarise the main features of each communication disorder.

At the end of each chapter, there are exercises along with answers which are designed to consolidate learning and suggestions for further reading. A glossary of key terms can be found at the end of the book. The website is a vitally important resource for student readers and for practitioners wishing to develop their knowledge. It contains 200 multiple choice questions and answers which examine every disorder discussed in the book. There is also an extensive array of audio and visual material on the website that covers everything from the speech of people who clutter to the numerous organic pathologies that cause voice disorders. The website can be accessed at **www.palgrave.com/language/ pml**. In short, this book provides its reader with a comprehensive treatment of communication disorders that is relevant to students, clinicians and researchers not only in speech and language therapy, but also in other disciplines, most notably linguistics.

LOUISE CUMMINGS

Acknowledgements

I wish to acknowledge with gratitude the assistance of the following people and organisations: Larry A. Sargent, MD (Medical Director, Tennessee Craniofacial Center), James P. Thomas, MD (laryngologist, Portland, Oregon), Bechara Y. Ghorayeb, MD (otolaryngologist, Houston, Texas), C. Richard Stasney, MD, FACS, Apurva A. Thekdi, MD and Jeremy Hathway, MS, CCC-SLP (Texas Voice Center), Alex Murphy (Director of stuttering video *Let Me Finish*), Trevor Pull (Learning Resources Manager, Nottingham Trent University), Rachel Eden (Subject and Programme Administrator, Nottingham Trent University), the Cleft Palate Foundation, the Cri Du Chat Support Group of Australia, the New York Eye and Ear Infirmary Voice and Swallowing Institute, the National Spasmodic Dysphonia Association, the National Association of Laryngectomee Clubs, InHealth Technologies, the National Stuttering Association, the Stuttering Foundation, RDF Television and Channel 4. The assistance of each of these individuals and organisations has been invaluable to me as I prepared this book. Jeremy Hathway has been particularly diligent in securing voice samples for me. I owe him and his colleagues at the Texas Voice Center considerable thanks.

I would also like to acknowledge Kitty van Boxel (Commissioning Editor, Humanities, Palgrave Macmillan) and Maggie Tallerman (Editor, Palgrave Modern Linguistics Series) for their positive response to the proposal of a book in the field of communication disorders. Their guidance from the outset is most gratefully acknowledged. The assistance of Aléta Bezuidenhout (Associate Editor, Palgrave Macmillan) has also been invaluable.

Finally, I have been supported in this endeavour by family members and friends who are too numerous to mention individually. I am grateful to them for their kind words of encouragement during my many months of writing.

LOUISE CUMMINGS

List of Abbreviations

AAC	augmentative and alternative communication
ADC	AIDS dementia complex
ADHD	attention deficit hyperactivity disorder
ALS	amyotrophic lateral sclerosis
AOS	apraxia of speech
ASD	autism spectrum disorder
BNT	Boston Naming Test
BDAE	Boston Diagnostic Aphasia Examination
CAPPA	Conversation Analysis Profile for People with Aphasia
CAPPCI	Conversation Analysis Profile for People with Cognitive Impairment
CAS	childhood apraxia of speech
CHI	closed head injury
CVA	cerebrovascular accident
DAS	developmental apraxia of speech
DDK	diadochokinesis
DPD	developmental phonological disorder
DS	Down syndrome
DVD	developmental verbal dyspraxia
EBD	emotional and behavioural disorder
EGG	electroglottography
EMG	electromyography
EPG	electropalatography
FAS	foetal alcohol syndrome
FTM	female-to-male
GER	gastroesophageal reflux
GID	gender identity disorder
HPV	human papilloma virus
IQ	intelligence quotient
LKS	Landau–Kleffner syndrome
LPR	laryngopharyngeal reflux
LSVT	Lee Silverman Voice Treatment
MDVP	Multi-Dimensional Voice Program
MLU	mean length of utterance
MS	multiple sclerosis
MTD	muscle tension dysphonia
MTF	male-to-female
OASES	Overall Assessment of the Speaker's Experience of Stuttering
OV	oesophageal voice

PD	Parkinson's disease
PCI	Predictive Cluttering Inventory
PNFA	progressive non-fluent aphasia
PPI	proton pump inhibitor
PROMPT	Prompts for Restructuring Oral Muscular Phonetic Targets
PSI	Perceptions of Stuttering Inventory
PWC	people who clutter
PWS	people who stutter
RLN	recurrent laryngeal nerve
SCA	Supported Conversation for Adults with Aphasia
SD	spasmodic dysphonia
SLI	specific language impairment
SLP	speech–language pathologist/pathology
SLT	speech and language therapist/therapy
SSD	speech sound disorder
TBI	traumatic brain injury
VFPP	vocal fold paralysis and paresis
VPI	velopharyngeal incompetence
WAB-R	Western Aphasia Battery-Revised
WS	Williams syndrome

The Study of Communication Disorders

1

1.1 Why study communication disorders?

A capacity for linguistic communication is a unique achievement of human evolution. No other species has the repertoire of linguistic and cognitive skills that are the basis of human communication. It is by virtue of these skills that people are able to develop complex social structures within their lives. These structures are the basis of our ability to co-exist with others and, accordingly, are integral to our mental and physical well-being. Given the centrality of communication to our existence, it is unsurprising that impairment of this important capacity should have many adverse consequences including social isolation, vocational and economic disadvantage and psychological distress. The severity of these consequences warrants serious consideration of the communication disorders that give rise to them. This book will examine these disorders and the child and adult clients who develop them.

The reader should be in no doubt that there is a very real need for academic and clinical studies of communication disorders. The Royal College of Speech and Language Therapists estimates that 2.5 million people in the UK have a communication disorder. Of this number, some 800,000 people have a disorder that is so severe that it is hard for anyone outside their immediate families to understand them. There is a high prevalence of communication disorders in children. Pinborough-Zimmerman et al. (2007) found the prevalence of communication disorder in 8-year-olds to be 63.4 per 1,000. In 2003, speech and language impairments accounted for 18.7 per cent of students aged 6 to 21 years who were receiving special education and related services in the US under the Individuals with Disabilities Education Act (US Department of Education, 2007). Speech and language impairments were the second largest disability category after specific learning disabilities. Communication disorders are an equally significant cause of disability amongst adults. Hirdes et al. (1993) examined the prevalence of communication disabilities among community-based and institutionalised Canadians. Among community-based individuals, the highest prevalences were found in subjects aged over 55 years with figures of 30 per 1,000 population and 42 per 1,000 population reported in subjects aged 75–84 years and 85+ years, respectively. The percentage of community-based individuals who were completely unable to make themselves understood when speaking to family and friends increased from 4.2 per cent to 7.0 per cent (family) and 10.4 per cent to 12.9 per cent (friends) in subjects between 55 years and 85+ years. Harasty and McCooey (1994) reviewed 22 studies which examined the prevalence of general communication impairment in adults. These investigators reported a range of prevalence figures from 0.8 per cent to 3.9 per cent.

Indicators of psychological distress and quality of life suggest that communication disorders are a significant burden for those who develop them. Hilari et al. (2010) report that at three months post stroke, 93 per cent of their subjects with aphasia experienced high psychological distress compared with only 50 per cent of stroke patients without aphasia. Manders et al. (2010) found that people with aphasia obtained significantly lower scores for quality of life measures compared with healthy controls and patients with brain lesions without neurogenic communication disorders. Plank et al. (2011) found a correlation between voice-related quality of life and physical and mental subscores on a general health-related quality of life questionnaire in 107 socially active people aged 65+ years. Nachtegaal et al. (2009) found that hearing status in young and middle-aged adults was negatively associated with higher distress, depression, somatisation and loneliness. There is also clear evidence that occupational and social disadvantage attends the development of communication disorders. Whitehouse et al. (2009) examined psychosocial outcomes in young adults with a childhood history of specific language impairment (SLI), pragmatic language impairment or high-functioning autism spectrum disorder (ASD). Participants with a history of SLI were most likely to pursue vocational training and work in jobs that did not demand a high level of language or literacy ability. ASD subjects had more difficulty obtaining employment than other subjects. All groups struggled to establish social relationships. The mitigation of the psychological distress and social and occupational disadvantage that attends communication disorders is a further reason why these disorders should be given serious academic and clinical consideration.

The high prevalence of communication disorders in the population and the distress and disadvantage caused by these disorders would be reason enough to justify the study of communication disorders. Yet, there is another reason why these disorders should be examined, a reason that is of particular relevance to linguistics. The study of how communication skills can be disrupted in children and adults often provides investigators with important insights into the nature of these skills in so-called 'normal' individuals. Models of language processing in particular have been developed and revised as information is gleaned from the study of language-impaired subjects. The properties of the semantic system have been directly based on the findings of studies conducted in subjects with aphasia. For example, Warrington (1981a) reports evidence for the vulnerability of subordinate compared with superordinate information in the verbal comprehension of individuals with aphasia. This pattern of impairment, she argues, indicates that 'the semantic representations of single words are hierarchical or ordered in their degree of specificity' (Warrington, 1981a: 411). Warrington (1981b) also reported a significant impairment in the ability to read concrete words compared with abstract words in a patient with an acquired dyslexia. This concrete word reading deficit, she argues, 'provides a further example of category specificity in the organization of the semantic systems subserving reading' (Warrington, 1981b: 175). The study of certain language skills and deficits in subjects with aphasia and other clinical subjects (e.g. individuals with language impairment in the presence of dementia) is thus of direct relevance to the generation of theoretical models of language processing within linguistics itself.

1.2 Human communication: processes and breakdown

Human communication is a remarkably complex process that draws upon a diverse set of linguistic, cognitive and motor skills. Before we even utter a single word, we must decide what message we want to communicate to a listener or hearer. Deciding what that message should be is itself a complex process that requires knowledge on the part of the speaker of the context in which a verbal exchange is occurring, the relevance of the message to that context and the goals of a particular exchange. Having successfully made these assessments, the speaker will have a clear *communicative intention* in mind which he or she will wish to convey to the hearer. In most communication between people, that intention is conveyed through language, although it may also be conveyed through non-verbal means. To the extent that a linguistic utterance is to be produced, the speaker needs to select the phonological, syntactic and semantic structures that will give expression to this intention in a stage of the communication cycle called *language encoding* (see Figure 1.1). A linguistically encoded intention is an abstract structure that still has some way to go before it is in a form that can be communicated to a listener. The speaker must select from the range of motor activities that the human speech mechanism is capable of performing those that are necessary to achieve the transmission of the utterance to a listener (one need only think of all the non-speech, oral movements and vegetative movements that the articulators are capable of performing to see that this is the case). It is during the stage of *motor programming* that these selections are made (subconsciously, of course) and certain motor routines are planned in relation to the utterance. Motor programmes can only be realised if anatomical structures (e.g. lips, tongue, vocal folds) receive nervous signals instructing them to perform particular movements. These movements are carried out during a stage in communication called *motor execution*. Assuming all preceding stages have been performed competently, the result of these various processes is audible, intelligible speech.

Thus far, we have only described the processes that lead to the production of a linguistic utterance. Yet, human communication is not just about producing utterances but receiving or understanding them also. The first step in this receptive part of the communication cycle is called *sensory processing*. This is

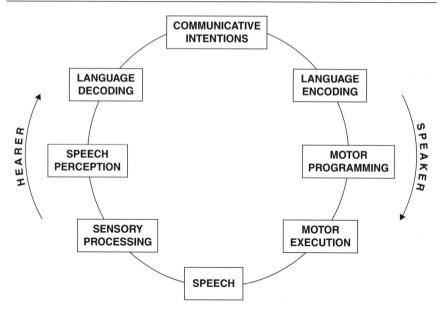

Figure 1.1 The human communication cycle

the stage during which sound waves are converted in the ear from mechanical vibrations into nervous impulses which are then carried to the auditory centres in the brain. The auditory centres are responsible for recognising or perceiving these impulses as speech sounds on the one hand or non-speech (environmental) sounds on the other hand (e.g. the bark of a dog). Having recognised certain speech sounds, the task of attributing significance or meaning to them within the utterance begins. By most accounts, rules begin to analyse the phonological, syntactic and semantic structures in the linguistic utterance in a stage called *language decoding*. Amongst other things, these rules tell the hearer the grammatical constructions used in the utterance (e.g. passive voice rather than active voice), as well as the semantic roles at play in the utterance (e.g. if a particular noun phrase is the agent in the sentence). The outcome of linguistic decoding of the utterance is not necessarily the particular communicative intention that the speaker intended to convey by way of producing the utterance (only sometimes is the literal meaning of the utterance the meaning that the speaker intended to convey). Quite often, further processing that is pragmatic in nature is needed to recover the particular intention that the speaker intended to communicate. Once that intention is recovered, for example, that the speaker who utters 'Can you open the window?' is requesting that the window be opened, only then is the communication cycle complete and the speaker's intended meaning manifest to the hearer.

The complex nature of the human communication cycle means that there is a multitude of ways in which this cycle may be disrupted in people with communication disorders. The adult with schizophrenia who has thought disorder may have difficulty formulating an appropriate communicative intention, that is, one which is relevant, fulfils the goals of a particular communicative exchange, and so on. The adult with non-fluent aphasia has impaired language encoding skills, one consequence of which is the use of syntactically reduced utterances. The child or adult with verbal dyspraxia may struggle to select specific motor routines during the motor programming of the utterance. The child with cerebral palsy or the adult who sustains a traumatic brain injury may both experience dysarthria, a disorder that disrupts the execution of speech on account of failure of nervous impulse transmission to the articulatory muscula-ture. Sensory processing of the speech signal may be disrupted in the individual with hearing loss. This loss may be either congenital (present from the time of birth) or acquired (as a result of an infection, for example) and may be conduc-tive or sensorineural in nature. The child with Landau–Kleffner syndrome, who experiences language impairment in the presence of a seizure disorder, has intact hearing but is unable to recognise or perceive spoken words. The result-ing auditory agnosia is often mistaken for deafness. The child with SLI and the adult with Down syndrome and intellectual disability or learning disabilities lack the language decoding skills required to understand the syntactic and semantic structures in the utterances spoken by others. Finally, the child with an ASD may have impaired pragmatic skills and may fail to recover a speaker's communicative intention in producing an utterance. These conditions and many others not mentioned here (stammering, dysphonia, etc.) form the com-plex array of communication disorders that will be examined in this book.

1.3 Significant clinical distinctions

The discussion of the communication cycle in section 1.2 introduced a number of terms that are central to the study of communication disorders. The cycle drew a distinction between the expression or production of utterances on the one hand and the reception or understanding of utterances on the other hand. This distinction pervades the assessment and treatment of communication dis-orders. For example, the clinician who is asking a client with aphasia to point to the picture in which 'The man who is crossing the road is tall' is assessing that client's understanding of relative clauses. The child with Down syndrome who is asked to describe a picture in which 'The ball is on top of the box' is having an aspect of his or her expressive syntax (viz., use of locative preposi-tions) assessed. Similarly, the clinician who is using exercises designed to elimi-nate the phonological processes of stopping (e.g. [tup] for 'soup') and fronting (e.g. [tat] for 'cat') in the speech of a 5-year-old child is working on expressive phonology, while the clinician who is asking the adult with dementia to organ-ise pictures according to semantic fields is focusing on an aspect of receptive semantics in therapy. The receptive–expressive distinction allows clinicians to characterise a number of different scenarios. One such scenario is where there is a mismatch in receptive and expressive skills in a client, that is, where one set of skills is significantly better than the other. For example, in the adult with non-fluent aphasia receptive language skills are typically superior to expressive language skills. Another scenario is where one set of language skills deteriorates more rapidly than the other in a client. For example, in the child with Landau–Kleffner syndrome receptive language skills are first to be affected. Expressive deficits usually occur later in the disorder and are thus considered to be secondary to the receptive impairment (Honbolygó et al., 2006).

A second important clinical distinction is that between a developmental and an acquired communication disorder. For a significant number of children, speech and language skills are not acquired normally during the developmental period. This may be the result of an anatomical defect or neurological trauma sustained before, during or after birth. The impact of these events on the development of speech and language skills varies considerably across the babies and children who are affected by them. The group of developmental communication disorders is thus a large and diverse one including children with cleft lip and palate (anatomical defect in the pre-natal period), with brain damage due to birth anoxia (neurological insult in the peri-natal period) or with cerebral palsy as a result of meningitis contracted at 6 months of age (neurological damage in the post-natal period). The group of acquired communication disorders is equally large and diverse. Previously.intact speech and language skills can become disrupted for a range of reasons including the onset of disease, trauma or injury affecting the anatomical and neurological structures that are integral to communication. An adult may develop a neurodegenerative condition like motor neurone disease, multiple sclerosis, Parkinson's disease (PD) or Alzheimer's disease. He or she may sustain a head injury in a road traffic accident, violent assault, sports accident or as a result of a trip or fall. A previously healthy adult may have a stroke (known as a 'cerebrovascular accident' – CVA). He or she may succumb to infection (e.g. meningitis) or develop benign and malignant lesions on any of the anatomical structures involved in speech production (e.g. larynx, tongue). Any one of these events will disrupt communication skills, leading to disorders such as acquired aphasia and dysarthria.

A third distinction that is integral to the study of communication disorders is that between a speech disorder and a language disorder. These are not the same thing notwithstanding everyday usage (people tend to use 'speech disorder' to refer to both speech and language disorders). The distinction between a speech and a language disorder can be best demonstrated by referring to the diagram of the communication cycle in Figure 1.1. Breakdown in the boxes in this diagram labelled *language encoding* and *language decoding* typically leads to a language disorder. So the adult with aphasia and the child with specific language impairment have a language disorder because they are unable to encode and decode aspects of language (e.g. syntax, semantics). However, breakdown in the boxes labelled *motor programming* and *motor execution* typically lead to speech disorders, verbal dyspraxia (or apraxia) and dysarthria, respectively. Traditionally, the speech–language distinction has been taken to reflect a distinction between non-symbolic and symbolic aspects of communication with only language dealing with symbolic aspects of communication (i.e. those that convey meaning). Crystal (1997: 267) explicitly articulates this distinction when he states that 'the former [language disorders] refer only to the "symbolic" aspects of communication, i.e. those concerned with the formulation and structuring of meaning…. The latter [speech disorders] refer to the "non-symbolic" aspects, that is, those concerned only with the use of sounds seen as a set of meaningless phonetic entities'. Although the distinction is still in widespread clinical use, it has attracted some criticism (e.g. it leaves the status of phonology somewhat indeterminate between speech and language). Of course, notwithstanding the distinction between speech and language disorders, it is not uncommon to find both types of disorder in a single client. For example, the adult who sustains a CVA may develop both aphasia and dysarthria.

1.4 Disciplines converging on the study of communication disorders

A large range of academic and clinical disciplines converge on the study of communication disorders. The study of language at each of its levels is pursued within linguistics. Linguistics is certainly a key area of knowledge for researchers and clinicians who study and treat communication disorders. Yet, it is by no means the only area of knowledge that is needed to understand the different ways in which communication can be disordered in children and adults. Various medical disciplines also play an important role. They include anatomy, physiology, neurology, psychiatry and otorhinolaryngology (known as Ear, Nose and Throat (ENT) medicine in the UK). As the part played by genes in the development of certain communication disorders (e.g. specific language impairment) becomes ever more apparent, disciplines such as genetics are assuming greater significance. Outside of medicine, a number of psychological disciplines contribute to the study of communication disorders. One cannot get far in understanding these disorders without encountering work in developmental psychology, cognitive psychology and neuropsychology. In the sections below, we examine the contribution of some of these disciplines to the study of communication disorders.

1.4.1 Linguistics

An understanding of communication disorders requires knowledge of all the main disciplines within linguistics. This includes phonetics, phonology, morphology, syntax, semantics, pragmatics and discourse. Phonetics is the study of speech sounds. Phoneticians examine not just the articulatory movements that are required to produce speech sounds (articulatory phonetics), but also physical dimensions of speech sounds such as amplitude and frequency (acoustic phonetics). The deviant speech of the child with cleft palate can be characterised in terms of phonetics. We will see in Chapter 2, for example, that cleft children struggle to achieve sufficient intra-oral air pressure to produce certain speech sounds (e.g. plosives). In an attempt to compensate for the loss of air pressure from the oral cavity, these children adopt a pattern of backed articulations. The oral plosives /p, b, t, d, k, g/ may be substituted by glottal stops /ʔ/ as the glottis is the only point in the vocal tract where the child can achieve a build-up of air pressure. Phonology is the study of the sound system of a language. Phonologists are interested in how sounds function contrastively to convey differences of meaning. For example, the single phonetic difference of voicing in the word initial bilabial plosives in 'pin' /pɪn/ and 'bin' /bɪn/ allows the speaker to convey the two meanings of *item used in sewing* and *receptacle for rubbish*. Knowledge of this branch of linguistics is vital to understanding disordered phonology in young children. We will see in Chapter 3 that a number of phonological processes may characterise the speech of children. These processes, which can markedly reduce the intelligibility of a child, include stopping ('five' pronounced as [paɪb]), fronting ('cap' pronounced as [tap]) and devoicing ('zip' pronounced as [sɪp]). Clinicians must have knowledge of phonology if they are to be successful in treating these various processes.

Morphology is the study of the internal structure of words. Morphologists examine how individual morphemes can be brought together to form words. For example, the word 'unhappiness' contains three morphemes including the root of the word ('happy'), a prefix (-un) and a derivational suffix (-ness). Morphology is disrupted in a number of clinical populations including children with specific language impairment and adults with schizophrenia. For example, the adult with schizophrenia who says 'I am being help with the food and the medicate' (Chaika, 1990: 24) displays problems with the use of both inflectional suffixes (help–*ed*) and derivational suffixes (medicate–*ion*). These morphological disturbances in clients can only be adequately assessed and treated by clinicians who have a detailed knowledge of this branch of linguistics. Words cannot come together in any order to form sentences. There is a specific order on their occurrence. For example, to form questions in English, the speaker must invert the subject pronoun and auxiliary verb (e.g. 'Are you going to school?'). Syntax is the study of sentence structure, which includes word order and the formation of phrases and clauses. Deficits in syntax are a prominent feature of many of the communication disorders that will be examined in this book. The client with agrammatic aphasia, for example, produces utterances in which syntactic structure can be severely reduced. Content words (e.g. nouns, verbs) are retained while function words (e.g. articles, prepositions) are omitted. The resulting utterances have the form of a telegram (hence, the name of this type of aphasia). The child with specific language impairment may use infinitive forms in finite positions (e.g. 'He fall off') or finite forms in verb phrase complement positions (e.g. 'He made him fell'). Knowledge of syntax is necessary in order to characterise, assess and treat these syntactic deficits.

Semantics is the study of linguistic meaning. Semanticists are concerned to explain a range of phenomena including the semantic components or primitives that make up the meaning of words (e.g. [MALE] [ADULT] [HUMAN] for 'man'), the lexical relations that exist between words (e.g. 'arm' is a meronym of 'body') and the conditions in the world under which sentences are true (in truth-conditional or formal semantics). Semantic deficits are commonplace in developmental and acquired communication disorders. The child with Down syndrome and intellectual disability may never acquire knowledge of the semantic fields to which words belong (e.g. 'apple', 'orange' and 'pear' are all types of fruit). The adult with aphasia may produce errors known as 'semantic paraphasias', in which the word uttered is related to the target lexeme. For example, during his naming of pictures, an adult with aphasia may say 'arm' when shown the picture of a leg. Pragmatics is the study of speaker meaning or meaning in context (Cummings, 2005). The utterance 'Can you tell me the time?' is rarely intended by speakers to be a question about someone's ability to tell the time. Rather, the question is uttered with a view to getting the listener to tell the speaker the time. This request meaning of the utterance is one of several types of context-based meaning examined by pragmatists. Pragmatics can be severely disrupted in children and adults with autism spectrum disorders (Cummings, 2011, 2012a, 2012b, 2014a, 2014b, 2014c). Individuals with these disorders struggle to recover the implicatures of utterances (that the utterance 'What lovely weather we're having!' uttered in the middle of a snow storm is ironic), to understand the illocutionary force of speech acts (that 'Can you tell me the time?' is a directive, not a question) and may produce irrelevant or verbose utterances during conversation. Knowledge of semantics and pragmatics is essential for the study of communication disorders.

Branches of linguistics such as syntax and semantics are concerned with analysing sentences. However, there are various interesting ways in which sentences can be related to other sentences within larger extracts of language. These ways are examined in discourse analysis. In recent years, the study of discourse has assumed increasing importance in both the assessment and treatment of clients with communication disorders. Investigations of discourse skills have revealed problems relating to coherence and cohesion in different clinical groups. The adult with schizophrenia, for example, may be able to establish cohesive links amongst his various utterances. We will see in Chapter 6, for example, how one such adult used a sequence of proper nouns, subject and object pronouns and possessives to establish cohesion between his utterances. However, his expressive output still could not be understood on account of a failure of coherence – the speaker's utterances failed to develop a particular theme or idea. Clinical discourse studies have also been used to examine the communication skills of adults with traumatic brain injury (TBI). Adults with TBI can often pass standardised language assessments and yet they can engage in conversations which are marked by repetitiveness, confusion and impoverished language content. This is related to the cognitive nature of their communication deficits (adults with TBI experience executive function deficits which are related to frontal lobe damage). A sound grasp of discourse and how discourse skills can be analysed is another essential part of the knowledge base in linguistics that people studying communication disorders must possess.

For further discussion of the application of linguistic concepts and theories to a range of communication disorders, the reader is referred to Cummings (2013a, 2013b).

1.4.2 Medicine

Several medical disciplines inform the study of communication disorders. These disciplines include anatomy, physiology, neurology, embryology, genetics, psychiatry and otorhinolaryngology. A sound knowledge is required of the anatomical structures that are the basis of speech production. How these structures function to produce speech and voice (physiology) is also an essential part of the working knowledge of those who study and treat communication disorders. This knowledge includes the pair of muscles (levator palatini) that raises the velum (soft palate) against the nasopharynx, the role of the intercostal muscles in respiration and the contribution of the arytenoid cartilages to voice production. Further, clinicians must understand how malformation or impaired functioning of these structures can adversely affect communication. For example, the levator palatini muscles are abnormal in the child with a cleft palate. These muscles are unable to raise the velum sufficiently to shut off the velopharyngeal port. The resulting velopharyngeal incompetence leads to the production of hypernasal speech, as air escapes from the oral cavity into the nasal cavities. Knowledge of anatomy and physiology is also required to understand the different ways in which communication disorders may be treated. For example, the sphincter muscle at the top of the oesophagus is formed by the cricopharyngeus muscle. This muscle can be vibrated to produce voice (oesophageal voice) in the patient who has undergone a laryngectomy (surgical removal of the larynx). Also, by drawing the thyroid and cricoid cartilages of the larynx closer together in a surgical procedure called cricothyroid approximation, the pitch of the voice can be elevated. This procedure may be used to achieve a female speaking voice in the client who has undergone gender reassignment surgery.

Neurology is fundamental to the study of communication disorders. An understanding of the structure and function of the central and peripheral nervous systems is an essential part of the working knowledge of clinicians. Clinicians must know, for example, the neuroanatomical structures of the brain that are involved in hearing, speech and language. This includes the neuroanatomical location of language centres in the left cerebral hemisphere, namely, Broca's area (inferior frontal gyrus) and Wernicke's area (planum temporale). The role of the primary motor cortex and cranial nerves in speech production is also an essential part of clinical knowledge. Damage to any one of these neurological structures may cause a communication disorder. For example, the adult who has a cerebrovascular accident (CVA or stroke) and sustains a lesion in the area of the inferior frontal gyrus may develop non-fluent aphasia. The adult with multiple sclerosis may develop dysarthria. This speech disorder is one of the sequelae of the neuropathology in multiple sclerosis, namely, the demyelination of the fatty sheath (myelin) that surrounds the axons of nerve cells. Adults with PD may also experience dysarthria which is caused by the loss of cells that produce dopamine (a neurotransmitter substance) in the substantia nigra in the brain. Adults who sustain traumatic brain injuries may have executive function deficits (e.g. difficulty with planning, impulse control) that are related to frontal lobe damage. These deficits cause cognitive communication problems that require knowledge on the part of clinicians of the type of brain damage sustained by this clinical population. Children born with Möbius syndrome may have lesions of a number of cranial nerves involved in speech production. Here, again, clinicians must understand the neurological basis of the dysarthria that is found in children with this syndrome.

Otorhinolaryngology is a further medical discipline which informs the study of communication disorders. In voice disorders clinics in particular,

ENT consultants and speech and language therapists work closely with each other in the assessment, diagnosis and treatment of patients with dysphonia. In conjunction with audiology, it is these medical specialists who diagnose hearing loss as conductive or sensorineural in nature. The child with a cleft palate, for example, is prone to repeated episodes of otitis media with effusion ('glue ear') on account of inadequate ventilation of the middle ear via the Eustachian tube. The conductive hearing loss that results can be a severe impediment to the phonetic inventory that the child with cleft palate is able to develop. Meningitis infection may leave children with hearing loss which is sensorineural in nature. This loss results from damage to the cochlea in the inner ear, the auditory pathways to the brain and the auditory cortices in the brain. Treatments for these hearing disorders range from the insertion of ventilating tubes in the tympanic membrane (ear drum) of the cleft child to the use of cochlear implants in the child with sensorineural hearing loss following meningitis. Otorhinolaryngologists also examine the structure and function of the laryngeal mechanism in patients who present with voice disorders. This examination may reveal an organic basis for a voice disorder such as vocal nodules and polyps, a malignant laryngeal tumour or paralysis of a vocal fold. However, it may also reveal that there is no organic basis for a voice disorder in which case a functional dysphonia (e.g. conversion aphonia) may be diagnosed. An understanding of these various communication disorders requires knowledge of the otological and laryngeal anomalies that underlie them.

Other medical disciplines that intervene on the study of communication disorders include embryology, psychiatry and genetics. Many communication disorders have their origin in events that occur during embryological development. One of these events is the malformations that give rise to cleft lip and palate. Delayed or inadequate fusion of the tissues that give rise to the structures of the face and oral cavity will result in clefting of various types. This defect occurs early in human development, generally during the sixth to ninth weeks of gestation. Neurodevelopment in the pre-natal period can be compromised by infections (e.g. rubella, cytomegalovirus) and exposure to noxious substances (e.g. alcohol, illegal drugs), amongst other events. Clinicians must have an understanding of the events that can disrupt embryological development and the implications of these events for the later acquisition of communication skills. Psychiatry makes a significant contribution to the study of communication disorders. The management of clients with schizophrenia, autism spectrum disorders and gender dysphoria has involved close interaction between psychiatrists and speech and language therapists for some years. Language and communication skills are now being examined in relation to specific symptom profiles (paranoid delusions, negative symptoms) in clients with schizophrenia (e.g. Corcoran and Frith, 1996). The recent attempt to characterise the language skills of children with emotional and behavioural disorders (e.g. attention deficit hyperactivity disorder) will develop yet further the contribution of psychiatry to the study of communication disorders. Finally, the genetic basis of several communication disorders (e.g. developmental verbal dyspraxia) is increasingly being revealed. Genetics promises to make an increasingly important contribution to the study of communication disorders in years to come.

SUGGESTIONS FOR FURTHER READING

Anderson, N.B. and Shames, G.H. (2010) *Human Communication Disorders: An Introduction* (Boston: Allyn & Bacon, 8th edn).

Cummings, L. (2008) *Clinical Linguistics* (Edinburgh: Edinburgh University Press), ch. 1.

Plante, E.M. and Beeson, P.M. (2007) *Communication and Communication Disorders: A Clinical Introduction* (Boston: Allyn & Bacon, 3rd edn).

EXERCISES

Exercise 1.1   The human communication cycle is depicted in Figure 1.1. It portrays communication as a complex process involving eight stages. Read each of the scenarios presented below. Then decide which of the eight stages in the communication cycle is impaired in the client described. Your answer may include one stage or more than one stage.

(a)   Sally is a sociable 5-year-old who attends primary school. The school's speech and language therapist has assessed Sally's communication skills and has found that her use of phonology is more typical of a 3-year-old child. In all other respects her communication skills are normal.

(b)   Bill is 49 years old and has been diagnosed with a brain tumour in his left cerebral hemisphere. Formal assessment of his language skills reveals that his comprehension and production of syntax is disrupted. His speech is also somewhat slurred and mildly unintelligible.

(c)   Frank is 65 years old and has been diagnosed with Alzheimer's disease. His participation in conversation has steadily diminished as he has found it increasingly difficult to make relevant contributions to verbal exchanges with others. An assessment of his communication skills reveals relatively intact structural language skills but marked difficulty in generating appropriate messages for communication.

(d)   Felicity is 6 years old. She was born with Möbius syndrome which has affected a number of the cranial nerves used in speech production. She is attending regular speech and language therapy where the focus of therapy is on improving the intelligibility of her speech.

(e)   Toby is 7 years old and is in recovery following severe bacterial meningitis. The infection has caused bilateral damage to the cochlea in his inner ear. Audiological assessment has revealed significant sensorineural hearing loss. His language skills are age-appropriate.

(f)   Rose is 50 years old and is two years post-onset a TBI that was sustained in a road traffic accident. Her expressive and receptive language skills are relatively intact. However, she has marked difficulty in sequencing the articulatory movements that are needed to produce speech and her vowels are severely distorted. The speech and language therapist diagnoses acquired verbal dyspraxia.

Exercise 1.2   This exercise is intended to get you thinking about three important distinctions in the study of communication disorders: (1) receptive versus expressive communication disorders, (2) developmental versus acquired communication disorders and (3) speech versus language disorders. Each of the scenarios below examines one of these three distinctions. You need to state which distinction applies within your answer.

(a)   Landau–Kleffner syndrome (LKS) is a rare disorder in children that has a peak incidence between 4 and 7 years of age (Temple, 1997). It leads to sudden or gradual loss of language skills in the presence of a seizure disorder (the children who develop LKS experience seizures as they sleep). Another term for LKS is 'acquired' epileptic aphasia'. Why is the term 'acquired' used of this disorder when it is exclusively children who develop the condition?

(b)   Patrick is 59 years old. He is aphasic following a CVA some six months earlier. His communication skills have been assessed by a speech and language therapist using the Boston Diagnostic Aphasia Examination (Goodglass et al., 2001), amongst other assessments. This has revealed that Patrick struggles to understand certain syntactic constructions (e.g. relative clauses and passive voice) and that he produces semantic paraphasic errors when asked to name pictures (i.e. his errors are semantically related to the target word, e.g. he says 'eye' for 'ear'). Are Patrick's difficulties with syntax and semantics expressive or receptive in nature?

(c)   Penelope is 8 years old and she has a severe communication disorder. Her problems with communication are so severe that she is unable to attend mainstream school and must attend a special school that has a team of speech and language therapists. Penelope's therapist has extensively assessed her communication skills and has noted the following: some slurring of speech, reports of unintelligibility from caregivers and teachers, age-appropriate performance on the Clinical Evaluation of Language Fundamentals (Semel et al., 2003). Does Penelope have a speech disorder, a language disorder, or both?

(d)   John is 27 years old and has schizophrenia. His communication skills are bizarre which has led to withdrawal and social isolation from everyone other than close family members. Informal observation by a speech and language therapist reveals marked impairment in the pragmatics of language. Specifically, John fails to understand humour and irony used by others and he interprets many utterances literally (e.g. he responds 'yes' to indirect speech acts such as 'Can you tell me the time?'). Also, he contributes many irrelevant utterances in conversation and produces utterances that are poorly related to each other. Are John's problems with pragmatics receptive or expressive in nature?

(e)   Frank is 45 years old. He is currently under the supervision of a speech and language therapist who is treating him for a speech disorder (dysarthria) that he developed as a result of a head injury sustained in a motorbike accident. This is not Frank's first contact with speech and language therapy. When he was 5 years old, he was diagnosed with grammatical delay by a therapist at the primary school he attended. Frank has experienced two communication disorders to date. Are these disorders developmental or acquired in nature?

(f)   Paul is a lively 6-year-old who has a number of cognitive and communication problems caused by his mother's excessive consumption of alcohol during pregnancy (he has been diagnosed as having foetal alcohol syndrome by a paediatrician). His expressive syntax is severely delayed – he is still only at the two-word stage of language production. An analysis of his expressive phonology reveals a number of immature phonological processes. However, his articulation skills are intact. Does Paul have a speech disorder, a language disorder or both?

Exercise 1.3 The study of communication disorders draws on a diverse knowledge base. Clinicians and researchers must have a sound understanding of a number of linguistic disciplines. However, they must also understand how a range of medical disciplines impact upon this field of work. The statements in (A) below describe linguistic features and errors in a range of child and adult clients. For each statement, name the branch of linguistics (e.g. phonology, syntax) that is used to characterise the feature in question. The statements in (B) below describe different aspects of the medical knowledge that clinicians and researchers draw upon in their work on communication disorders. Name the branch of medicine (e.g. neurology, psychiatry) to which each of these statements relates.

Part A: Linguistics

(a) An adult with aphasia is asked by a therapist to describe a picture in which an elderly man is walking a dog. The patient struggles to say 'Man...walk...dog'.

(b) A 5-year-old child says to his mother 'Can we go in the [tar]?' when he wants to be taken for a drive in the car.

(c) A child with an autism spectrum disorder starts to talk about his friends when he is asked what school he attends.

(d) An adult with Down syndrome cannot categorise pictures of objects according to the fields *fruit*, *clothing* and *furniture*.

(e) The child with SLI says to his teacher 'Bobby make a mess'.

(f) During an articulation test, the child with cleft palate says [ʔa] for 'cat'.

(g) An analysis of the verbal output of a patient with TBI reveals a lack of cohesion and extensive repetitiveness.

(h) An adult with aphasia is describing a picture in which a young girl is building a snowman. He says 'She builds a stowcan'.

(i) An adult with autism is asked by a social worker 'Can you close the door?'. He responds 'Yes' but does not get up to close the door.

(j) The child with language delay is asked by a therapist to point to a picture in which a girl is being hit by a boy. The child points to a picture showing a girl hitting a boy.

Part B: Medicine

(a) An undersized mandible (micrognathia) is a feature of both Treacher Collins syndrome and Pierre Robin syndrome.

(b) A vocal polyp is detected on the left vocal fold during laryngoscopy.

(c) Following surgical repair of a cleft in the palate, the velum may be insufficiently mobile to achieve the elevation that is needed to make contact with the posterior pharyngeal wall.

(d) If fusion of the maxillary processes does not occur, a child will be born with a cleft in the upper lip.

(e) Aphasia is associated with a lesion in the inferior frontal gyrus (Broca's area) of the left cerebral hemisphere.

(f) Oro-nasal fistulae can appear in the palate after surgical repair of a cleft. Some fistulae can compromise speech production.

(g) A diagnosis of schizophrenia is based on the identification of positive symptoms (e.g. thought disorder) and negative symptoms (e.g. social withdrawal).

(h) In families with children with SLI, two regions on chromosomes 16 and 19 have been linked to language-related measures.

(i) The facial nerve (cranial nerve VII) innervates the orbicularis oris, the sphincter muscle that encircles the lips.

(j) A patient with hyponasal speech is referred by his general practitioner to the regional hospital for further investigation. Examination of his nasal cavities reveals a well-developed nasal polyp.

ANSWERS TO EXERCISES

Exercise 1.1

(a) language encoding
(b) language encoding; language decoding; motor execution
(c) communicative intentions
(d) motor execution
(e) sensory processing
(f) motor programming.

Exercise 1.2

(a) The term 'acquired' in *acquired* epileptic aphasia relates to the fact that a significant amount of language acquisition has taken place prior to the onset of Landau–Kleffner syndrome.
(b) Patrick's problems with syntax are receptive in nature. His difficulties with semantics are expressive.
(c) Penelope has a speech disorder.
(d) John has receptive and expressive pragmatic problems.
(e) Frank's grammatical delay is developmental, while his dysarthria is acquired.
(f) Paul has a language disorder.

Exercise 1.3

Part A:

(a) syntax, (b) phonology, (c) pragmatics, (d) semantics, (e) morphology, (f) phonetics, (g) discourse, (h) phonology, (i) pragmatics, (j) syntax.

Part B:

(a) anatomy, (b) otorhinolaryngology, (c) physiology, (d) embryology, (e) neurology, (f) anatomy, (g) psychiatry, (h) genetics, (i) neurology, (j) otorhinolaryngology.

Developmental Speech Disorders

2

2.1 The classification of developmental speech disorders

A significant number of children fail to develop speech along normal lines. In some cases, this developmental failure may be little more than a mild speech delay which has few, if any, implications for the child's ability to communicate effectively with family members and friends. In many other cases, children may experience a severe speech disorder which renders them highly unintelligible even to those closest to them. The clinicians who assess and treat these disorders must do so with an understanding of the aetiology of speech disorders. They must be aware, for example, that some speech disorders are related to structural anomalies of the anatomy used in articulation (e.g. speech in cleft palate), while other speech disorders arise from damage to the nerves and muscles that are involved in speech production (e.g. dysarthria). They must also appreciate the implications of this aetiology for the prognosis of a speech disorder. The neurogenic speech disorder dysarthria may worsen over time in the child with a progressive condition like muscular dystrophy. Alternatively, dysarthria may improve in the child with a traumatic brain injury (TBI) as the underlying neurological injury begins to resolve. The differing aetiologies and prognoses of speech disorders directly impact upon the clinical management of children with these disorders. Clinicians and therapists will seek to institute an augmentative or alternative communication (AAC) system in a child with progressive dysarthria or dysarthria in which there is severe, but static, neurological damage and speech intelligibility is severely compromised. From aetiology and prognosis to assessment and treatment, the group of developmental speech disorders spans a large and varied population of children. It is this population which will be the focus of the current chapter.

It should be emphasised from the outset that not all developmental speech disorders are readily classified along structural and neurological lines. This reflects the fact that many speech disorders in children lack a single, clearly identifiable aetiology. The exact aetiology of developmental verbal dyspraxia is still unknown, although a neurological aetiology may be presumed. The child with an intellectual disability may be slow to acquire speech sounds on account of his or her learning disability. Ultimately, this disability is the result of anomalies in neurodevelopment even if specific brain lesions cannot be identified in a particular case. In still other children, there is a mixed or complex aetiology for their speech disorder such as when structural and neurological problems combine to cause a disorder. A child with cleft palate may sustain neurological damage related to birth anoxia during a complicated labour. This child's speech disorder has a complex aetiology which includes structural components (e.g. a cleft of the hard and soft palates) alongside neurological deficits (e.g. cranial nerve damage). In most developmental speech disorders, it appears possible to distinguish between proximal and distal aetiologies involved in a disorder, with different causal factors falling within one or other main type of aetiology. In the child with Down syndrome and speech disorder, for example, learning disability or intellectual disability may be the proximal aetiology of the child's speech disorder. However, ultimately, factors relating to abnormal neurodevelopment and aberrant genetics (namely, the trisomy of chromosome 21) constitute the distal aetiology of this child's speech disorder.

A further difficulty surrounding the classification of speech disorders concerns the extent of the developmental period. It seems unproblematic to classify any speech disorder which is linked to an event in the pre-, peri- and early post-natal periods as developmental in nature. So the child who is born with a structural anomaly of the speech anatomy or who contracts meningitis at 6 months of age and sustains brain damage has a developmental speech disorder, in that these events have interrupted the processes that are involved in the acquisition of speech sounds. But classification becomes more difficult in the case of the child of 3;6 years who sustains a TBI. Clearly, by 3;6 years of age, this child has already acquired a sizeable repertoire of speech sounds. To the extent that the child may no longer be able to produce these sounds, it seems correct to say that there is an acquired component to his or her speech disorder – previously acquired phonetic skills have been lost as a result of brain injury. However, phonetic development is not complete by 3;6 years of age. Many more sounds still have to be acquired before a child may be said to have anything resembling the complete phonetic repertoire of his or her native language. To the extent that the acquisition of these sounds may be delayed or even permanently disrupted following brain injury, this same child also has a clear developmental component to his or her speech disorder. A simple, binary distinction between developmental and acquired speech disorders overlooks these complicated cases which are more appropriately characterised as a combination of both types of speech disorder. Finally, the developmental – acquired distinction has also become associated, somewhat unhelpfully, with a distinction between children and adults. It is, of course, possible for adults to have a developmental speech disorder (e.g. the adult with cerebral palsy who has developmental dysarthria).

In this chapter, three main types of developmental speech disorder will be examined. The class of structural articulation disorders includes any speech disorder that is related to (usually) a congenital malformation of the speech anatomy. The example we will discuss in the next section is the child with cleft lip and palate. However, the class of structural articulation disorders might equally well be represented by the child with Pierre Robin syndrome who has speech problems related to severe micrognathia (small jaw) and glossoptosis (retraction of the tongue). In both cases, major structural anomalies in the speech anatomy are the basis of the child's articulation defects. The production of speech may also be impaired in children as a result of neurological damage to the motor pathway that innervates the speech musculature. Also, the muscles that form the articulators may be diseased or damaged. Where a neurological or muscular problem is the basis of a speech disorder, the term 'dysarthria' is used. Dysarthria is found in a large range of children including, amongst others, those with cerebral palsy and muscular dystrophy, children who have sustained a head injury in a fall, road traffic accident or as a result of abuse and children who have sustained brain damage on account of an infection such as meningitis. The last of the speech disorders to be examined in this chapter is developmental verbal dyspraxia (DVD). This disorder may be found as part of a wider dyspraxia or it may exist on its own. DVD is often a severe speech disorder in which affected children can be highly unintelligible. Its features will be discussed at length in section 2.4.

2.2   Cleft lip and palate

In some children, the tissues that form the upper lip, upper gum and hard and soft palates do not fuse properly during early pre-natal development. The result is a cleft of one or more of these structures (see Figures 2.1, 2.2 and 2.3). Although there is some small variation in the rate of occurrence of cleft lip and palate, figures suggest that this birth defect is found in between 1 in 700 births (Sargent, 1999) and 1 in 750 births (American Cleft Palate-Craniofacial Association, 2000). The disorder affects males and females in a ratio of 2:1 (Sargent, 1999). Cleft lip and palate is believed to have a multifactorial aetiology

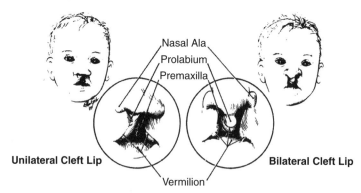

(Reprinted with permission from the Cleft Palate Foundation, www.cleftline.org)

Figure 2.1   The cleft lip and nose

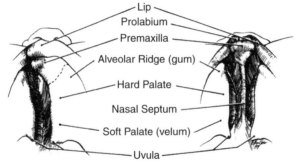

(Reprinted with permission from the Cleft Palate Foundation, www.cleftline.org)

Figure 2.2 Unilateral and bilateral cleft lip and palate

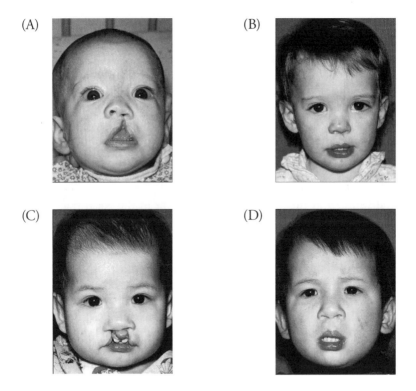

Figure 2.3 Diagrams showing unilateral cleft lip (A) pre-operatively and (B) post-operatively, and bilateral cleft lip (C) pre-operatively and (D) post-operatively. These excellent surgical results appear in the *Craniofacial Surgery Book*, which is authored by Larry A. Sargent, MD, the operating surgeon in both cases. Dr Sargent's permission to reproduce these images is gratefully acknowledged.

which includes genetic factors (evidenced by aggregation within families), certain medications (e.g. anticonvulsive drugs), heavy alcohol consumption and smoking. Another indication that genetic factors are involved in cleft lip and palate is that over 150 syndromes, many of which are genetic or chromosomal in nature, have the defect as part of their differential diagnosis. Two such syndromes are velocardiofacial syndrome (the syndrome most commonly associated with cleft palate) and Pierre Robin syndrome (Sargent, 1999). Whatever factors cause the embryological malformations that give rise to cleft lip and palate to occur, what is clear is that they have their effect in the first trimester of pregnancy (see Cummings (2008) for a detailed discussion of embryological processes). Sargent (1999) reports that 21 per cent of all orofacial clefts have a cleft lip only (unilateral and bilateral), 46 per cent have a cleft lip and palate, and 33 per cent have a cleft palate alone. Stengelhofen (1993) states that an isolated cleft of the palate is the only type of cleft which occurs more commonly in females.

The child who is born with a cleft lip and palate faces considerable feeding, hearing, speech and language problems (the reader is referred to Cummings (2008), for a detailed discussion of feeding, hearing and language problems). The principal speech defect in cleft palate stems from failure to achieve sufficient intra-oral pressure for speech production. Even when the cleft in the palate is surgically repaired in a procedure known as 'palatoplasty', pulmonary air may escape into the nasal cavities on account of inadequate closure of the velopharyngeal port (a surgically repaired soft palate may lack the mobility and length required to close this port). The result is excessive nasal resonance during speech production (hypernasal speech). The cleft child engages in a number of compensatory strategies in order to achieve the necessary build-up of air pressure for speech. These strategies involve a general backward shift in the place of articulation of speech sounds as the child attempts to gain closure at other locations in the vocal tract. The oral plosives /p, b, t, d, k, g/ may be substituted by glottal stops /ʔ/ as the glottis is the only point in the vocal tract where the child can achieve a build-up of air pressure. There may be substitution of palato-alveolar fricatives /ʃ, ʒ/ with palatal /ç, j/, velar /x, ɣ/ or pharyngeal /ħ, ʕ/ fricatives. Secondary articulations (e.g. pharyngealisation, velarisation and nasalisation) and double articulations (e.g. alveolar and glottal contacts) are common. The result of these various phonetic defects is a marked reduction in the intelligibility of the cleft child's speech. The exit of air from the nasal cavities during speech can produce audible nasal emissions. These emissions may mask articulations in the oral cavity, further reducing the intelligibility of the child's speech.

These phonetic features are evident in the speech of a child known as JW who was studied by Harding and Grunwell (1998). JW had undergone a one-stage palate repair to treat a bilateral cleft lip and palate (see Table 2.1).

At 5;0 years, JW displayed a marked backing pattern that affected all alveolar sounds. The alveolar fricative /s/ was substituted by palatal, velar, uvular and pharyngeal fricatives. The alveolar stop /t/ and the alveolar nasal /n/ underwent backing to become a velar stop and velar nasal, respectively. By 5;6 years, alveolar realisation had become more stable with only /s/ consistently backed to velar position. Glottal articulation had resolved by 5;6 years. Double articulations and lateralisation persisted throughout this six-month period.

Table 2.1 Phonetic features of the speech of a child with a repaired bilateral cleft lip and palate

Process	5;0 years	5;6 years
Pharyngeal, glottal articulation	ð→h s→ħ	———
Backing to uvular	s→χ	———
Backing to velar	n→ŋ, t→k, s→x	s→x
Double articulation	t→t͡k d→d͡g	t→t͡k
Palatal fricatives	s→ç	———
Lateralisation/palatalisation	t→tˡ kˡ	t→tˡ

Source: Based on Harding and Grunwell (1998).

Although most of the cleft palate literature has assumed a phonetic perspective, it is clear that there are also phonological influences on the speech disorder. Morris and Ozanne (2003: 461) state that many cleft speech characteristics could be considered to be phonological processes as they commonly affect more than one consonant in any given place or manner class. Also, sounds which are not considered difficult for the speaker with a cleft palate, such as nasals and liquids, are also affected. Phonological processes which have been reported in the speech of children with a cleft palate include initial and final consonant deletion, nasalisation, velar and nasal assimilation, backing and glottal insertion (Morris and Ozanne, 2003). Harding and Grunwell (1996) contend that cleft palate speech should be conceived in terms of an articulatory disorder with phonological consequences.

KEY POINTS: Cleft lip and palate

- Found in approximately 1 in 700 births with males and females affected in a ratio of 2:1
- Compromises speech, language, hearing, feeding and dentition
- Chief communication defect is hypernasal speech which is due to velopharyngeal incompetence
- Backed articulations are common as child attempts to compensate for loss of air pressure through the velopharyngeal port by finding a position further back in the vocal tract where closure can be achieved
- Speech disorder in cleft palate also has phonological components as evidenced by the presence of phonological processes such as backing

2.3 Developmental dysarthria

Hodge and Wellman (1999: 209) define developmental dysarthria as 'a general diagnostic term used for a group of speech disorders that result from disruption or damage to those parts of the immature central (brain and spinal cord) and peripheral (cranial and spinal nerves) nervous systems that control the muscles used to speak'. The population of children and adults with developmental dysarthria is aetiologically diverse. It includes individuals with speech disorder in the presence of cerebral palsy. Other, less common causes of developmental dysarthria are head injury, infections such as meningitis, brain damage related to metabolic disorders such as phenylketonuria and cranial nerve damage in certain syndromes. For example, lesions to cranial nerves V, VII and XII can produce a marked dysarthria in Möbius syndrome (see Murdoch and Horton (1998: 415–19) for a discussion of speech production in a 12-year-old girl with Möbius syndrome). In a retrospective study of motor speech disorders at the Glenrose Rehabilitation Hospital, Hodge and Wellman (1999) found that of the children diagnosed with dysarthria, 50 per cent had some type of cerebral palsy, 23 per cent had some other type of congenital condition, 21 per cent had a later onset condition (e.g. TBI), 3 per cent had a neuromuscular disorder (e.g. muscular dystrophy) and 3 per cent did not have a neurological diagnosis in their medical records. On account of these diverse aetiologies, it is difficult to obtain figures for the prevalence and incidence of developmental dysarthria. Typically, such figures are reported in relation to particular clinical groups within the dysarthria population. In this way, Morgan et al. (2009) reported a low incidence of dysarthria (1.2 per cent) in a cohort of 1,895 children following TBI. In children with severe TBI, this incidence figure rose to 20 per cent.

In developmental dysarthria, one or more of the following speech production subsystems is compromised: articulation, resonation, phonation, respiration and prosody. The dysarthric child may be unable to round his lips to produce the vowel /ɔ/, elevate the tip of his tongue close to the alveolar ridge to articulate the fricative sound /s/ or bring the back of his tongue into contact with the velum to produce the stop consonant /k/. Normal resonation requires the proper functioning of the velopharyngeal port. The velum must be raised and lowered with considerable speed during speech with any aberration of this movement perceived as hypernasality or hyponasality. In the severely dysarthric child, there may be limited movement of the velum and speech may exhibit marked hypernasality. Phonatory disturbances are commonplace in developmental dysarthria. The initiation of voicing may be problematic or the dysarthric child may be unable to cease voicing at the appropriate point during speech production. These problems in phonation may be perceived as the devoicing of voiced sounds and the voicing of voiceless sounds, respectively. Also, phonatory problems may occur as the dysarthric child attempts to compensate for weaknesses in other aspects of speech production. The child may increase vocal intensity in an effort to compensate for the loss of air through the velopharyngeal port. Respiratory patterns that are shallow or mistimed will have an adverse effect on speech production. The dysarthric child may produce short speech units and use frequent inhalations if the pulmonary airstream is escaping through the velopharyngeal port. Finally, prosodic features such as stress and intonation are often disordered in dysarthria. The dysarthric child may place stress incorrectly on some words and fail to use stress on other words. Speech may be monotonous or display other aberrations in intonation.

These clinical features of dysarthria are confirmed by Morgan et al. (2009) in their study of children following TBI. The 22 children with dysarthria in this study had deficits across all speech subsystems. Problems with respiration, primarily reduced breath support for speech, occurred in 18 per cent of children. Some 23 per cent of children displayed phonatory or voicing disturbances, which often involved a hoarse, harsh or breathy voice. Articulation defects, primarily imprecise phonemes, were found in 32 per cent of the dysarthric children in the study. Resonance problems, which were largely characterised by hypernasality, were present in 18 per cent of children. Prosodic disturbances were found in 55 per cent of children and involved monopitch, and reduced loudness or volume. In total, 36 per cent of the children in this study displayed reduced intelligibility or a lack of naturalness of speech. Reflecting the neurological nature of these children's speech disorder, Morgan et al. reported cranial nerve anomalies in 13 of the dysarthric children in the study. These anomalies included facial nerve dysfunction (62 per cent) which was characterised by unilateral facial weakness and lip musculature deficits, and hypoglossal nerve dysfunction (39 per cent) which involved lingual weakness or discoordination. A smaller number of cases displayed reduced overall rate and coordination of oral motor movement (15 per cent) and impaired jaw movement (8 per cent).

A detailed articulatory assessment of dysarthric speech reveals a number of deviant features. Harris and Cottam (1985: 66–7) undertake such an assessment in the case of a child of 4;11 years called Mike. Mike was born one month prematurely and has a congenital heart lesion which has necessitated long periods of hospitalisation. He has no structural abnormalities of the lips and tongue. However, at rest both structures appear lax: the lips are parted and the tongue tip protrudes slightly. The same general laxness is evident when Mike performs movements during non-verbal tasks. On the basis of these findings, it was concluded that developmental dysarthria is a major contributory factor in Mike's speech unintelligibility. An articulation test was performed and yielded the data presented in Table 2.2 for analysis.

Three features of the south Yorkshire urban vernacular to which Mike is exposed should not be attributed significance within the analysis: (1) the presence of 'h-dropping' (the absence of historical /h/ in words such as 'house'); (2) monophthongal realisations of the nuclei in words such as 'nice' (/aɪ/→[æ]); and (3) the loss of historical /r/ in preconsonantal and prepausal position (south Yorks vernacular is non-rhotic), for example, 'horsie', 'chair'. Two further features in Mike's speech are cluster reduction and fronting. Cluster reduction is evident in 'brush' and 'smoke' where /br/ and /sm/ are realised as [b] and [m], respectively.

Table 2.2 Single-word productions of a child with developmental dysarthria

Target word	Production	Target word	Production	Target word	Production
boat	[bo: ʔs̬]	hoof	[u:f]	pool	[pɸu:]
bottle	[bɒs̬ʊ]	hoop	[u:pʰ] ~ [u:pɸ]	sail	[s̬e:ʊ]
brush	[bəs̬]	horsie	[ɔ:s̬ɪ]	sew	[s̬o:]
cake	[kʰe:ʔs̬]	house	[aʊs̬]	smoke	[mo:ʔs̬]
car	[kʰɑ:] ~ [xɑ:]	marching	[mɑ:s̬ɪn]	sock	[s̬ɒʔs̬]
cat	[kʰaʔs̬]	matches	[mas̬ə]	sugar	[s̬əs̬ə]
chair	[ts̬e:]	milk	[mɪʊx]	tail	[s̬e:ʊ]
chimney	[s̬ɪns̬ɪ]	nice	[næ:s̬]	tea	[ts̬i:]
cotton	[kxɒs̬ən]	night	[næ:ʔs̬]	teeth	[tʰi:s̬]
cuff	[xəf] ~ [kxəf]	nothing	[nəs̬ɪn]	three	[fɔi:]
fin	[fɪn]	paper	[pʰe:ɸə]	toe	[s̬o:]
hiss	[ɪs̬]	penny	[ɸɛɫɪ]	watch	[wɒʔs̬]
hit	[ɪʔs̬]	pin	[pɸɪn]	water	[wɔ:s̬ə]

With permission from John Harris. See also 'Phonetic Features and Phonological Features in Speech Assessment', *British Journal of Disorders of Communication*, 20, 61–74 (1985), table 1.

Fronting of palato-alveolars to alveolar position occurs in all positions: initial ([s̬]at the start of 'sugar'), medial ([s̬] in the middle of 'matches') and final ([s̬] at the end of 'brush'). However, the fronting of velar sounds is more restricted, as it occurs only in non-initial positions and then only variably (e.g. fronting occurs at the end of 'sock' but not at the end of 'milk'). Cluster reduction and fronting are common in the speech of young children. However, in a child of Mike's age they are symptomatic of delayed development. Two further features relating to the place of articulation are the production of alveolar fricatives with a slit articulation [s̬] rather than the grooved articulation that is the adult form, and the use of [f] for dental fricatives in word initial position (e.g. 'three') and [s̬] for these fricatives in other positions (e.g. 'nothing', 'teeth').

Mike's speech also contains a number of deviant articulatory features that are not seen either in adult speech or as part of normal development. This is Mike's tendency to realise voiceless plosives as affricates or fricatives, and for affricates to be realised as fricatives. The former feature is the reverse of the normal developmental pattern of stopping in which fricatives and affricates are realised as stops. Mike substitutes affricates or fricatives for voiceless plosives in word initial position ([ɸ] at the start of 'penny'), medial position ([s̬] in the middle of 'cotton') and final position ([s̬] at the end of 'boat'). Affricates are realised as fricatives in all word positions ([s̠] is used in place of /ʧ/ in 'chimney', 'matches' and 'watch'). These deviant features sometimes combine with a developmentally normal feature in Mike's speech. In 'smoke', for example, word final /k/ is realised as [s̠] which is a combination of fronting and Mike's tendency to replace voiceless plosives with fricatives. A further deviant feature of Mike's speech is his use of heavily aspirated plosives. The tendency in Mike's local northern English vernacular is for voiceless plosives to be unaspirated. Mike makes his most extensive use of aspirated plosives in word initial position, which is where some other types of English also show some degree of aspiration. In conclusion, Mike's production of voiceless plosives and affricates is compromised by a combination of aspiration, affrication (plosives are realised as homorganic affricates, particularly in word initial position) and spirantisation (the realisation of plosives and affricates as homorganic fricatives, in Mike's case in all positions).

The combined effect of impairments across different speech production subsystems is a reduction in the intelligibility of the dysarthric speaker. This may be a minimal reduction so that the affected child or adult may remain intelligible to all apart from when speaking in adverse conditions such as in the presence of considerable background noise. Alternatively, the reduction in intelligibility may be so great that the dysarthric speaker is unintelligible even to close family members and carers. In the latter case, speech and language therapists will seek to institute an appropriate alternative form of communication so that the speaker will be able to communicate basic needs to those in his or her environment (see section 2.5). Also, some speech features may contribute more to an individual's (un)intelligibility than other features. Murdoch and Hudson-Tennent (1994) studied 19 children aged 4;5 to 16;10 years who developed dysarthria following excision of a posterior fossa tumour. The most commonly identified deviant speech dimensions were imprecise production of consonants and hypernasal/hyponasal speech, which were exhibited by 72.7 per cent of these subjects. Reduced overall intelligibility was present in 63.6 per cent of these children. Intelligibility levels of 52 per cent and 47 per cent have been reported in children and adults with Down syndrome and speakers with cerebral palsy, respectively (Cleland et al., 2010; Hunter et al., 1991). Liu et al. (2005) examined speech intelligibility in Mandarin-speaking young adults with cerebral palsy. These investigators found that cerebral palsy subjects had smaller vowel working space areas than age-matched controls and that these areas were significantly correlated with vowel and word intelligibility.

KEY POINTS: Developmental dysarthria

- A speech disorder with a neurological aetiology (damage to the central and/or peripheral nervous systems)
- Developmental dysarthria is most commonly found in cerebral palsy, but may also occur in traumatic brain injury, muscular dystrophy and in a number of syndromes (e.g. flaccid dysarthria is a feature of Down syndrome and Prader-Willi syndrome)

- One or more aspects of speech production is compromised: articulation, resonation, phonation, respiration and prosody
- The speaker with developmental dysarthria may lack the tongue movements required to produce oral consonants (articulation), display hypernasal speech related to velopharyngeal incompetence (resonation), have a breathy voice due to inadequate adduction or closure of the vocal folds (phonation), have inadequate breath support for speech (respiration) and place stress inappropriately on certain words (prosody)
- The dysarthric child may be mildly unintelligible or so severely unintelligible that some form of augmentative and alternative communication is required

2.4   Developmental verbal dyspraxia

Developmental verbal dyspraxia (DVD), also known as developmental apraxia of speech (DAS) and childhood apraxia of speech (CAS), is a motor speech disorder that can seriously compromise intelligibility in affected individuals. Most definitions of DVD attempt to distinguish this disorder from developmental dysarthria, another motor speech disorder. In this way, Strand (1995: 127) remarks that '[i]n DAS, a child has difficulty carrying out purposeful voluntary movement sequences for speech in the absence of a paralysis of the speech musculature'. As well as highlighting the absence of paralysis in DVD (a neuromuscular impairment must be present in developmental dysarthria), Strand's definition gives emphasis to another feature of this speech disorder: there is a distinction between volitional and automatic speech, with the former usually posing greater difficulty for the affected child or adult. Other definitions of DVD locate the breakdown in speech production at the planning and programming stages. Caruso and Strand (1999: 16–17) claim that '[i]t is our view that the term developmental apraxia of speech is a motor level of impairment. Specifically, we posit that the speech characteristics of these children are due to disruption of sensorimotor planning or sensorimotor programming'. Whatever is ultimately shown to be the true status of this disorder, what is clear is that DVD is one of the less common communication disorders in the developmental period. Shriberg et al. (1997a) state that DAS affects between 1 and 2 per 1,000 children. DVD is more commonly found in boys. Hall et al. (1993) found an average male:female ratio of approximately 3:1 in a review of 24 group studies and 11 single-subject studies. The aetiology of this disorder is still unknown, although neurological, genetic and metabolic factors have all been argued to play a role in the development of this disorder (see Cummings (2008), for further discussion).

A detailed characterisation of the features of DVD is important in establishing a differential diagnosis of the disorder. Like developmental phonological disorder (see section 3.2), children with DVD produce many consonant errors. These errors include the deletion of initial and final consonants, cluster reductions, voicing errors and substitutions. Lewis et al. (2004) reported that initial and final consonant deletion, syllable deletion and cluster reduction occurred in higher proportions in children with childhood apraxia of speech

(CAS) than in children with isolated speech sound disorders (S group) or in children with combined speech sound and language disorders (SL group). Specifically, 100 per cent of CAS subjects produced final consonant deletion errors, compared with 25 per cent and 38 per cent of the S and SL groups, respectively. In relation to syllable deletion and cluster reduction, it was found that 90 per cent of CAS subjects deleted syllables and 60 per cent simplified clusters. This compared with 8 per cent and 15 per cent for the S and SL groups, respectively, for syllable deletion and 0 per cent and 8 per cent of the S and SL groups for cluster reduction. In a study of three children with CAS, Jacks et al. (2006) found that omissions and substitutions were the most frequent error types, occurring with a mean frequency across sessions of 42 per cent and 34 per cent, respectively. Final consonants were omitted more often than either initial or medial consonants. Retroflex and cluster errors were less frequent, occurring with mean frequencies of 14 per cent and 9 per cent, respectively.

The vowel system in DVD is often severely disordered. Lewis et al. (2004) found that 100 per cent of the CAS children in their study produced vowel errors. This compared with only 1 per cent of children with isolated speech sound disorders and 1 per cent of children with combined speech sound and language disorders. These findings were based on an examination of the children when they were preschool age (4–6 years). When these same children were re-examined at 8–10 years of age, a similar distribution of vowel errors emerged. An analysis of conversational speech samples revealed that 90 per cent of CAS children produced vowel errors compared with 8 per cent and 0 per cent of children with speech sound disorders and combined speech and language disorders, respectively. Davis et al. (2005) charted the vowel inventory and accuracy patterns of three children with suspected DAS over a three-year period. The children were aged between 4;6 and 7;7 years and received treatment during the study. Vowel accuracy was impaired in all children, although accuracy did show a moderate increase from a range of 61–75 per cent at the first data recording to 71–85 per cent at the final data recording. Errors consisted mainly of vowel substitutions and de-rhoticisation. No consistent pattern of errors was found in the substitutions (a lack of error consistency is a feature of DVD). Also, errors that involve small changes in vowel quality in the same area of vowel space (e.g. tensing/laxing) were also observed to occur more commonly than other errors. Although other studies have reported extensive diphthong reduction in DVD children (Davis et al., 1998; Pollock and Hall, 1991), substantial diphthong reduction was not found in this investigation. Vowel accuracy did not decrease with increasing utterance length and there was only a slight trend towards decreasing accuracy with increasing syllable and word complexity. These findings challenge the length and complexity effects that are frequently reported in DVD.

Stackhouse and Snowling (1992: 42) studied two children with DVD, Michael and Caroline, who were aged 10;7 and 11;9 years, respectively, at the start of their study. Amongst the speech errors examined in this study were a number which were unique to the DVD children (i.e. they were not found in 10 normally-speaking control children used in the study) (see Table 2.3).

Table 2.3   Single-word productions of two children with DVD

biscuits	[ˈbɪsɪʔ]
treasure	[ˈstɛrəz]
caravan	[ˈkxærəˌvaen]
burglar	[ˈbɜɡləx]
crab	[kəˈʋaeb]
slipper	[s sə ˈlɛpə]
treasure	[s ˈst ˈstɛrə ˈstɛvə ˈdʒɛvə ˈstɛrə ˈdʒɛlɪʃ ˈdʒɛdə]

Based on: Stackhouse and Snowling (1992).

The consonant and vowel errors exemplified by the above productions include the glottal replacement of clusters, with [ʔ] used in place of /ts/ in 'biscuits'. Two consonant distortions – flapping and frication – are also present. In the word 'treasure' the child with DVD has used a voiced alveolar tap [r] or 'flapped r' in place of the voiced palato-alveolar fricative /ʒ/. The second distortion, frication, is evident in 'caravan' and 'burglar' with the voiceless velar fricative [x] used in word initial and final positions, respectively. Vowels also intrude into these children's productions. Two examples of epenthesis occur in which a schwa vowel [ə] is inserted into the consonant clusters /kr/ and /sl/ in 'crab' and 'slipper', respectively (there is also reduction of the first of these clusters). Caroline in particular engaged in repeated attempts at articulating target words, as can be seen in her production of 'treasure'. During her struggle to produce the target word, Caroline used deviant speech features (e.g. flapping), as well as features that are found in normal development (e.g. stopping in the use of [d] for the fricative /ʒ/). However, in a child of Caroline's age, the persistence of stopping is also markedly deviant.

Prosodic disturbances, including anomalies of rate, intonation and stress, have been reported in children with DVD. It has been argued that slowed speaking rates in DVD serve a compensatory function with the child decreasing his or her rate in an attempt to increase the intelligibility of speech. Shewan (1980: 4) remarks of this point as follows: 'Some children demonstrate normal prosodic aspects of speech; however, at a normal speech rate they are frequently unintelligible. Others modify prosodic aspects, using a slow rate and equalized stress'. Morgan Barry (1995b) studied four children with speech disorder, two of whom displayed features consistent with DVD. The two children in question, who were both aged 9 years, demonstrated variable rate with rapid bursts of speed over longer utterances. A number of studies have investigated intonation in children with DVD. Morgan Barry (1995c) compared the intonation of the two children with dyspraxic features discussed in Morgan Barry (1995b) with that of an adult who had acquired dyspraxia. While the adult's pitch and range were high and moderate, the children's were low and narrow. The children displayed predominantly falling tones, while the adult's were predominantly rising. Probably the most extensively investigated area of prosody in DVD is stress. Shriberg et al. (1997b) compared the speech and prosody-voice profiles of 14 children with suspected DAS and 73 children with speech delay. These investigators found that inappropriate stress was the only linguistic domain that differentiated these two groups of children. Odell and Shriberg (2001) compared prosody-voice patterns in adults with apraxia of speech (AOS) and children with suspected apraxia of speech (AOSci). Compared with speakers with AOS, speakers with AOSci had significantly more utterances meeting criteria for inappropriate stress.

Other features of diagnostic significance in DVD include poor oromotor skills, as evidenced by reduced diadochokinetic (DDK) rates. These rates are calculated by timing how long it takes the child with DVD to produce words (real and nonsense) and syllables (e.g. /pə, tə, kə/) in quick succession over several repetitions. As well as exhibiting reduced rates, children with DVD can also have difficulty with the sequencing of sounds and syllables on DDK tasks. Moriarty and Gillon (2006) studied three children with CAS: Katie (6;3 years), Paul (6;10 years) and Derek (7;3 years). All three children displayed poor sequencing during DDK tasks. Additionally, Derek and Paul had reduced DDK rates. An oral dyspraxia is present in a significant number of children with DVD. Alcock et al. (2000) investigated oral dyspraxia in 12 members of a family (the 'KE' family) which suffers from an inherited form of DVD. These investigators found marked difficulties among these subjects on a test of non-verbal oral movements, leading them to conclude that these members of the KE family made dyspraxic errors not just in speech, but in oral movements generally. Children with DVD also display 'soft' neurological signs such as drooling, early feeding difficulties and clumsiness on gross and fine motor tasks (Stackhouse, 1992). Children with DVD can also display language problems with receptive skills generally superior to expressive skills. Aziz et al. (2010) found that the children in their study with suspected CAS had significantly lower language scores only in their expressive abilities. A 3-year-old boy with CAS, who was studied by Grigos and Kolenda (2010), attained language test scores that were one standard deviation below the mean for receptive skills and two standard deviations below the mean for expressive skills.

KEY POINTS: Developmental verbal dyspraxia

- A motor speech disorder that occurs in the developmental period in the absence of any neuromuscular impairment; often characterised as a speech motor programming disorder
- Aetiology is unknown; males are more commonly affected than females
- Consonant and vowel errors are common and can have a severe adverse effect on speech intelligibility

- Prosodic disturbances involving speech rate, intonation and stress are routinely present in DVD
- An oral dyspraxia is often present as are 'soft' neurological signs and language (particularly expressive) difficulties

2.5 Assessment and treatment

The population of children with developmental speech disorders is so diverse that it is difficult to capture the many different assessment and treatment techniques that may be used with these children. However, a number of general observations relating to the assessment and treatment of this clinical population can nevertheless be made. By taking an extensive case history, the clinician can establish whether factors known to disrupt speech sound development may have played a role in a child's failure to develop speech along normal lines. For example, the child with cleft palate often experiences repeated episodes of otitis media ('glue ear') and the resulting conductive hearing loss can compromise the acquisition of speech sounds. A case history will reveal whether a child achieved general and communication-related developmental milestones (e.g. walking, first words) at a delayed rate compared with his or her age peers. It will also reveal any illnesses (e.g. meningitis), injuries (e.g. head trauma) or other factors (e.g. intellectual disability, craniofacial anomalies) that may account for the child's delayed or deviant speech-sound development. The clinician will also use a case history to establish the presence of communication disorders in other family members, as this may also shed light on the aetiology of the speech disorder (see Alcock et al. (2000) in section 2.4, for discussion of an inherited developmental verbal dyspraxia in the KE family). It will also be relevant to establish whether the child has experienced situations that may have contrived to limit his or her exposure to linguistic stimuli. For example, the child with complex medical needs may have endured prolonged periods of hospitalisation. Finally, it will be relevant to establish the presence of early feeding difficulties, as such difficulties are often associated with the later development of speech problems.

Having taken an extensive case history, the speech and language therapist will perform an assessment of the structure and function of the speech anatomy. An oral examination may reveal a previously undetected submucous cleft palate, a short velum that fails to make adequate contact with the posterior pharyngeal wall or various anomalies of dentition. These structural anomalies may ultimately be shown to be asymptomatic (i.e. have no effect on speech production). Nonetheless, their presence should be recorded on account of their potential, either singly or in combination, to compromise speech production. The anatomical structures used in speech production may be intact, but may nevertheless function poorly. An oral examination will seek to examine the strength and range of tongue movements, the ability of the lips to round and spread and the range of jaw movements. Apart from the articulators, the function of the phonatory and respiratory mechanisms should be examined. This examination may reveal poor breath support for speech, as well as possible compensatory behaviours such as forceful vocal fold adduction during phonation. The results of the oral examination will help the therapist identify key areas for intervention and further investigation. For example, if a child with cerebral palsy presents with limited movement of the velum, the therapist can expect to investigate the part played by velopharyngeal incompetence in the child's speech disorder. It may also be necessary to undertake instrumental investigation (e.g. nasendoscopy) to establish the full extent of the child's difficulty with velar movement and to assess the child's suitability for prosthetic intervention (e.g. the use of a palatal lift).

An assessment of the function of individual articulators performing single movements, usually in imitation of the therapist, must be followed by an examination of how these same articulators operate when performing speech-related movements. These movements may be required to articulate a series of syllables which vary in their place of articulation (e.g. /pə, tə, kə/) or as used in multisyllabic words (e.g. 'sellotape'). The use of DDK tasks is an important part of the assessment process and can contribute to a differential diagnosis of motor speech disorders. So the child with DVD may struggle to sequence the syllables used in DDK tasks and may slow his or her rate of production in an effort to attain an intelligible target. Of course, the therapist will need to establish the full extent of the child's phonetic inventory. To this end, articulation tests may be used which examine the child's production of speech sounds in a range of phonetic contexts. One long-standing articulation test is the Goldman–Fristoe Test of Articulation 2 (GFTA-2; Goldman and Fristoe, 2000), which examines 39 consonant sounds and clusters in word initial, medial and final positions. This test requires the respondent to name pictures of objects that are culturally appropriate and are within the language level of most children. These tests may present some challenges to the assessing clinician. For example, the child with Down syndrome and learning disability may be unable to name certain test items that are not yet part of his or her vocabulary. Similarly, the child with cerebral palsy who has visual impairment may struggle with the visual demands of this task. These difficulties are usually easily overcome by the resourceful clinician. Time permitting, the clinician may be able to supplement the results of an articulation test with an analysis of the speech sounds that the child uses in more spontaneous contexts.

Having established that a child has marked difficulties with particular classes of sounds (e.g. fricatives) or that he or she cannot produce sounds with a certain place of articulation (e.g. alveolar consonants), the clinician will want to establish the impact of these phonetic anomalies on the intelligibility of the child's speech. An assessment of articulation must always be followed by a phonological assessment in order to establish the presence of any processes that are reducing the child's ability to use sounds contrastively and thereby signal differences of meaning. Like articulation tests, there are many commercially available phonological assessments that can be used for this purpose. One such assessment which has been developed to be used alongside the GFTA-2 is the Khan-Lewis Phonological Analysis (KLPA-2; Khan and Lewis, 2002). Grigos and Kolenda (2010) used the KLPA-2 to assess phonological processes in the speech of their 3-year-old subject with CAS.

These investigators found that the following processes had an occurrence greater than 20 per cent and had the greatest impact on the child's intelligibility: final consonant deletion, cluster simplification, syllable reduction and initial voicing. Intelligibility is a function of many different factors, only some of which relate to features of the child's speech. For example, familiar listeners such as parents and carers will always assess a child to be more intelligible than unfamiliar listeners. Also, a child may appear more intelligible when telling a story to a wordless picture book, where the listener can see the pictures and knows the target words, than in spontaneous conversation. For these reasons, the therapist should aim to supplement an assessment of intelligibility based on single-word productions with an assessment of intelligibility across these other contexts.

With the results of assessment in hand, the therapist can proceed to implement a suitable course of therapy for the child. Once again, many different intervention techniques may be used with children who have developmental speech disorders and so this account cannot be exhaustive. For children who have a severe speech disorder in the presence of a neurological impairment that will remain unchanged or even deteriorate (e.g. in a progressive condition like muscular dystrophy), speech intelligibility may not improve and should not be the focus of therapy. In such cases, an augmentative or alternative communication (AAC) system may need to be instituted. Developments in computer technology have seen a proliferation of high-tech systems, although a well-designed communication board mounted onto the wheelchair of a child or adult with cerebral palsy may be equally effective in serving the individual's communication needs. The selection of an appropriate system requires consideration of a client's motor and visual skills, as well as cognitive level. The individual with cerebral palsy may lack the motor skills that are needed to point with an extended forefinger at signs on a communication board but may have sufficient head and body control to use a head stick as an alternative form of pointing. Visual disturbances may limit an individual's ability to scan signs on a communication board or computer screen. Cognitive limitations will also be important in determining the type of AAC system that can be used with a particular client. Efforts to teach Blissymbols to subjects with learning disability, for example, have been largely unsuccessful owing to the complex graphic formation and similarity in form of many of these signs (von Tetzchner and Martinsen, 2000). A system selected in the absence of full consideration of these factors is likely to be greeted by communicative failure and frustration.

Where there is a reasonable prospect of achieving an improvement in speech intelligibility, therapy should address those sounds and phonological processes that are most likely to bring this about. The child with cleft palate may have a well-established pattern of backed articulations which have developed as a compensatory adjustment to his or her anatomical limitations. By addressing this overriding articulatory tendency in the speech of the child with cleft palate, significant gains in intelligibility may be achieved. Some clinicians argue that sounds which are targeted first in intervention must be stimulable. In testing for stimulability, the clinician provides a model of the target sound which the child is then encouraged to imitate. If a sound is not immediately stimulable, additional cues (e.g. visual and tactile information) may be used to encourage production. Some speech gains are only achievable if underlying anomalies in speech anatomy and musculature have been successfully addressed through surgical or prosthetic means. For example, no reduction in hypernasality is possible if a client's velum exhibits paresis or paralysis, or if the soft palate is too short to make contact with the posterior pharyngeal wall. In these cases, the fitting of a palatal lift and posterior wall augmentation surgery may enable a paretic velum or a short velum, respectively, to close the velopharyngeal port. Even as speech gains are being targeted in therapy, it may be necessary to pursue simultaneously an AAC intervention. For example, the highly unintelligible child with DVD may be encouraged to make extensive use of gestures, manual signs or a range of AAC aids (e.g. voice output communication aids) to communicate basic needs even as an oral speech intervention is being pursued.

Speech intervention consists in quite different techniques and approaches for each of the developmental speech disorders that we have examined in this chapter. There is widespread agreement amongst clinicians that a motor speech intervention for DVD should involve repeated production drills with sounds treated in combination rather than in isolated phoneme training (Strand, 1995). Intervention must be particularly intensive to achieve improvement in this speech disorder. Campbell (1999) reported that children with apraxia of speech required 81 per cent more individual treatment sessions than children with severe phonological disorders to achieve a similar functional outcome in terms of improvement in speech intelligibility. Isolated phoneme training may be required, at least initially, to establish articulation of particular sounds that are missing from the phonetic inventory of the child with cleft palate. Alongside establishing the correct articulation of individual speech sounds, the therapist may need to focus on diminishing maladaptive patterns of articulation that the child may have developed as compensatory strategies (e.g. nasal friction). Once established in isolation, these sounds can be integrated into a range of syllable structures and, eventually, phrases and sentences. Drills that target improving the strength, range and tone of the speech musculature in developmental dysarthria are of dubious value. For example, although they are extensively used, there is little evidence to support the adoption of blowing and sucking exercises as a means of diminishing hypernasality during speech production. Hodge and Wellman (1999: 222) remark that 'the efficacy of behavioural treatments that attempt to normalize pathokinesiologies underlying dysarthric speech in children is by and large unknown'.

As well as playing a role in the assessment of developmental speech disorders, instrumental techniques can also contribute to the treatment of this clinical population. One prominent technique is electropalatography (EPG). Gibbon (2004: 286) describes EPG as 'a visual feedback facility that provides a real time display of tongue–palate contact patterns that can be used as part of a speech therapy programme'. The visual displays produced in EPG help to make subconscious and hidden lingual misarticulations concrete and real for children with speech disorders. Once observed, these abnormal lingual patterns are more readily modified in therapy. Of course, EPG is not suitable for every individual with developmental speech disorder. Some children and adults are unable to tolerate the artificial palate that must be worn in this procedure (e.g. the child with cerebral palsy who displays oral hypersensitivity). If a child or adult has a learning disability, it will be difficult for him or her to translate the visual displays of tongue–palate contacts into altered motor speech patterns. Notwithstanding these difficulties, the technique has been successfully used in children with cleft palate, and children with DVD and developmental dysarthria (Gibbon, 2004; Gibbon and Wood, 2003; Morgan Barry, 1995a, 1995b, 1995c). Gibbon and Wood (2003) describe the case of an 8-year-old boy with cerebral palsy who consistently fronted velar targets and who did not respond to conventional speech therapy techniques. EPG analysis revealed two aberrant features – an unusually asymmetrical pattern of tongue–palate contact and unusually long stop closure durations. After 15 sessions of EPG therapy over a period of four months, there was a significant improvement in the boy's ability to produce velar sounds.

SUGGESTIONS FOR FURTHER READING

Hodge, M.M. (2014) 'Developmental dysarthria', in L. Cummings (ed.) *Cambridge Handbook of Communication Disorders* (Cambridge: Cambridge University Press), pp. 26–48.

Watson, A.C.H., Sell, D.A. and Grunwell, P. (eds) (2001) *Management of Cleft Lip and Palate* (London: Whurr).

Yorkston, K.M., Beukelman, D.R., Strand, E.A. and Hakel, M. (2010) *Management of Motor Speech Disorders in Children and Adults* (Austin, TX: Pro-Ed, 3rd edn).

EXERCISES

Exercise 2.1 Harding and Grunwell (1996) report the findings of six studies that have examined the consonants which are most often affected in cleft palate speech. These studies are presented with the most adversely affected consonants listed beside them. You should (a) state the two main classes of consonants that are affected in cleft palate speech on the basis of these studies, and (b) explain in articulatory terms why these particular classes are most severely affected.

Study	Consonants	
Subtelny and Subtelny (1959)	s z	p b f v k g t d l
Morley (1970)	s	t d p b k g
Van Demark et al. (1979)	s z ʃ ʒ ʧ ʤ	t d l k g
Albery (1991)	s z ʃ ʒ ʧ ʤ	p b t d k g
Eurocleft Speech Group (1993)	s	t d n
Harding and Grunwell (1993)	s ʃ ʧ	t d n

Exercise 2.2 Morgan Barry (1995a) studied a child of 12 years known as J, who was diagnosed as having congenital suprabulbar paresis (Worster-Drought syndrome). J presents with severe developmental dysarthria. A summary of J's perceptually-based speech assessments is given in the table below alongside his chronological age. Consider the information in this table and then answer questions (a) to (e):

(a) Instrumental investigations conducted at 9;8 years revealed velopharyngeal incompetence (VPI) in J. However, what features prior to these investigations would have suggested the presence of VPI?

(b) J has responded to his VPI by engaging in compensatory articulation. Name two such articulations in J's speech.

(c) Double articulation is also a feature of J's speech. Give an example of such articulation.

(d) Apart from VPI, which other articulatory defect is responsible for J's failure to produce oral stops?

(e) Which of the techniques used to examine J's VPI involves passing a flexible endoscope transnasally?

CA	Summary comments based on perceptual speech assessments
2;8 yrs	J's system contains two consonants only and a limited range of vowels; regurgitation through the nose was noted
3;10 yrs	The vowel system is increasing; nasals and approximants are now present; nasal friction occurs for /s, z, ʃ/
5;4 yrs	J has poor phonatory control; there are no tongue movements; palatal movements can be seen but there is incomplete nasopharyngeal closure
5;9 yrs	Therapy consists of continuing work on all consonants
6;0 yrs	J has a broad palate which lifts well; hypernasality is a problem of control rather than structure
7;0 yrs	Phonatory-respiratory problems exist with prosodic features of dysrthymia and variable loudness
9;8 yrs	Radiology, videofluoroscopy and nasendoscopy (with his cooperation for these being less than optimal) showed palatal movement but insufficient closure to the pharyngeal wall
10;8 yrs	Full range of (nasalised) vowels and diphthongs, nasals /m, n/ and glottal stop [ʔ] which he uses in place of oral stops; demonstrated lip movements for /f, v/ but these sounds heard as having nasal friction

Exercise 2.3 The speech of children with developmental verbal dyspraxia contains numerous consonant and vowel errors. Grigos and Kolenda (2010) and Morgan Barry (1995b) both studied children with DVD who were aged 3 years and 9 years, respectively. A number of these children's single-word productions are transcribed

below. For each production, describe the consonant and/or vowel errors that have occurred:

(a) 'round' [waʊ̃ŋg]

(b) 'sun' [kʌŋ]

(c) 'cut' [bai]

(d) 'red' [wɛk]

(e) 'shark' [xak]

(f) 'Christmas' [kɪxmək]

(g) 'eat' [ɪt]

(h) 'elephant' [eɪfəŋk]

(i) 'train' [geɪŋ]

(j) 'cot' [gɒk]

(k) 'fish' [fɪx]

(l) 'fight' [jɛ]

(m) 'tent' [kʰɛŋk]

(n) 'salt' [gəʊk]

(o) 'skirt' [gɜk]

ANSWERS TO EXERCISES

Exercise 2.1

The two consonant classes most adversely affected in cleft palate speech are stops (plosives) and fricatives. The production of stops requires a build-up of air pressure behind two articulators that are in direct contact with each other. In the child with cleft palate, this build-up of air pressure is not easily achieved. A surgically repaired soft palate (velum) may be short and immobile, and fail to make contact with the posterior pharyngeal wall. As a result, there may be a loss of air through the velo-pharyngeal port. Fistula (small holes) may develop in the area of the palate repair and let air pass into the nasal cavities. In both cases, stops will be weak and accompanied by excessive nasal resonance. In order to articulate fricative sounds, the speaker must achieve the constriction of the airstream between two articulators. For this constriction to be achieved, there must be no loss of air at any other point in the vocal tract (e.g. through the velopharyngeal port). If pulmonary air is lost before the area of constriction in the oral cavity, the resulting fricative sounds will be weakly produced.

Exercise 2.2

(a) nasal regurgitation and hypernasality

(b) the substitution of oral stops by the glottal stop [ʔ] and the use of nasal friction for the fricatives /s, z, ʃ/

(c) J uses nasal friction at the same time as he assumes the labiodental position for /f, v/

(d) absence of tongue movements

(e) nasendoscopy

Exercise 2.3

(a) 'round': gliding, backing (velarisation)

(b) 'sun': stopping, velarisation

(c) 'cut': fronting, voicing, diphthongisation

(d) 'red': gliding, backing, devoicing

(e) 'shark': velarisation
(f) 'Christmas': cluster reduction, velarisation, stopping
(g) 'eat': vowel lowering
(h) 'elephant': weak syllable deletion, velarisation
(i) 'train': cluster reduction, backing, voicing, velarisation
(j) 'cot': voicing, backing
(k) 'fish': velarisation
(l) 'fight': backing, voicing, diphthong reduction, final consonant delection
(m) 'tent': velarisation
(n) 'salt': stopping, voicing, cluster reduction, backing
(o) 'skirt': cluster reduction, voicing, backing.

Developmental Language Disorders

3

3.1 The classification of developmental language disorders

For the large majority of children, language is effortlessly acquired along with other skills in the developmental period. However, there is a sizeable number of children for whom the process of language acquisition is anything but unproblematic. Some of these children have been neurologically compromised by events in the pre-, peri- or post-natal period. For example, a child may have a syndrome that is related to a chromosomal or genetic abnormality (e.g. fragile X syndrome). A baby may sustain oxygen deprivation (birth anoxia) during labour or develop meningitis at 6 months of age. These events can cause brain damage with resulting intellectual disability (or learning disability). The child with intellectual disability experiences considerable difficulty with language acquisition and may never acquire the language skills of normally-developing peers. Even in the absence of neurological compromise some children can fail to acquire language. A child may exhibit a specific deficit in the acquisition of language in the absence of intellectual disability and a range of other conditions that are known to compromise language development. Children with so-called 'specific language impairment' (SLI) lack a clear aetiology for their language disorder and display normal development in other areas. Alternatively, language may be one of several areas in which the child is failing to develop along normal lines. Children with autism spectrum disorders exhibit deficits in language and communication alongside problems in socialisation and imagination. Finally, a child may begin to acquire language normally only for this process to be interrupted. The child who sustains a traumatic brain injury (TBI) or who develops Landau–Kleffner syndrome (LKS) may lose previously acquired language skills. The language disorders that attend these various conditions will be examined in this chapter.

As well as classifying language disorders by aetiology, these disorders may also be characterised by their linguistic features. In some developmental language disorders several language levels are simultaneously compromised. For example, the child with Down syndrome (DS) is likely to experience difficulty with the acquisition of phonology, syntax and semantics. There may also be impairment of discourse and pragmatic skills. However, in other developmental language disorders, some language levels are relatively intact while others can be severely disordered. The child with phonological disorder, for example, has pronounced deficits in phonology and impaired lexical acquisition, while morphosyntax is particularly compromised in the child with SLI. Receptive and expressive language skills can be equally compromised or one may be more adversely affected than the other. The child with LKS, for example, has a severe auditory comprehension deficit which is related to auditory agnosia with expressive language skills only deteriorating subsequent to the comprehension deficit (see section 4.5 in Cummings (2008)). Also, a language disorder may affect all modalities including spoken, written and signed language. Traditionally, speech and language therapists have tended to concentrate on the assessment and remediation of spoken language skills to the exclusion of written language. However, it is important to remember that disorders of written language are most likely to compromise the academic performance of children. With language compromised at different levels (phonology, syntax, etc.), in different modalities (speech, writing) and across input (comprehension) and output (expression) modes, it is clear that any assessment of language skills in developmental language disorders must address these various dimensions. We will return to issues of assessment in section 3.6.

3.2 Developmental phonological disorder

A significant number of children may fail to acquire knowledge of the sound system of their native language. Diagnosed as having developmental phonological disorder (DPD), these children can be highly unintelligible and yet fail to exhibit any medical or other cause for their evident failure to acquire the phonology of language. In specific terms, these children do not have a neurological disorder that affects their ability to articulate speech sounds. They do not have intellectual disability, hearing loss or a craniofacial abnormality, all conditions that might be expected to compromise a child's ability to produce speech sounds. Due to the use of different diagnostic criteria, prevalence figures for DPD vary considerably. However, Shriberg (1994) reports how he and his colleagues have found that approximately 60 per cent of the preschool children in their local populations have speech delay without associated involvements. They calculate that this translates to a population estimate of 1–2 children per 100 with a form of DPD called 'speech delay'. Males are more commonly affected than females. Shriberg (1994) reports a figure of 75 per cent of boys in their samples. Studies are increasingly revealing the presence of speech and language impairments amongst the biological relatives of individuals with DPD (e.g. Felsenfeld et al., 1995). Such findings suggest that there may ultimately be a genetic explanation of DPD: 'Converging evidence supports the hypothesis that the most common subtype of childhood speech sound disorder (SSD) of currently unknown origin is genetically transmitted' (Shriberg et al., 2005: 834).

In DPD, consonants can be severely disordered in the presence of an intact vowel system. The phonological errors that children produce can be analysed in terms of distinctive features and phonological processes. For example, the child who pronounces 'sock' as [tɔk], 'five' as [paɪb], 'very' as [bɛri] and 'nose' as [nod] has substituted fricative sounds with plosive sounds. Fricative sounds possess the distinctive features [continuant] and [strident], while plosive sounds lack these features. In terms of phonological processes, the child who pro-duces these forms has engaged in stopping. In keeping with the dominant use of process analysis in clinical phonology, several processes will be discussed here. Stoel-Gammon et al. (2002) describe three basic types of phonological process. The first type affects the syllable structure of words and includes final consonant deletion ('bat' pronounced [bæ]), cluster reduction ('swim' pronounced [wɪm]) and weak syllable deletion ('banana' pronounced [nænə]). The second type of process involves changes in the place, manner or voicing of consonants and includes velar fronting ('gun' pronounced [dʌn]), palatal fronting ('sheep' pronounced [sip]), stopping ('sun' pronounced [tʌn]), glid-ing ('red' pronounced [wɛd]), prevocalic voicing ('pen' pronounced [bɛn]) and final devoicing ('bag' pronounced [bæk]). In the third type of process, one consonant assimilates to (i.e. becomes like) another consonant in the word. Assimilatory processes include velar assimilation ('dog' pronounced [gɔg]) and labial assimilation ('top' pronounced [bɑp]). These processes, alongside a number of others, can be used to characterise the errors produced by sev-eral children with phonological disorder who were studied by Powell et al. (1999):

Keith (5;2 years): 'comb' [toʊm] 'duck' [dʌk]
Sally (3;10 years): 'soup' [tup] 'teeth' [ti] 'nosy' [noʊdi]
Suzy (3;10 years): 'vase' [tɛt] 'ice' [aɪ] 'glove' [tʌt] 'yawn' [hɔn]
 'cheese' [ti] 'jeep' [tip] 'leafy' [hiti] 'drum' [nʌm]
John (5;0 years): 'laugh' [væf] 'leg' [ðeɪg]

The oldest child, Keith, engages in velar fronting (/k/→[t]) in word initial position but not in word final position. Sally uses stopping of fricatives both in word initial position (/s/→[t]) and intervocalically (/z/→[d]). She also omits fricatives (/θ/) in word final position. Suzy also uses stopping of fricatives but she does so in word initial position (/v/→[t]), word final position (/z/→[t]; /v/→[t]) and intervocalically (/f/→[t]). Fricatives are optionally omitted in Suzy's speech in word final position (see 'cheese' and 'glove'). The affricates in word initial position in 'cheese' and 'jeep' are both realised as [t]. Suzy also engages in devoicing of voiced consonants both in word initial position (/v/→[t]) and in word final position (/z/→[t]). In prevocalic position, Suzy uses [h] instead of the liquid /l/ and the glide /j/. When a word ends in a nasal sound, Suzy uses nasal assimilation (/dr/→[n]). John's substitutions are some-what unusual. In the context of /f/, the liquid /l/ becomes the fricative [v]. In other contexts, he uses [ð] in place of /l/.

A number of the phonological processes discussed above are to be found in the speech of children who will go on to develop normal phonology. The issue for clinicians is therefore how to distinguish children for whom these various simplifications are simply part of the normal maturational process in terms of phonology from children who are struggling to acquire the sound system of their language. Yavaş (1998) describes several characteristics that researchers have proposed in order to make this identification. The first of these characteristics is the persistence of normal processes. Processes such as prevocalic voicing and consonant harmony (assimilation) are normally expected to resolve by 3 years of age (Stoel-Gammon and Dunn, 1985). However, in children with disordered phonology, these processes may persist to 4 years and beyond (Yavaş, 1998). A second characteristic is the presence of a chronological mismatch in the child's phonological errors. The expression 'chronological mismatch' was used by Grunwell (1981) to describe a child who uses very early normal processes alongside later normal processes. Such a pattern occurs, for example, if syllable initial cluster reduction persists while the use of complex syllable final clusters has become well-established. A third characteristic is the variable use of processes in relation to one and the same target structure. A child, for example, may delete final consonants on some occasions but replace them with a glottal stop [ʔ] on other occasions. A fourth characteristic is the presence of a systematic sound preference. For example, a child may use only one or two sounds to replace a whole group of sounds that share the same manner of articulation. A fifth characteristic is the presence of unusual, idiosyncratic or atypical processes in the child's speech. We saw an example of unusual substitutions in John's productions above. Yavaş (1998) lists a number of other processes that are rarely found in children's speech: backing of alveolars, gliding of fricatives, glottal insertion, frication of stops, unusual cluster reduction and initial consonant deletion.

KEY POINTS: Developmental phonological disorder

- Production of speech sounds is impaired in the absence of an underlying aetiology; more common in boys than girls
- Phonological errors can be analysed in terms of distinctive features or phonological processes; process analysis is widespread in clinical phonology
- Simplification processes can be extensive and can compromise intelligibility of child
- Phonological processes can affect syllable structure of word (e.g. final consonant deletion), the place, manner or voicing of consonants (e.g. velar fronting) or one consonant can assimilate to another consonant (e.g. velar assimilation)
- Disordered phonology can be distinguished from normal phonology in terms of (1) persistence of normal processes, (2) presence of chronological mismatch, (3) variable use of processes, (4) presence of systematic sound preference, and (5) presence of idiosyncratic processes

3.3   Specific language impairment

For some children, there is a severe and specific deficit in the acquisition of language. Other aspects of development (e.g. motor skills) are normal and there is no known cause for the impairment in language. Although a number of terms have been used in the past to describe this population of children, the diagnostic label 'specific language impairment' is now in widespread clinical use. The SLI label has been called a diagnosis by exclusion. Thus, Craig (1991: 166) remarks that 'the SLI diagnostic label is applied on the basis of well-accepted exclusion criteria'. These criteria include a range of conditions (e.g. hearing loss, neurological damage, anatomical defects) that are known to cause language impairment in children. Leonard (1998: 10) defines criteria for the application of the SLI label. Children with SLI must have language test scores of -1.25 standard deviations or lower and a performance IQ of 85 or higher. Their poor language skills must place them at risk for social devalue. They must pass hearing screening at conventional levels and have no recent episodes of otitis media with effusion. There should be no neurological dysfunction (no evidence of seizure disorders, cerebral palsy or brain lesions) and the child must not be taking medication for the control of seizures. There must be no structural anomalies in the oral cavity and the child must pass screening for oral motor function using developmentally appropriate items. The child must not exhibit symptoms of impaired reciprocal social interaction or restriction of activities (this criterion excludes children with an autism spectrum disorder). Despite intact skills and performance in each of these areas, the child with SLI exhibits a language disorder that is so severe that he or she may receive education within special language units.

Deficits may occur at all language levels in SLI, but are most pronounced in syntax and semantics. Phonology may be disrupted in SLI but should not be the only impaired language level – Leonard (1998: 13) states that 'children with phonological disorders are included in the category of SLI only if they perform poorly on other measures of language'. Aguilar-Mediavilla et al. (2002) examined the phonology of 3-year-old children with SLI and found, amongst other things, that children with SLI used more syllabic and nonsyllabic cluster reduction and initial and final consonant deletions than age controls. They also deleted medial consonants significantly more often than age controls and deleted unstressed syllables in initial position significantly more than control subjects. Aguilar-Mediavilla et al. (2002: 573) state that these results suggest that 'the development of SLI phonology is deviant'.

There are extensive reports of deficits in morphosyntax in children with SLI with tense-marking morphemes particularly vulnerable to impairment. Rice et al. (1998) found that morphemes which share the property of tense marking (third person singular –s; past tense –ed; 'be' and 'do') are mastered by the age of 4 years in typically developing children and after the age of 7 years in children with SLI. Other grammatical findings in SLI are also noteworthy. They include higher production and acceptance rates of past-tense over-regularisations (e.g. he falled) than in age-matched controls, greater use and acceptance of infinitive forms in finite positions (e.g. he fall off) and greater acceptance of finite form errors in verb phrase (VP) complement positions (e.g. he made him fell) (Redmond and Rice, 2001). Rice et al. (1995) found that children with SLI used non-finite forms of lexical verbs and omitted 'be' and 'do' more frequently than controls matched for age and mean length of utterance (MLU). Moore (2001) studied 12 children with expressive SLI. Some of the grammatical errors produced by these children are shown below:

Child A (4;10 years): Her's painting a flower.
Child B (5;4 years):   He eating.
Child C (3;11 years): Her painting.
Child D (4;6 years):   She building block.
Child E (4;9 years):   Why he fall in the car?
Child F (4;2 years):   And her painting now.
Child G (4;2 years):   He's marrying my dad.
Child H (4;1 years):   Yeah, he sleeping right here.

The auxiliary verb 'is' is omitted by children B, C, D, F and H, while child E omits the auxiliary verb 'did'. The indefinite article 'a' is omitted in the utterance produced by child D. A number of pronoun errors are present. Child G selects the incorrect subject pronoun ('he' instead of 'she'). An object pronoun ('her') is used instead of a subject pronoun ('she') by children A, C and F. Child E has used an immature grammatical pattern to form a question – the interrogative adverb 'why' is placed at the front of a sentence in the declarative form. Areas of intact grammatical use include the inflectional morpheme *–ing* on verbs, the possessive determiner 'my', definite and indefinite articles (notwithstanding child D's utterance), the locative preposition 'in' and contraction of the auxiliary verb 'is' to the preceding (albeit incorrect) pronoun.

The semantics of language is also disrupted in children with SLI. These children have been found to produce more errors in naming pictures than children with no language impairment, with proportionally more of these errors being in the names of objects associated with the pictured object (e.g. shoe/foot) and phonologically related to the target (Lahey and Edwards 1999). McGregor et al. (2002) found that children with SLI made significantly more errors when naming age-appropriate objects than normally developing age-matched controls, with semantic misnaming and indeterminate responses (e.g. 'don't know' or non-specific responses) forming the predominant error types for both groups of subjects. McGregor et al. (2002: 998) state that 'this study demonstrates that the degree of knowledge represented in the child's semantic lexicon makes words more or less vulnerable to retrieval failure and that limited semantic knowledge contributes to the frequent naming errors of children with SLI'.

The issue of whether children with SLI experience pragmatic difficulties is an area of considerable debate. Traditionally, it has been assumed that if pragmatic difficulties do exist, these must be secondary to the child's structural language impairment (the child who lacks the grammatical competence to achieve inversion of the subject pronoun and auxiliary verb in 'Can you open the window?' will not be able to form the indirect speech act of request, for example). Recently, Bishop and co-workers have argued that there exists a subgroup of children with SLI in whom pragmatic difficulties are not simply the consequence of poor structural language skills (Bishop, 1998, 2000; Bishop et al., 2000). Formerly known by the diagnostic label 'semantic pragmatic disorder', children with pragmatic language impairment are described as being poor at inferencing, over-literal, neglectful of their listener's perspective and as displaying a tendency to use socially inappropriate and/or stereotyped conversational responses (Bishop, 2000). For further discussion of pragmatics in SLI, the reader is referred to section 2.2 in Cummings (2009). A detailed characterisation of the linguistic and cognitive deficits in SLI can be found in section 4.4 in Cummings (2008).

KEY POINTS: Specific language impairment

- Severe language disorder in children: language skills −1.25 standard deviations or greater below mean
- Diagnosis by exclusion: language disorder in the absence of hearing loss, psychiatric disturbance, intellectual disability, etc.
- Deficits particularly evident in syntax and semantics; errors in morphosyntax are common
- Phonology may be disrupted but should not be the only impaired language level
- Debate surrounds status of pragmatic deficits, primary or secondary in nature (latter related to structural language problems)

3.4   Language disorder in intellectual disability

For a considerable number of children, language is not normally acquired because there is an underlying cognitive, intellectual or learning disability. Traditionally, clinicians used intelligence quotient (IQ) scores to determine an individual's level of learning disability or intellectual disability. These scores are the basis of four degrees of severity of intellectual disability: mild learning disability (IQ range 50–55 to about 70), moderate (IQ range 35–40 to 50–55), severe (IQ range 20–25 to 35–40), and profound (IQ level below 20–25). However, factors other than IQ are now as likely to be taken into consideration in determining the level of support that individuals with learning disability should receive: 'the presence of a low intelligence quotient, for example an IQ below 70, is not, of itself, a sufficient reason for deciding whether an individual should be provided with additional health and social care support' (Department of Health, 2001). A wide range of conditions is associated with intellectual disability. Some of these conditions include genetic and chromosomal anomalies such as fragile X syndrome and DS, exposure to alcohol (foetal alcohol syndrome – FAS) and maternal infections (congenital rubella) in the pre-natal period, birth anoxia, and brain damage due to meningitis. With so many diseases and events causing intellectual disability in children, it should not be surprising to learn that the population of persons with learning disability is very large indeed. The Department of Health in the UK estimates that some 1.2 million people in England alone have mild/moderate learning disabilities and a further 210,000 people have severe/profound learning disabilities, 65,000 of which are children. As part of the Metropolitan Atlanta Developmental Disabilities Surveillance Program, the Centers for Disease Control in the US estimated that, between 1991 and 1994, on average about 1 per cent of children between the ages of 3 and 10 years had intellectual disability.

Intellectual disability can compromise the acquisition of language in a multitude of ways. There is considerable evidence of phonological delay and deviance in children with intellectual disability. Kumin et al. (1994) found that the order of phoneme emergence in 60 children with DS was unlike that of typically developing children. Even when norms for the emergence of certain phonemes were missed by the DS children, they nevertheless went on to acquire these phonemes. One DS child, for example, was 8 years old before he began to produce /b/, a sound that is typically acquired by 3 years of age. Van Borsel et al. (2004) recorded the frequencies of 13 phonological processes in the speech of a 10-year-old girl with Wolf–Hirschhorn syndrome. Cluster reduction and final consonant deletion were the most frequently occurring syllable structure processes in this girl's speech. The most common substitution processes were fronting and gliding, while assimilation also occurred quite frequently. The acquisition of morphosyntax also does not proceed along normal lines in children with intellectual disability. Bellugi et al. (2003) used a sentence repetition task to examine morphosyntax in typically developing children and children with Williams syndrome (WS) and DS. Children with WS and DS were functioning at the same level of general cognitive ability. While typically developing children showed decreasing morphosyntactic errors between 3 and 8 years of age, with a perfect score achieved on average between ages 8 and 9, morphosyntactic errors in children with WS decreased from 4 to 14 years of age with near perfect scores achieved between 14 and 16 years. Morphosyntactic errors decreased most slowly in the children with DS, with these children still committing such errors at 16 years of age.

Grammatical development has been examined in a range of syndromes associated with intellectual disability. Carney and Chermak (1991) assessed grammar among other language skills in 10 American Indian children with FAS. Seventeen normally developing American Indian children served as controls. The mean performance of the children with FAS was significantly poorer than that of the control children on three of five subtests on a test of language development. These subtests – sentence combining, word ordering and grammatical comprehension – relate to grammatical aspects of language development. McCardle and Wilson (1993) examined language skills in a boy (JB) of 5;6 years with intellectual disability in the presence of FG syndrome with callosal agenesis. (FG syndrome was named using the surname initials of the first family diagnosed with this syndrome.) JB's limited grammatical skills were evident in the production of telegraphic sentences, which were usually clear in content. For example, when asked what one should do when tired, JB replied: 'I go sleep uncle room, I sleep uncle bed'. The telegraphic nature of this utterance derives from JB's omission of the preposition 'in' (sleep *in* uncle room), and the genitive form's (uncle's room; uncle's bed). During his assessment at 67 months, the following exchange unfolded between JB and the examiner (E):

E: Tell me about your dog.
JB: It go woof woof.
     I have a doggie, yep.
E: What's your doggie's name?
JB: Spot.
     Spot doggie puppy dog.
     They go pee-pee.
     Go pee-pee (pointing to the floor)
     Smell (holding nose, laughing)
     I go fight doggie (kicking the air)
     Puppy dog go bite. (McCardle and Wilson, 1993: 95)

JB's utterances reveal a number of grammatical immaturities for a child of this age. He omits the inflectional suffix *–es* in his first utterance. His utterances are short, sometimes only a single word, and contain nouns (Spot) and verbs (smell) to the exclusion of other grammatical categories. There are no conjunction words (e.g. 'and') linking his utterances. JB has quite possibly selected an incorrect pronoun form 'they' if he is intending to refer to his own dog Spot (the most obvious referent) rather than to dogs in general. Other features include his use of immature lexical items, such as the onomatopoeic form *woof woof* instead of the verb 'bark'. Finally, JB makes extensive and effective use of gesture to compensate for his limited grammatical skills.

The rate of lexical acquisition is considerably delayed in children with intellectual disability. Oliver and Buckley (1994) studied vocabulary development in 17 children with DS, all of whom were between 1 and 4 years of age at the start of the study. These investigators found that an expressive vocabulary of 10 words was achieved by these children at 27.3 months, a delay of around 12 months. These early acquired words are similar to those used by typically developing children, with Daddy, Mummy, bye-bye and a person's name the four most commonly produced. As in typically developing children, some children with DS experienced a 'vocabulary explosion'. The mean age of this explosion was 30 months when an average vocabulary of 24.4 words had been acquired. At this point, children with DS acquired around 10–30 new words per month compared with 30–50 words per month in typically developing children. Although vocabulary development has been most extensively studied in DS, lexical acquisition has also been investigated in other children with intellectual disability. Angelillo et al. (2010) studied an Italian boy with Floating-Harbor syndrome and borderline intellectual disability. At 48 months, this child's understanding of words was equivalent to a language age of 36 to 41 months, while his ability to name pictures representing body parts and common objects was equivalent to a language age of less than 30 months. Axelrad et al. (2007) studied 16 subjects with Costello syndrome. These subjects had a mean full-scale IQ score of 57, placing them in the range of mild intellectual disability. Both receptive and expressive vocabulary abilities were tested and were found to be in the extremely low range.

There is now considerable evidence that children with intellectual disability experience deficits in pragmatics and discourse skills. Laws and Bishop (2004) observed significant levels of pragmatic language impairment in 17 of their 19 subjects with WS. The Children's Communication Checklist (Bishop, 1998) was completed for each of these subjects as well as for children and adolescents with DS, children with specific language impairment and typically developing children. Only subjects with WS achieved a pragmatic composite score below the 132 cut-off indicative of impairment. Annaz et al. (2009) examined the comprehension of metaphor in 10 children with WS aged between 6;0 and 10;08 years. Metaphor comprehension was significantly poorer in these children than in typically developing children and fell below receptive vocabulary level in subject with WS. Reilly et al. (2004) examined the production of narratives in 36 children with WS. These children ranged in age from 4;9 to 12;9 years and had a mean full-scale IQ of 55, which placed them in the mild to moderate range of intellectual disability. The wordless picture book *Frog, where are you?* (Mayer, 1969) was used to elicit narratives from these subjects with WS and from typically developing children. In order to demonstrate how aspects of narrative production were disordered in the subjects with WS in this study, the attempts of some of these children to describe one of the pictures in this story are reproduced below. The picture in question depicts a young boy looking into a hole in the ground in search of his frog. Meanwhile, in the background, his dog is jumping at a beehive that is hanging from the branch of a tree. Utterances produced by age-matched, typically developing children are also presented for comparison:

Williams syndrome children:

A   (7;11 yrs) And then all of a sudden the dog finds some bees flying.
B   (9;5 yrs) The beehive is down and the bees are all over him and the boy is sitting down.
C   (9;10 yrs) So many bees! The boy said "Ow! Somebody stung me!"
D   (9;11 yrs) I think that the beehive may fall onto the boy.

Typically developing children:

E   (7;0 yrs) The dog knocked down the hive and the little boy went looking in the tree for the frog.
F   (8;2 yrs) They looked in the beehive and in the hole but could not find the frog.
G   (9;8 yrs) The boy started calling for the frog and the dog was barking at the bees.
H   (9;10 yrs) The boy stuck his head in a hole, looking for the frog, while the dog was barking at some bees.

The typically developing children have little difficulty establishing the 'search' theme of the story. All these children describe the boy as engaged in some type of search activity. Indeed, three of these children – F, G and H – give prominence to the boy's search by describing it first in the utterance (even if F incorrectly describes the boy as looking in the beehive). The utterances produced by the children with WS, however, make no reference whatsoever to the boy's search for his frog. In their descriptions of the same scenario, these children have focused on a background detail – the dog jumping at the beehive – to the complete exclusion of establishing the story's 'search' theme. The neglect of theme is particularly evident in the utterance produced by child B. The boy is described by this child as sitting down, when in fact he is crouched down in order to search a hole in the ground. The children with WS also describe actions that are not shown in the picture (e.g. the boy is stung) and speculate about things which may happen but are not actually depicted (e.g. the beehive falling onto the boy). In short, the children with WS produce narratives that contain information peripheral to the story, while the theme is largely neglected.

KEY POINTS: Language disorder in intellectual disability

- Children may fail to acquire language on account of cognitive or intellectual disability; these children are described as having a learning disability in the UK
- Intellectual disability is diagnosed on the basis of intelligence quotient (IQ) scores; an individual with an IQ score less than 70 is diagnosed as having intellectual disability
- Intellectual disability is associated with a range of conditions: genetic and chromosomal syndromes (e.g. Down syndrome), infections (e.g. meningitis), pre-natal exposure to cocaine and alcohol (e.g. foetal alcohol syndrome), oxygen deprivation during birth, metabolic disorders (e.g. phenylketonuria), etc.
- Language can be compromised at all levels (e.g. phonology, syntax) both receptively and expressively
- In severe cases of intellectual disability, language may not emerge at all

---

3.5 Language in autism spectrum disorders

In this section, we examine the language and communication skills of a sizeable and growing population of children and adults with autism spectrum disorders (ASDs). In the fifth edition of the *Diagnostic and Statistical Manual of Mental Disorders* (American Psychiatric Association, 2013), the diagnostic category of autism spectrum disorders results from the merger of three earlier categories: autistic disorder (autism), Asperger's syndrome and pervasive developmental disorder, not otherwise specified. This is not the place to give a detailed characterisation of these disorders (see section 3.3 in Cummings (2008), for an extended discussion). However, some features of the ASDs are noteworthy in this context. Much is now known about the epidemiology of these disorders. In its review of autism research, the Medical Research Council found that the average prevalence from all studies published by the year 2000 is

10 per 10,000 for autistic disorder and 2.5 per 10,000 for Asperger's syndrome (Medical Research Council, 2001). ASDs affect many more males than females. Boys with the autism phenotype typically outnumber girls by at least four to one (Skuse, 2000). There is also evidence that the number of children being diagnosed with ASDs is increasing, a development that may reflect changing diagnostic thresholds and better case ascertainment. Powell et al. (2000) found that incidence rates for classical childhood autism increased by 18 per cent per year between 1991 and 1996. Much less is known about the aetiology of ASDs. Genetic, neurobiological and psychological factors have all been advanced as possible aetiologies of the ASDs.

Approximately 50 per cent of individuals with autistic disorder do not develop functional speech (O'Brien and Pearson, 2004). For those individuals with autism who do become verbal communicators, language can be markedly deviant. Although linguistic deficits are most pronounced at the level of pragmatics, studies have also found evidence of impairments in prosody and structural aspects of language. Paul et al. (2005) examined the production and perception of three prosodic elements (stress, intonation and phrasing) in a group of 27 subjects with ASD (average age = 16.8 years). Each of these elements was examined in two prosodic functions: a grammatical function and a pragmatic/affective function. These investigators found significant differences between subjects with ASD and a group of typically developing subjects in the grammatical production of stress, as well as in the pragmatic/affective perception and production of stress. In a case study of the phonology of an 8-year-old boy with autism, Wolk and Edwards (1993) found that stops, nasals and glides were generally present and fricatives, affricates and the liquid /r/ were absent. Several phonological processes (e.g. velar fronting) were observed to persist beyond the expected age and some unusual sound changes (e.g. extensive glottal replacement and segment coalescence) also occurred. There was also evidence of chronological mismatch and restricted use of contrasts in this child's speech. Kjelgaard and Tager-Flusberg (2001) found significant impairments of vocabulary, syntax and semantics in a subgroup of children with autism whose language was defined as borderline or impaired. This finding led these investigators to conclude that there is a distinct subgroup of autistic children with SLI, a conclusion that is contrary to the standard use of the SLI diagnostic label (see section 3.3).

Pragmatic deficits in individuals with ASD include difficulties in the production and comprehension of speech acts, in the use and understanding of non-literal language and in the ability to draw upon contextual information during language interpretation. Martin and McDonald (2004) found that individuals with Asperger's syndrome performed significantly more poorly than controls on tasks requiring the interpretation of ironic jokes. These subjects were more likely to conclude that the protagonist in stories was lying rather than telling an ironic joke. Surian (1996) examined the detection of utterances that violate Grice's maxims by children with autism. It was found that most of the children with autism in the study performed at chance on this detection task, while normal children and children with SLI performed above chance. Emerich et al.

(2003) investigated the ability of adolescents with high-functioning autism or Asperger's syndrome to comprehend humorous material. Results confirmed the presence of a breakdown in the comprehension of humorous material in subjects with autism. Loukusa et al. (2007) found that children with Asperger's syndrome or high-functioning autism engaged in certain types of error when asked contextually demanding questions. These children's errors revealed that they had tried to use contextual information, but had done so incorrectly. Other errors involved topic drifts. An example of the former type of error is given below. A 10-year-old boy with Asperger's syndrome is told a story which is followed by a question. The boy's response to the question reveals that he has gleaned from the wider context that the dog is misbehaving for the woman. However, this rather general interpretation of the events in the story overlooks the altogether more specific focus of the woman's command, which is to get the dog to come to her:

> The woman runs over and calls the dog to come to her. However, the dog doesn't obey the woman. Two boys are standing near the dog watching them. The woman shouts 'Help!' to the boys and 'Here!' to the dog.
>
> *Question*:   What does the woman mean when she shouts 'Here!' to the dog?
>
> *Response*:   The woman has problems with the dog.

The topic drift in the response of this 11-year-old boy with Asperger's syndrome occurs after he has successfully answered the question posed to him. However, he very quickly strays from the content of the passage to begin talking about the railways in Finland (the boy is Finnish):

> A family is about to start eating their dinner soon. A girl is standing near the oven. The mother says to the girl: 'Be careful'.
>
> *Question*:   What does the mother mean?
>
> *Response*:   That she won't burn herself by the way yet another odd thing (points to the table in the picture) here there is perspective, but inside the oven there isn't any. This is a bit like when it when er-er- when Finland's biggest wait, they were building railroads when an inspect-, wait, inspect-, an official came to inspect, that-that- they did. Why are those rails narrowing over there (mimicking a haughty official)? See Mr. official something, it-it-it- is this thing called perspective Finland's railways will have none of this perspective, remove it (mimicking a haughty official).

Pragmatic disorders in ASD are increasingly being linked to theory of mind (ToM) deficits in this clinical population. Theory of mind describes the cognitive capacity to attribute mental states both to one's own mind and to the minds of others. To the extent that pragmatic interpretation involves the exchange and recovery of a particular type of mental state (viz., communicative intentions), it is unsurprising that pragmatic skills should be disrupted in children and adults with ASD. At least one of the responses given in Loukusa et al.'s (2007) study suggests a ToM deficit on the part of the child concerned.

This 7-year-old boy with Asperger's syndrome is unable to conceive of another person as having mental states that are different from his own. He has enjoyed the experience of climbing a tree and thus reasons that the boy in the picture must feel likewise:

The boy sits up in the tree and a wolf is at the bottom of the tree.

Question: How does the boy feel?

Response: Fun because he climbs up the tree. I always have fun when I climb up a tree.

Studies have confirmed the presence of a ToM component in pragmatic deficits in ASD. Ziatas et al. (2003) examined assertive speech acts in children with autism and children with Asperger's syndrome. It was found that children with autism used significantly lower proportions of assertions involving explanations and descriptions than children with SLI or normally developing children. When mental assertions were analysed further, it was found that children with autism and Asperger's syndrome referred predominantly to desire and made few references to thought and belief. Ziatas et al. relate these findings to ToM impairments in the children with autism. In their study of the interpretation of ironic jokes by individuals with Asperger's syndrome, Martin and McDonald (2004) found that second order ToM reasoning was significantly associated with the ability to interpret non-literal utterances. Studies such as these indicate the importance of considering cognitive factors within any discussion of pragmatic impairments in the ASD population.

Discourse skills, including the production of narratives and the ability to participate in conversational exchanges, are also compromised in children and adults with ASD. Diehl et al. (2006) analysed the narratives of 17 children with high-functioning ASDs. The narratives produced by these children were significantly less coherent than the narratives of typically developing children. Volden (2004) examined the conversational repair abilities of nine high-functioning children with ASD when they were confronted with requests for clarification. Children with ASD were significantly more likely than language age-matched controls to use an inappropriate response when faced with a request for clarification. Dobbinson et al. (1998) examined the conversations of Mary, a 28-year-old woman with autism. Among several conversational difficulties, Mary was often unable to maintain a topic that she introduced into an exchange. This is evident in the following exchange between Mary (M) and a researcher (R). All transcription conventions have been removed with the exception of micropauses (.) and timed pauses:

1   M: it was a surprise yes
2   it was a (.) it was a very nice birthday cake (.)
3   R: what was it like (1.27)
4   M: I had a look at it (.) and it was pink and it was very nice (.)
5   and Gloria (1.19) wh gl- gl- Gloria came down to the day centre she says to
6   me what's that (.)

7		she says to Amy wh- what's that is that- is that a- (1.01) is that a cake or- (.)
8		is that a pi- (.) is that (.) cake or piece of or or is it a rabbit (1.03)
9	R:	why was it- why did she say that (.)
10	M:	just a joke (.)
11	R:	why- (.) what was (.) why
12	M:	when I was walking up with Katy Post (2.09)
13	R:	aah right
14		why did she make a joke like that
15		why was that
16	M:	she was just saying it (1.72)
17	R:	what did the cake look like
18	M:	it looked very nice (.)

At turn 8, Mary makes a comment about a rabbit. This comment appears bizarre in the context of a conversation about a birthday cake and so leads the researcher to push Mary for an explanation of it. Having made the comment, Mary is clearly unable to give an adequate account of it. Initially, in turn 10, she attempts to justify it in terms of a joke. When this explanation still fails to satisfy the researcher's curiosity, she adds an utterance about when the rabbit comment was made in turn 12. However, the researcher continues to press Mary for a satisfactory explanation in turns 14 and 15. This elicits a further utterance from Mary in turn 16 which still fails to explain her statement about the rabbit. Eventually, after a pause of 1.72 seconds, the researcher clearly decides that she is not going to get a satisfactory explanation from Mary and decides to return to the topic of the birthday cake in turn 17.

Perhaps unsurprisingly, researchers are increasingly linking discourse impairments in children and adults with ASD to ToM deficits. Hale and Tager-Flusberg (2005) examined discourse skills – specifically, the use of topic-related contingent utterances – and ToM in 57 children with autism. Over one year, these children made significant gains in the ability to maintain a topic of discourse. Theory of mind contributed unique variance in the contingent discourse skills of these children beyond the significant contribution made by language skills. Capps et al. (2000) found that the narrative abilities of 13 children with autism were linked to performance on measures of ToM and to an index of conversational competence. Understanding the relationship between ToM and pragmatic and discourse deficits in ASD will be an important step in the development of effective communication interventions for clients with ASD.

KEY POINTS: Language in autism spectrum disorders

- A diagnosis of autism spectrum disorder is made on the basis of criteria in the fifth edition of the *Diagnostic and Statistical Manual of Mental Disorders* (American Psychiatric Association, 2013)

- Autistic disorder has a prevalence of 10 per 10,000 population; ASDs significantly more common in males than in females; a genetic aetiology appears likely
- Individuals with ASDs have marked impairments in social communication and social interaction. There are also restricted, repetitive patterns of behaviour, interests or activities
- Approximately half of children with autism become verbal communicators
- Prosodic disturbances are common; structural levels of language can also be impaired
- Most significant deficits are found in pragmatics and discourse skills
- Pragmatic and discourse deficits are increasingly being linked to ToM impairments

3.6   Assessment and treatment

The assessment and treatment of language across the different populations that we have considered in this chapter involve a range of techniques and skills. Although it is not possible to examine each of these in detail, we can nevertheless tease out a number of general principles that guide assessment and treatment. Firstly, assessment must consider both the structure and use of language. Assessment should include some component of formal language testing, the traditional means of assessing language structure. But it must go on to examine language skills – principally, pragmatic and discourse skills – that are not well assessed by means of a battery of language tests. It is not unusual to find cases of children whose performance on language tests does not reflect their everyday communicative skills. A child may complete a language test with only moderate difficulties. Yet, in a less structured context which places greater demands on his social use of language, his language disorder may be altogether more severe. Similarly, a child may exhibit an auditory comprehension deficit on formal testing which is compensated to a large extent using contextual cues in more naturalistic communicative interactions.

Secondly, the timing of assessment should reflect the fact that developmental language disorders do not stand still. In the case of a child with significant intellectual disability, the child's language status may remain relatively static. However, for other children language skills may improve or deteriorate over time. The language skills of a child with TBI may improve as the underlying neurological injury begins to resolve. A child with LKS may experience a rapid or more gradual decline in his or her language skills. In cases such as these, assessment must keep pace with changes in a child's language functioning.

Thirdly, assessment should reveal not just a child's linguistic weaknesses, but also his or her linguistic strengths. Knowing that certain syntactic constructions are intact while others are impaired, or that certain phonemic contrasts are present while others are absent, gives therapists a more complete picture of a child's language skills than is possible if assessment seeks only to list language problems. There are several advantages in characterising linguistic strengths as well as weaknesses. Intact language skills can serve as important indicators of the linguistic gains a child is likely to make. For example, if a child with DS and delayed expressive language can understand certain prepositions, there is a reasonable likelihood that he will go on to produce these same prepositions in his linguistic output. Another advantage of documenting linguistic strengths as well as weaknesses is that the former can be used as a guide as to what structures to target initially in therapy. For example, many clinicians subscribe to the view that sounds which are poorly discriminated or are not stimulable (i.e. the child cannot imitate a sound that is absent from his inventory immediately following the therapist's model) are poor initial targets for phonological therapy. If a therapist knows that a child with phonological disorder can at least discriminate /p/ from /b/, then this area of intact linguistic skill may be used as a basis for establishing this particular phonemic contrast in the child's spoken language. A further benefit of documenting linguistic and communicative strengths is that a weakness at one language level may be compensated by stronger or intact skills at another level. We saw in section 3.4, for example, how a child with FG syndrome was able to compensate for his poor expressive language skills through the effective use of gesture.

Fourthly, assessment should also examine non-linguistic skills as many of these skills relate indirectly to language and communication. For many of the children examined in this chapter, language is only one of several areas of impaired functioning. The child with intellectual disability in the presence of a syndrome, for example, may experience sensory problems (e.g. impaired vision) and memory and attention deficits, as well as impaired language skills. A language-disordered child with cerebral palsy may have difficulty controlling the movement of his or her arms. These additional problems, while not linguistic in nature, impact very directly on the type of language and communication intervention that may be appropriate for a child and should be thoroughly examined during assessment. A child with visual field problems may be unable to scan the symbols on a communication board attached to his wheelchair. A child with memory and attention deficits may struggle to learn even the simplest augmentative and alternative communication (AAC) systems. And a child with limited control of his or her arms may have to use head sticks instead of arm movements to point to symbols on a communication board or a computer screen. These additional deficits, which are commonplace in certain populations of children with language disorder, are by no means insignificant and must be comprehensively examined as part of the assessment process.

Such are the interconnections between assessment and treatment that each of these principles of assessment has a direct correlate in terms of treatment. Firstly, intervention must do more than merely target the comprehension and production of certain linguistic structures. It must also give children the means of putting those structures to effective communicative use within a range of different contexts. This will necessitate the use of treatment techniques in which pragmatic and social communication skills are emphasised alongside the training of specific linguistic structures. On some occasions, it may even mean neglecting to treat an impaired aspect of syntax or semantics where this aspect is unlikely to achieve a significant improvement in a child's overall communicative functioning. With the use of language an equally dominant consideration in intervention, sentence-level treatments that target syntactic and semantic structures must be justified in terms of the wider communicative gains that they achieve for a child.

Secondly, like assessment, treatment must keep pace with the changing nature of developmental language disorders. The child with a TBI may require AAC intervention in the weeks immediately following injury. As his neurological status improves, his dependence on an AAC system may diminish, at which point therapeutic activities with a focus on expressive language may become more prominent. A quite different treatment approach may need to be taken with the child who is gradually losing his expressive language skills. The child who is experiencing a regression of language skills as part of an autism spectrum disorder or in LKS will need therapy to reflect the courses of these conditions. In these cases, an alternative communication system must be instituted well before the point of mutism has been reached.

Thirdly, treatment should aim to exploit any areas of linguistic strength that have been identified during assessment. A child who displays skills in using world knowledge or contextual cues to compensate for an auditory comprehension deficit may gain more from an intervention that directly draws upon these skills than from one which targets aspects of receptive syntax and semantics as isolated linguistic structures. This is directly borne out in a study conducted by Kim and Lombardino (1991) who attempted to train the comprehension of two semantic constructions in four preschool children with intellectual disability. A script-based and a nonscript-based treatment were used. (A script or schema represents knowledge of the typical behaviour of people, etc. in a range of scenarios, for example, that people normally order food and pay a bill in a restaurant.) The constructions in question were agent-action-object (e.g. 'Make Mickey kiss the cup') and action-object-locative (e.g. 'Put the cup on top of the ice box') which were trained in three routines (popcorn-making, pudding-making and milkshake-making). In three of the four subjects in this study, the script-based treatment was more effective than the nonscript-based treatment in facilitating comprehension of the targeted semantic constructions. Clearly, the ability to draw upon real-world knowledge in the form of scripts served as a catalyst for language learning in most of the children in this study.

Finally, the non-linguistic features recorded during assessment have a direct influence upon the types of treatment that are appropriate in a particular case. These features include visual skills and deficits, the presence and extent of any cognitive or intellectual disability and physical disabilities (e.g. limb dyspraxia). The intellectual disability, that is a feature of many of the syndromes examined in this chapter, may preclude the use of Blissymbols as an AAC system in children who have language disorder – the content of the pictures is not readily understood by these children. However, the good visual and motor skills found in children with DS are generally credited with explaining the relative ease with which these children can acquire manual signs in an AAC system such as the Makaton vocabulary. A child's skills and deficits across a range of non-linguistic areas have a direct impact upon the type of treatments that can be beneficially pursued and must be considered an integral part of the intervention process.

SUGGESTIONS FOR FURTHER READING

Abbeduto, L. (ed.) (2003) *Language and Communication in Mental Retardation* (San Diego, CA: Academic Press).

Hulme, C. and Snowling, M.J. (2009) *Developmental Disorders of Language and Cognition* (Chichester, West Sussex: Wiley-Blackwell), ch. 4 (specific language impairment) and ch. 8 (autism).

Rvachew, S. (2014) 'Developmental phonological disorder', in L. Cummings (ed.) *Cambridge Handbook of Communication Disorders* (Cambridge: Cambridge University Press), pp. 61–72.

EXERCISES

Exercise 3.1 Below is a list of phonological processes which were used by Crary (1983: 136) to analyse the spontaneous speech of 20 children selected from the caseloads of practising speech-language clinicians. A description of each process is provided. Match each of the items in List A to the correct phonological process in List B:

List A:

(a)	'sun':	sʌn→tʌn	(j)	'baby':	bebɪ→beʔɪ
(b)	'toes':	toz→koz	(k)	'cup':	kʌp→tʌp
(c)	'daddy':	dædɪ→bætɪ	(l)	'run':	rʌn→wʌn
(d)	'light':	laɪt→jaɪt	(m)	'sun':	sʌn→hʔn
(e)	'dog':	dɔg→dɔ	(n)	'two':	to→do
(f)	'elephant':	ɛləfənt→ɛfənt	(o)	'telephone':	tɛləfon→tɛfon
(g)	'cut':	kʌt→ʌt	(p)	'puppy':	pʌpɪ→pʌi:
(h)	'sea':	si→zi	(q)	'go':	go→do
(i)	'do':	du→gu	(r)	'dog':	dɔg→dɔʔ

List B:

(1) **Final consonant deletion:** Syllable final consonant deleted or replaced by glottal stop
(2) **Stopping:** Fricatives or affricates replaced by stops
(3) **Gliding:** Liquids replaced by glides
(4) **Fronting:** Velar or palatal sound produced at a more anterior point of articulation
(5) **Backing:** Alveolar sound produced as a velar sound
(6) **Weak syllable deletion:** Unstressed syllable omitted from polysyllabic word
(7) **Prevocalic voicing:** A voiceless obstruent becomes voiced in the prevocalic position

(8) **Initial consonant deletion:** Initial consonant omitted
(9) **Labialisation:** Replacement of a lingual consonant by a labial consonant
(10) **Glottal replacement:**
    (a) Replacement of an oral consonant by /ʔ, h/
    (b) Deletion of intervocalic consonants

Exercise 3.2 Errors in morphosyntax are common in the expressive language of children with specific language impairment. Reilly et al. (2004) recorded the following utterances produced by children with SLI during the narrative production task *Frog, where are you?* (Mayer, 1969). For each utterance, describe the type of morphosyntactic error committed by the child.

Child A (4;3 years): Frog going to sleep with the dog.
Child B (4;4 years): The dog get in the bowl.
Child C (4;4 years): He growl.
Child D (6;4 years): The little boy putted his shirt on.
Child E (7;6 years): Then when they woked up in the morning they saw the frog was gone.
Child F (9;3 years): The frog is jumping out of the jar and the dog and the boy is sleep.
Child G (12;9 years): The dog and the boy are looking on the frog.

Exercise 3.3 The utterances in the table below are produced by children with Williams syndrome (WS) and Down syndrome (DS) who were studied by Singer Harris et al. (1997). The utterances were collected when these children had productive vocabularies of approximately 430 words and 600 words, respectively (you will note the children have different chronological ages when their productive vocabularies are the same). Your task is to contrast the quite different language skills of these children at these two points in language development.

WS (3;5 years; 434 words):	**DS (4;2 years; 426 words):**
Karen read a book with Daddy.	Baby go bye-bye.
Karen go on turtle in the pool.	Stop baby don't.
I like a bottle please.	Three, four, five.
WS (3;3 years; 610 words):	**DS (3;10 years; 601 words):**
Mamma, need to pick up toys, vacuum floor.	Gonna go car.
I go my room get one book bring out here.	Matt want bottle.
Please have some grapes in my cup right now.	Here-ya-go/Hold me.

Exercise 3.4 Approximately half of all children with autism fail to develop verbal communication. For those children who do acquire spoken language, problems are most pronounced at the pragmatic and discourse levels of language. These problems are particularly evident during conversational exchanges with others. In the following exchange from Crystal and Varley (1998: 161), a therapist (T) is talking to a child (P) with autism during play. Describe in detail why this exchange is not particularly satisfactory:

T: What are you going to do with that car now?
P: I like my car (pushing it on the floor)
T: Look. I've got one like that.
P: In here it goes (pushing car into garage)
T: Don't forget to shut the doors.
P: Find the man now (looking about)

ANSWERS TO EXERCISES

Exercise 3.1

(a)	stopping	(j)	glottal replacement (part a)
(b)	backing	(k)	fronting
(c)	labialisation	(l)	gliding
(d)	gliding	(m)	glottal replacement (part a)
(e)	final consonant deletion	(n)	prevocalic voicing
(f)	weak syllable deletion	(o)	weak syllable deletion
(g)	initial consonant deletion	(p)	glottal replacement (part b)
(h)	prevocalic voicing	(q)	fronting
(i)	backing	(r)	final consonant deletion

Exercise 3.2

Child A: Omission of definite article 'the' and auxiliary verb 'is'
Child B: Omission of inflectional suffix –s
Child C: Omission of inflectional suffix –s
Child D: Use of inflectional suffix –ed when it is not required
Child E: Inflectional suffix –ed is attached to irregular past tense verb 'woke'; auxiliary verb 'was' used instead of 'had'
Child F: Use of auxiliary 'is' instead of 'are'; omission of inflectional suffix –ing
Child G: Use of preposition 'on' instead of 'at'

Exercise 3.3

The most noticeable difference between the children with WS and DS is that children with WS are producing significantly longer sentences than children with DS at both points in language development. When productive vocabulary is approximately 430 words, the average number of words in the sentences produced by children with WS is six. This compares with an average of only three to four words in the sentences produced by children with DS at the same stage. When a productive vocabulary of approximately 600 words is reached, the average length of sentences produced by children with WS has increased to nine words, while the average length of the sentences produced by children with DS remains at just three words. This difference in sentence length reflects a considerably greater grammatical capacity on the part of the children with WS.

At both productive vocabulary points, there are considerable differences in the grammatical structure of the sentences produced by children with WS and DS. Children with DS use content words such as nouns (e.g. car, bottle, baby) and lexical verbs (e.g. want, go, stop) to the almost complete exclusion of words from other grammatical categories. Because content words convey most meaning in language, the children with DS are still able to communicate quite effectively notwithstanding their obvious grammatical limitations. As well as omitting words such as prepositions (*in* car) and articles (*a/the* bottle), the children with DS also omit inflectional morphemes on main verbs (Matt wants bottle; Baby goes bye-bye). The children with DS also use sentences which are learned, automatic forms. These sentences are *Three, four, five* and *Here-ya-go*.

As well as producing longer sentences than the children with DS, the children with WS also use words from a greater range of grammatical classes than the children with DS. These classes include prepositions (*on* turtle; *in* my cup), articles (*a* book; *the* pool), quantity and possessive determiners (*some* grapes; *my* cup) and adverbs (*right now*). There are still occasions when words from these classes are omitted (e.g. a preposition is omitted in 'I go (into) my room' and an article is omitted in 'Karen go on (the) turtle'). Other omissions include pronouns (e.g. bring (it) out here) and conjunctions (e.g. I go my room (and) get one book). Nevertheless, the greater range of grammatical classes in evidence in the utterances of the children with WS reflects the superior grammatical skills of these children. Even within grammatical classes, children with WS use a greater range of words than children with DS. For example, across the six utterances produced by the children with DS, only four verbs are used. However, the children with WS use nine verbs across their six utterances. The children with WS use inflectional morphemes on nouns (toys; grapes), but omit inflectional morphemes on lexical verbs (Karen read a book; Karen go on turtle).

Exercise 3.4

On first sight, it may seem that a proper conversational exchange is taking place – the child with autism is taking turns with the therapist at appropriate points in the exchange. However, upon further examination, it is clear that the child's utterances are not responses to the therapist's utterances and even fail to engage meaningfully with those utterances. Each response fails to address the therapist's question (What are you going to do with that car now?), statement (I've got one like that) or imperative (Don't forget to shut the doors). The child is essentially conducting a monologue that just happens to be broken up by the therapist's utterances.

Acquired Speech Disorders

4

4.1 Acquired speech disorders and their causes

Previously intact speech production skills can become disordered in adults. An adult may sustain a head trauma in a road traffic accident, violent assault or fall. He or she may develop a brain tumour, sustain a stroke (or cerebrovascular accident – CVA) or acquire a cerebral infection (e.g. meningitis). In later life, adults may develop a neurological disorder like Parkinson's disease (PD), multiple sclerosis (MS) or motor neurone disease. Malignant tumours or injuries may necessitate the surgical removal of all or part of an articulator (e.g. the tongue in glossectomy). Additionally, surgery may inadvertently result in damage to the network of nerves that innervate the speech musculature. A speech disorder is a common (though not inevitable) consequence of each of the events just described. If a speech disorder does result from the events described, its impact can be significant, affecting all aspects of an individual's personal, social and occupational functioning. It is in an effort to mitigate these adverse effects that speech and language therapists assess and treat the disorders that will be examined in this chapter. In order to do so effectively, however, they must understand the epidemiology, aetiology and clinical features of acquired speech disorders. While this chapter cannot give an exhaustive account of all acquired speech disorders along each of these parameters, it will nonetheless present the reader with a detailed introduction to this diverse group of communication disorders. In doing so, the reader will become aware of the complex considerations that must be countenanced by clinicians and therapists who are involved in the clinical management of adults with acquired speech disorders.

The population of acquired speech disorders can be subclassified into disorders that have a structural aetiology and those with an aetiology that is neurological in nature. If any part of speech production anatomy is compromised in an adult through disease or injury, an acquired speech disorder will result. In Chapter 7, we will examine the effects on the production of voice of laryngeal trauma and disease. However, in this chapter we will examine one particular speech disorder that is caused by the removal, either in whole or in part, of a key articulator. The articulator in question is the tongue and its removal during a surgical procedure called a 'glossectomy' is necessitated by the presence of a malignant tumour. Although this is a little known (but highly specialised) area of work in speech and language therapy, the implications of a glossectomy for speech production are considerable (the impact of this surgical procedure on feeding will not be examined in this chapter). The speech disorder in a patient who has undergone glossectomy is not discussed with a view to representing all the different ways in which speech production may be disrupted in adults with impaired anatomy. Quite different speech anomalies may occur in adults who have experienced surgical removal of parts of the palate and jaw or serious trauma to one of these structures. Nevertheless, a discussion of glossectomy will serve to demonstrate how speech can become disordered in adults who have no prior communication difficulties as a result of structural anomalies.

A number of the diseases and injuries described above can compromise the central and peripheral nervous systems and give rise to neurogenic speech disorders such as dysarthria and apraxia of speech. A CVA may cause dysarthria by damaging the parts of the primary motor cortex that control the speech musculature or one or more of the cranial nerves that innervate the articulators and other structures involved in speech production. In PD, dysarthria is related to a pathological process in which cells responsible for the production of the neurotransmitter dopamine in the substantia nigra of the brain are depleted in substantial numbers. In MS, a quite different pathological process known as demyelination (destruction of the myelin sheath of neurones) can interrupt nerve impulse transmission and, in so doing, cause dysarthria. An adult may have a cranial nerve severed inadvertently during laryngectomy or thoracic and thyroid surgery. The extent and severity of any resulting dysarthria will depend on the particular group of speech muscles that was innervated by the severed nerve. Infections such as meningitis and encephalitis may cause permanent damage to the brain's motor cortex. If this damage involves areas that control speech production, dysarthria will likely be one of the neurological sequelae. Finally, an adult may sustain brain damage of varying degrees in a traumatic brain injury (TBI). This damage may be restricted to a particular neuroanatomical site or may involve several such sites, as is often seen in a TBI that is caused by a road traffic accident. The motor speech areas in the brain may be so severely damaged that intelligible speech is no longer possible. In a case of severe TBI, a patient may be given a diagnosis of anarthria rather than dysarthria.

Although the acquired speech disorders examined in this chapter mirror the developmental speech disorders discussed in Chapter 2, it would be wrong to assume that acquired disorders have the same clinical features as developmental disorders. There are several reasons why such an assumption is incorrect. Firstly, although developmental and acquired speech disorders have certain aetiologies in common (e.g. CVA), there are many other aetiologies that distinguish them. For example, genetic and chromosomal syndromes can only be within the aetiology of developmental dysarthria, while neurological conditions such as PD can only be part of the aetiology of acquired dysarthria.

Secondly, it is to be expected that the impact of disease and injury on the developing nervous system will be different from the impact of the same events on the mature nervous system. The young child's brain has greater plasticity than the brain of an adult. This means that it can adapt to disease and injury in ways that are largely foreclosed to the adult. The result of increased plasticity in children is that while children may emerge from a stroke with negligible impairment, a similar stroke may cause a severe impairment of functioning in adults. We can therefore expect to see different manifestations of brain damage in children and adults, even when this damage is of the same type and extent in both child and adult clients. Thirdly, adults – unless in cases of very severe damage – have access to some residual speech capacity that will be absent in the child who has not acquired this capacity in the first place. This residual capacity will play a largely facilitative role in the recovery of speech function in the adult. Its absence in the child is a further reason why it is not possible simply to 'read off' the features of an acquired speech disorder from its developmental counterpart.

4.2 Glossectomy

'Glossectomy' is the partial or total surgical removal of the tongue and is undertaken as a form of treatment for a malignant carcinoma of the tongue. On account of the wide-ranging implications of this procedure for speech and feeding, this operation is performed as a last resort when it is clear that chemotherapy and radiotherapy alone will not treat the carcinoma in question. In the US, the National Cancer Institute's SEER statistics reveal that 7,690 men and 3,300 women will be diagnosed with cancer of the tongue in 2010 (Altekruse et al., 2010). In the same year, 1,990 people will die of the disease. The incidence rate of tongue cancer is 2.9 per 100,000 men and women per year. As might be expected, survival rates are directly related to the stage of disease at diagnosis. SEER statistics show that five-year relative survival is 77.3 per cent if a tumour is localised (confined to primary site) at diagnosis, 55.2 per cent if a tumour is regional (spread to regional lymph nodes) at diagnosis and 29.5 per cent if it is distant (cancer has metastasised) at diagnosis. The most common type of tongue cancer is a squamous cell carcinoma. Less commonly found carcinomas of the tongue include adenoid cystic carcinoma and mucoepidermoid carcinoma (Leong et al., 2007; Luna-Ortiz et al., 2009). As well as tobacco smoking and alcohol consumption, other risk factors for tongue cancer include certain viruses (e.g. Epstein-Barr virus and human papilloma virus (HPV) 16 and 18), cultural practices – prevalent in parts of India – such as reverse smoking (the burning end of cigars is within the mouth) and dipping (placing a mixture of Khaini tobacco and slaked lime in the lower gingival groove), and sexual behaviours including oral sex (although this is likely to be related to HPV infection) (Heck et al., 2010; Stich et al., 1992; Zheng et al., 2010).

WEBSITE: Carcinoma of the tongue

View the images of squamous cell carcinoma of the tongue on the website. These images have been reproduced with the kind permission of Bechara Y. Ghorayeb, MD (www.houstonoto.com/PicturesLarynx.html). Squamous cell carcinomas are associated with chronic smoking and can occur in a range of positions on the tongue.

The loss of so central an articulator as the tongue has serious implications for a patient's speech function. Unusual labial, mandibular and pharyngeal speech compensations can result in relatively good intelligibility (Kazi et al., 2007). Some of these compensations are described by Morrish (1988) in a study of the speech of a 69-year-old male patient known as GS. GS had undergone a total glossectomy following a diagnosis of invasive squamous cell carcinoma at the base of the tongue. His speech was rated as 58 per cent and 65 per cent comprehensible according to auditory tests that involved phonetically naïve students rating the intelligibility of a passage of conversation and sentences, respectively. GS had developed a number of compensatory strategies involving the jaw and lips for the articulation of plosive consonants. Specifically, bilabial and alveolar plosives were distinguished by jaw lowering (/p, b/ had a consistently lower posture than /t, d/), jaw protrusion (/p, b/ were more protruded than /t, d/) and bilabial protrusion (/t, d/ were more protruded than /p, b/). Alveolar and velar plosives were not similarly distinguished. Notwithstanding GS's compensatory adjustments, only /p, b/ were correctly perceived by listeners at a rate better than chance. The perception of alveolar and velar plosives was largely in the direction of /p, b/. Compensatory articulations were also observed in GS's production of vowels. During videofluoroscopy, GS was found to differentiate between the production of high and low vowels through compensatory use of the epiglottis and the grafted flap that re-lined the floor of the mouth. The epiglottis and grafted flap were particularly active during the production of low vowels with strong retraction of the epiglottis and extreme raising and bunching of the flap serving to narrow the pharynx.

Patient GS had undergone a total glossectomy. However, patients who have parts of their tongues removed in a partial glossectomy may also experience speech difficulties and develop a range of compensatory articulations. Barry and Timmermann (1985) studied seven patients who underwent partial glossectomy for the treatment of carcinoma of the tongue. Surgery in these patients, who were aged 32 to 62 years, ranged from removal of two thirds of the tongue to removal of a small part of tongue tissue. In some patients, additional surgical procedures were performed including partial removal of the jaw or fixation of the tongue body to the floor of the mouth. These patients, who were all German speakers, received an assessment of their speech. A narrow phonetic transcription of some of their single-word productions is given in Table 4.1.

These productions, which were uttered by different glossectomy speakers, reveal a number of articulatory anomalies, as well as efforts to compensate for those anomalies. Plosive sounds involving the tongue (i.e. /t, d, k, g/) are not used by these speakers. In the data presented below, they are substituted by fricatives

Table 4.1 Single-word productions of German speakers with glossectomy

Word	Meaning	Phonemic norm	Speaker production
stritten	quarrelled	/ˈʃtʁɪtən/	[ʁ·ɪʔn]
Nordwind	north wind	/ˈnɔːtvɪnt/	[ˈnɔːʔvɪnʔ]
stärkere	stronger	/ˈʃtɛəkəʁə/	[ˈfpɛ·χ·ʁə]
warmen	warm	/ˈvaːmən/	[ˈvaːm̃m]
Mantel	overcoat	/ˈmantəl/	[ˈmamʔl]
gehüllt	wrapped	/gəˈhYlt/	[ɣəˈɦYlʔ]
einig	united	/ˈaenɪç/	[ˈaɪnɪə]
stärkeren	stronger	/ˈʃtɛəkəʁən/	[ˈʃpɛʁəʁn]
Weges	way	/ˈveːgəs/	[ˈveˑɣəs]
daherkam	came along	/daˈheəkaːm/	[s̃aˈɦɛəxam]

Source: Based on Barry and Timmermann (1985).

(/g/→[ɣ] in 'gehüllt'), glottal stops (/t/→[ʔ] in 'stritten'), or bilabial stops (/t/→[p] in 'stärkeren'). These substitutions have compensatory qualities. The speaker who is unable to use the tongue to achieve closure at the alveolar ridge for /t/ uses a glottal place of articulation instead (blockage of the pulmonary airstream at the glottis is possible). Similarly, [p] is used in place of /t/, because the bilabial plosive achieves the required blockage of the airstream when an alveolar place of articulation is not possible. The patient who cannot elevate the back of the tongue to make contact with the velum in order to produce the voiced velar plosive /g/ approximates this articulation by using the voiced velar fricative [ɣ]. This lack of velar closure was confirmed by electropalatography (EPG) in the patient who uttered 'gehüllt'. The voiceless equivalent of this articulatory pattern is evident in /k/→[x] in 'daherkam'. A similar lack of closure, this time involving the alveolar place of articulation, accounts for /d/→[s] also in 'daherkam'. This, too, was confirmed by EPG. In this last example, there is also some voicing confusion. The voiced alveolar plosive /d/ is replaced by the voiceless alveolar fricative. The lost voicing seems to be displaced onto the voiceless glottal fricative producing its voiced counterpart (i.e. /h/→[ɦ] in 'daherkam').

In two further substitutions, the voiceless velar plosive is replaced, not by velar fricatives, but by uvular fricatives. This can be seen in /k/→[χ] in 'stärkere' and /k/→[ʁ] in 'stärkeren'. This retracted pattern of articulation is explained by Barry and Timmermann (1985) as follows. The speaker who produces one of these substitutions had one third of the tongue removed. The remaining part of the tongue was sewn to the floor of the mouth. The fixed tongue body made palatal contact impossible. Back closures were consequently shifted back to a point where the mandibular–maxillar angle provided natural proximity of the tongue and soft palate. As a result, uvular sounds came to substitute velar sounds. Several other features of the above data are noteworthy. Consonant clusters that contained /t/ were either reduced (/ʃtʁ/→[ʁ] in 'stritten') or /t/ in these clusters was replaced by a bilabial plosive (/ʃt/→[ʃp] in 'stärkeren'). The difficulty with the alveolar place of articulation extends beyond plosives to include nasals with /n/→[m] in 'warmen'. Once again, a bilabial articulation is taking the place of alveolar articulation in the patient with compromised lingual movement. Other evidence of attempts by these patients to replace problematic lingual articulations with other articulations include /ʃ/→[f] in 'stärkere' where a labiodental fricative takes the place of a palato-alveolar frica-tive, and /ç/→[θ] in 'einig' where a dental fricative replaces a palatal fricative. The second of these substitutions was produced by a patient whose tongue tip remained mobile but who had relative immobility of the tongue body. This set of tongue movements made dental friction possible where palatal friction could not be achieved.

Articulatory studies of patients who have undergone glossectomy have ena-bled researchers to draw conclusions about the type of tongue structure after surgery which leads to the best speech outcomes. Bressmann et al. (2009) assessed speech acceptability in 22 patients with partial glossectomies. These investigators found that the amount of tongue tissue resected predicted 41 per cent of the variance in post-surgical speech acceptability. Moreover, a defect size of more than 20.4 per cent of tongue tissue was found to be the critical cut-off point for poorer speech acceptability. According to Barry and Timmermann (1985), post-operative lingual mobility is more related to speech acceptability than the amount of tongue mass remaining after surgery. One of the seven patients studied by these investigators had very little of his tongue mass removed, but experienced post-operative paralysis of the back of his tongue. This patient's speech acceptability was judged to be less than that of two patients who had undergone more extensive surgical procedures involving the removal of larger amounts of tongue tissue (one quarter of the tongue and the right side of the mandible in one case, and the right side of the tongue and the mandible in the other case). Morrish (1988: 19) appears to concur with Barry and Timmermann when she claims that the motility of the remaining oral structures was the crucial factor in GS's recovery of speech function: 'We propose that the preservation of the hypoglossal nerve, the epiglottis and the extrinsic musculature of the tongue and larynx is more critical than an attempt to spare tongue tissue or to replace the surgical defect with a bulky flap'.

WEBSITE: Glossectomy

Listen to the audio file on the website of two patients who have undergone glossec-tomy. These speakers – a man and a woman – were studied by Morrish (1984, 1988). These patients can be heard reciting numbers from 1 to 20, producing the vowel sounds /i, u, a/ in isolation and engaged in connected speech. Rate how intelligible these speakers are during these respective tasks. What factors account for these different ratings? Note any compensatory articulations used by these patients.

KEY POINTS: Glossectomy

- Carcinomas of the tongue are the most common type of oral cancer; squamous cell carcinoma is the most common type of tongue cancer but other types (e.g. mucoepidermoid carcinoma) also exist
- Tongue cancer is more commonly found in men than women; risk factors include smoking, alcohol consumption, viruses (e.g. human papilloma virus – HPV), cultural practices (e.g. reverse smoking and dipping in parts of India) and oral sex (related to HPV infection)
- Removal of the tongue can be total (total glossectomy) or partial (partial glossectomy) and may be performed alongside other procedures (e.g. mandibulectomy); a range of flaps may be used to correct the oral cavity defect
- Speech of varying levels of intelligibility and acceptability is possible after glossectomy; compensatory articulations often develop spontaneously or as a result of therapy
- The best speech outcomes appear to be related more to the mobility of the tongue tissue that remains after surgery than to the amount of this tissue

---

4.3 Acquired dysarthria

Acquired dysarthria is a motor speech disorder that arises when illness, injury or disease damages the motor speech pathway. This pathway sets out from the primary motor cortex in the brain and terminates in the innervation of the different muscle groups that achieve speech production. In section 4.1, a number of the medical conditions and other events that can disrupt this pathway were described. They include cerebrovascular accidents (CVAs or strokes), brain tumours, TBI, cerebral infections such as meningitis and neurological disorders like PD and MS. Not all these conditions are equally significant causes of dysarthria in adults. While most cases of acquired dysarthria are related to the onset of a CVA, a much smaller number of dysarthria cases are caused by disorders such as MS, for example. This merely reflects the fact that many more people sustain CVAs than develop disorders such as MS – the prevalence of stroke can be as high as 833 per 100,000, while the average prevalence of MS is estimated to be 110 per 100,000 population (Bonita et al., 1997; Richards et al., 2002). However, although CVAs are a more common cause of dysarthria than a disorder like MS, dysarthria is less commonly one of the neurological sequelae of stroke than it is of MS. Hartelius et al. (2000) examined 77 individuals drawn from an MS population. In this cohort, the prevalence of mild to severe dysarthria was 51 per cent. Melo et al. (1992) studied 255 patients who sustained a first stroke. These investigators found dysarthria in 29 per cent of patients. This figure is likely to be higher than that found in other stroke populations, as Melo et al.'s subjects all displayed isolated hemiparesis (dysarthria is more likely to occur in the presence of this motor impairment).

The type and severity of dysarthria is related to the location and extent of a neurological lesion. Spastic and flaccid dysarthria is caused by damage to the upper and lower motor neurones, respectively. Spastic dysarthria is characterised by increased muscle tone (hypertonia), weakness, limited range of movement and slowness of movement. In flaccid dysarthria, there is decreased muscle tone (hypotonia), weakness, atrophy, reduced reflexes and fasciculations. Hypokinetic and hyperkinetic dysarthria are associated with damage to the basal ganglia and associated brainstem nuclei. 'Hypokinetic dysarthria' is a term that was originally used to characterise the speech features of PD: 'hypokinetic dysarthria is generally considered to be essentially synonymous with the dysarthria of (idiopathic) PD' (Adams and Dykstra, 2009: 166). Hyperkinetic dysarthria is found in a range of (quick and slow) hyperkinetic syndromes. The most common quick forms include chorea, myoclonus, tic disorders and ballismus; athetosis, tardive dyskinesia and dystonia are the most common slow forms. Tremor may occur in either form (Zraick and LaPointe, 2009). Ataxic dysarthria occurs when there is damage to the cerebellum and/or the nerve fibres leading to and from it. The main neuromuscular deficits associated with this type of dysarthria include inaccuracy of movement, irregular rhythm of repetitive movement, discoordination, slowness of individual and repetitive movements and hypotonia of affected muscles (Murdoch and Theodoros, 1998). Finally, mixed dysarthria is caused by damage to more than one of the neuroanatomical sites mentioned above. If both upper and lower motor neurones are damaged, as is the case in motor neurone disease, a flaccid-spastic dysarthria occurs. A mixed type, largely ataxic-spastic dysarthria, occurs in MS (Duffy, 1995).

One or more of the following speech production components is disordered in the client with acquired dysarthria: articulation, resonation, phonation, respiration and prosody. Such a client may be unable to spread his or her lips to articulate the vowel /i/ or may be unable to raise the back of the tongue to make contact with the velum for the articulation of /k/. Aside from articulatory disturbances, the adult with dysarthria may experience problems with resonation due to inadequate valving of the pulmonary airstream at the velopharyngeal port. If the velum is weak or paralysed, it may fail to elevate to the degree needed to close off the velopharyngeal port. In this case, too much air may pass through this port into the nasal cavities leading to the production of hypernasal speech. The production of voice during phonation may be compromised in the adult with dysarthria. Inadequate innervation of the vocal folds may lead to the production of a weak, breathy voice as the folds fail to adduct normally (see section 7.2.2 in Chapter 7, for a discussion of neurogenic voice disorders). The adult with dysarthria may experience shallow or erratic breathing and may need to take frequent inhalations to produce sufficient breath support for speech. The result of these respiratory disturbances may be a much reduced speaking volume or abrupt changes in volume during speech. Finally, the adult with dysarthria may also experience prosodic disturbances. Such disturbances may manifest as problems with intonation, rate and stress. In this way, the adult with dysarthria may speak with a monotone voice or may stress unstressed syllables and words in utterances. These prosodic problems should not be overlooked as they can have a substantial, adverse effect on the intelligibility of speech.

Studies of speech production in a range of dysarthric clients confirm the type of anomalies described above. Tjaden et al. (2005) investigated the vowel space area formed by the lax vowels /ɪ/, /ɛ/ and /ʊ/ in normal controls, speakers with PD and speakers with amyotrophic lateral sclerosis (ALS; another term for motor neurone disease). Only vowel space areas for ALS speakers differed from those of controls. Specifically, ALS speakers did not show the same adjustments of the vowel space area under different speaking rates as controls. Goozée et al. (2000) examined consonant imprecision in the speech of an individual with dysarthria following severe TBI. Kinematic analysis revealed that this subject had difficulty decelerating tongue movements on the approach to the palate during consonant production. Holmberg et al. (1996) studied 23 adult patients with myotonic dystrophy. All nine patients with dysarthria had a hypernasal resonatory problem. Yamout et al. (2009) examined vocal symptoms and acoustic changes in 82 patients with MS. Vocal breaks and vocal fatigue were the most common vocal symptoms in these patients. Male patients with MS displayed a significant decrease in fundamental frequency, habitual pitch and maximum phonation time, while female patients only evidenced a decrease in maximum phonation time. De Letter et al. (2007) studied three respiratory parameters – vital capacity, sustained vowel phonation and phonation quotient – in 25 patients with idiopathic PD. The main respiratory disturbance was vital capacity, which was abnormal in 18 patients. Wang et al. (2005) studied prosody in 12 subjects who developed dysarthria after TBI. These subjects, who were aged 18 to 51 years, displayed a slow speaking rate and reduced ability to convey intended stress.

The speaker with disarthria may develop a range of strategies to compensate for his physiological limitations during speech production. Vance (1994) describes a number of such strategies in the use of prosody by a 30-year-old male with MS. This client, known as 'D', presented with a mild to moderate ataxic dysarthria. The Frenchay Dysarthria Assessment (Enderby, 1983) was used to assess D's speech production. D displayed reduced respiratory control (his breathing was shallow and irregular), reduced but adequate functioning of the lips and jaw, reduced palatal function (D displayed moderate hypernasality) and reduced but adequate tongue function. D was most impaired on the laryngeal subtests of the assessment. His use of pitch and volume range and control was compromised. Although speech production was relatively clear, D produced speech in short, irregularly spaced phrases with limited pitch and volume variation. At least some of the prosodic anomalies in D's speech could be seen to be adjustments to the physiological difficulties D experienced in speech production. To see this, consider the following utterances produced by D:

(1)   ... ¦what they refer to as the béd^w but/ ____
       in (laugh) ¦actual fáct it's/ ____
       ¦just a ____ platform really that's/ ____

cóvered with/ ___
sponge rúbber and/ ___
plástic/
on 'top of thát and/ ...

(2)   ...'just so 'long 'as ___ they 'know I'm hére I'll/
hòpefully get brought 'in to mé/

Key to symbols: '= stress; ʷ= widened pitch range; ' = rising tone; / = tone
unit boundary; ___ = long pause; ⁻ = level tone; ↑ = rise in pitch

In normal speech production, tone unit boundaries typically occur at the end
of phrases and clauses. (A tone unit is the part of an utterance over which a single intonation contour extends.) It can be seen that D's tone unit boundaries do
not conform to this normal pattern. Specifically, D includes conjunctions such
as 'but' and 'and' in (1) at the end of a tone unit where these would normally
be found at the beginning of the next tone unit. Also, he completes a tone unit
with the subject and verb of the following clause, where again these elements
would be expected to be found at the start of the next tone unit. This can be
seen in the use of 'it's' and 'that's' in (1) and in 'I'll' in (2). These anomalies of
phrasing can be explained by D's difficulties with pitch control alongside his
respiratory problems. D's reduced respiratory control during speech production meant that he had to take frequent inhalations. The above utterances,
which contain a number of clauses, could not be produced on a single exhaled
breath and were broken up by D through his use of long pauses at the end of
tone units. However, D's reduced pitch control often resulted in a levelling
out of tones towards the end of these units. This may be perceived by D's listener as a signal to take the next turn. To ensure that this did not happen, D
had developed a strategy of using a grammatical element from the next clause
within his current tone unit in order to signal to the listener his unwillingness
to relinquish the current turn. What appeared to be an impairment of phrasing
was, in fact, a conscious adjustment by D to his problems with pitch variation
and respiration during speech. A further compensatory strategy is evident in
D's utterances below:

(3)   I won't pur'sue her ___ ↑ iǹnocent little 'comments/
(4)   'the ___ ↑ pòrter will call 'round for me/
(5)   well I must say Ì had 'hoped/
        ___ ↑ ỳou young 'ladies ...

As well as pausing at the end of tone units, D also made extensive use of mid-
tone unit pauses. Once again, D's impaired respiratory control made these
mid-tone unit pauses for frequent inhalations necessary. However, the placing
of these pauses has significance beyond D's need to take frequent inhalations
for speech production. In (3) and (4), it can be seen that mid-tone unit pauses
precede an item that carries a nuclear tone. D is attempting to coordinate his
need to take frequent inhalations with those parts of the utterance which carry
emphasis. Most of D's mid-tone unit pauses preceded a marked falling tone
with a wide range or a rise–fall tone. Long pauses at the end of tone units, such

as in (5), were generally followed by a high fall tone. D's limited physiological resources meant that it was difficult for him to achieve emphasis of elements within his utterances. His strategic placement of pauses served his increased need to take inhalations while also preparing him to place emphasis on the elements that followed those pauses.

KEY POINTS: Acquired dysarthria

- A motor speech disorder which has its onset in adulthood; speech may be minimally disrupted or so severely impaired that only basic vocalisations are possible (in the latter case, the term 'anarthria' is used)
- Acquired dysarthria is caused by damage to the central and/or peripheral nervous systems; aetiologies include CVAs (strokes), brain tumours, cerebral infections, TBI, and neurological disorders such as MS and PD
- One or more speech production subsystems may be compromised in dysarthria: articulation, resonation, phonation, respiration and prosody
- Speakers may produce distorted vowels and consonants (articulation), exhibit hypernasal speech due to velopharyngeal incompetence (resonation), produce a breathy or strained-strangled voice (phonation), display shallow and erratic breathing (respiration) and present with problems related to intonation, stress and rate (prosody)
- Many clients with dysarthria attempt to compensate for speech production difficulties in certain areas (e.g. respiration, phonation) by making adjustments to other areas of speech production (e.g. prosody). Sometimes, these compensations can be beneficial (i.e. they lead to improvements in overall intelligibility); on other occasions, they contribute to increased perceptual deviance of speech

---

4.4 Apraxia of speech

Apraxia of speech (AOS) is a motor speech disorder in which the ability to coordinate sequential, articulatory movements is compromised. The disorder is generally thought to result from a breakdown in motor speech programming. Unlike dysarthria, speech production difficulties in AOS are not caused by any muscle weakness. Also unlike dysarthria, volitional speech is more adversely affected than automatic speech. AOS reduces the intelligibility of adults who experience this disorder. Of the speakers with AOS examined by Haley et al. (1998), 70 per cent obtained intelligibility scores below the normal range. AOS is caused by many of the same diseases and injuries that give rise to dysarthria. Although CVAs (strokes) are the most common cause of AOS, other causes include TBI, brain tumour, and progressive non-fluent aphasia, a type of frontotemporal dementia that is consistently associated with AOS (Rohrer et al., 2010). Figures for the incidence and prevalence of AOS in adults do not exist. However, some idea of the prevalence of this disorder following CVA can be obtained from studies of oral apraxia in the stroke population (oral apraxia and apraxia of speech often co-occur). Pedersen et al. (2001) examined the prevalence of oral apraxia in 618 acute stroke patients. Oral apraxia occurred in 6 per cent of these patients. Studies are increasingly investigating the neuroanatomical basis of AOS. The severity of AOS correlated with left posterior inferior frontal lobe atrophy in the patients with progressive non-fluent aphasia studied by Rohrer et al. (2010). Ogar et al. (2006) found lesions in the left superior precentral gyrus of the insula in the 18 patients with AOS examined in their study. On rare occasions, the disorder results from lesions in the right hemisphere (Balasubramanian and Max, 2004).

The speech features of AOS have been extensively characterised. They include sound substitutions and additions, transposition of sounds and syllables, and perceived voicing errors (Yorkston et al., 1999). Bilabial and lingual-alveolar phonemes are more often in error than phonemes involving other places of articulation (Peach, 2004). Affricates and fricatives are more problematic than stops or nasals and there is greater difficulty with consonant clusters than singleton consonants (Yorkston et al., 1999). Errors are greater for infrequently occurring sounds and as the distance between successive points of articulation increases. Errors occur in both imitative and spontaneous speech but are more common in spontaneous speech (Peach, 2004). The number of speech errors increases as the length of words and linguistic complexity of utterances increases. AOS speakers display greater difficulty on novel or less practised utterances than well-practised utterances, and more errors on nonsense words than real words (Yorkston et al., 1999). Vowel distortions are commonplace. Prosodic disturbances, such as stress errors (a tendency towards equal stress), inappropriate phrasing and slow speech rate, are also in evidence in AOS. Groping, silent posturing and trial-and-error movement behaviour are also common in AOS (Yorkston et al., 1999). Articulatory groping, as well as inconsistency in speech errors (another feature that distinguishes AOS from dysarthria), are evident in the following attempt by a speaker with AOS to repeat the word 'catastrophe' five times (Ogar et al., 2006: 343):

catastrophe, patastrofee, t , catastrophe, katasrifrobee, aw sh-, ka, kata, sh-, sh-. I do not know

Many of these speech features are confirmed in clinical studies of speakers with AOS. Peach and Tonkovich (2004) examined a 71-year-old man who developed apraxia of speech following a left frontal brain haemorrhage. These investigators found significantly more substitution errors than other types of errors. In order of decreasing frequency, other errors included additions, repetitions, instrusive schwa and omissions. Significantly more errors occurred in word initial position than in the medial and final positions of words. Errors affecting consonant clusters, fricatives and nasals accounted for between 5 and 10 per cent of total errors. Only stops accounted for less than 5 per cent of total errors. Odell et al. (1991) examined single-word imitations by apraxic speakers. Errors were found in low, tense and back vowels. There were more vowel distortions than other types of vowel error, and errors occurred predominantly in initial position of words and in monosyllabic words. Apraxic speakers also produced syllabic stress errors and had more difficulty initiating than completing word production. Odell and Shriberg (2001) examined prosody-voice characteristics in 14 adults with AOS. Speakers with AOS had significantly more utterances meeting criteria for inappropriate phrasing and inappropriate speech rate than children with suspected AOS. Strand and McNeil (1996) found length and linguistic complexity effects on temporal acoustic characteristics of the imitative speech of speakers with AOS. Vowel duration and two between-word segment durations were examined in a range of conditions that manipulated the length of the apraxic speaker's response, and also the linguistic complexity of that response. In apraxic speakers, vowel and between-word segment durations were consistently longer in sentence contexts than in word contexts. These speakers also displayed greater intra-subject and inter-subject variability for between-word segment durations in sentence than in word conditions.

Several of the speech features described above can be seen in Table 4.2 which presents the single-word and phrase productions of a speaker with AOS who was studied by Morgan Barry (1995c). The speaker, known as Mr T, was 48 years of age and had developed AOS following a left-sided CVA. Alongside a phonetic assessment of Mr T's speech, EPG was performed to obtain an appreciation of Mr T's tongue–palate contacts. Two of these productions are indicated with (EPG) in Table 4.2.

Almost all consonant clusters in the data in Table 4.2 are reduced. This includes /fr/, /str/ and /gr/ in word initial position in 'frustrated', 'stroke' and 'gradually', and /str/ in word medial position in 'frustrated'. Consonants are inserted in 'knot' ([k]), 'key' ([s]) and 'dart' ([g]) (Morgan Barry suggests

Table 4.2   Single-word and phrase productions of a speaker with AOS

frustrated	[fʌsteɪtɪd]	Kim	[k\k\k\kɪm]
stroke	[srɐʊk]	gradually	[g::ædʒəli:]
shop	[sɒp] (EPG)	my	[m\m\m:aɪ]
shocking	[sɒkɪn]	a key	[əs.ki:]
dodgy	[dɒdi:]	a dart	[eig.dat]
chain	[teɪn] (EPG)	knot	[ənɒkt]
one minute	[ˈwʌˈmɪʔ]	a fish	[eɪs:p:fɪ]
shark	[əs::.ʧ.a:k]	speech	[p:s:pi:ʧ]
sheep	[əs:ç:i:p]	nurse	[n\nɜpnɜsnɜp]
brush	[əbɹʌʔʃ]	a leg	[əlɛglɛg]

Source: Based on Morgan Barry (1995c).

that the first of these insertions may be the result of confusion created by the orthography of 'knot'). The palato-alveolar fricative /ʃ/ is fronted to [s] in word initial position in 'shop', 'shocking', 'shark' and 'sheep', while it is omitted word finally in 'fish'. There is also affrication of this fricative word initially in 'shark' and word finally in 'brush'. Glottal insertion occurs in 'brush' and there is glottal replacement of an unstressed syllable in 'minute'. There is stopping of the affricates /tʃ/ and /dʒ/ in 'chain' and 'dodgy', respectively. The nasal /n/ is omitted in 'one' while /ŋ/ is fronted to [n] in 'shocking'. The word initial consonant is repeated in 'Kim', prolonged in 'gradually' and repeated and prolonged in 'my'. Word repetition occurs in 'nurse' and 'leg' with the former production varying between correct and incorrect forms. There is evidence of Mr T searching for the target sound word initially in both 'fish' and 'speech'. There is considerable variability in the production of target forms with 'chain' realised on different occasions as [teɪn], [əz.t.leɪn] and [eɪˈteɪn], 'shark' as [əs:ː.ʧ.aːk] and [slak] and 'sheep' realised as [əs:ç:iːp] and [s\s:iːp]. Extensive use was made of the schwa vowel /ə/ at the start of words. This may merely reflect the speaker's attempt to say '*a* shark', etc. However, it is even more likely to be a strategy on the part of the speaker to ease himself into the production of the often problematic initial consonant of the target word. When he used a slow speaking rate, Mr T was able to produce some targets correctly (e.g. compare 'the nurses' [ˈðə__ˈnɜːː_ˈsːɪz] to 'nurse' above).

KEY POINTS: Apraxia of speech

- Motor speech disorder that compromises the sequential, articulatory movements that are required to produce speech; believed to result from a breakdown in motor speech programming
- Distinguished from dysarthria in that there is no muscle weakness, volitional speech is more impaired than automatic speech and speech errors are inconsistent
- Results from many of the same diseases and injuries that cause dysarthria in adults; CVAs are the most common cause of AOS
- Speech features include consonant errors (substitutions, additions, omissions, etc.), vowel errors (mainly distortions), prosodic anomalies (e.g. stress errors, rate problems), greater difficulty with consonant clusters than singleton consonants and articulatory groping
- AOS speakers show word length and linguistic complexity effects

4.5 Assessment and treatment

Acquired speech disorders are assessed using a range of perceptual, acoustic and instrumental techniques. Perceptual analysis of speech continues to be the mainstay of assessment. An extensive range of published assessments exists for this purpose. One of the most widely used perceptual assessments of dysarthria is the Frenchay Dysarthria Assessment-2 (FDA-2; Enderby and Palmer, 2008).

This assessment contains eight sections that examine reflexes, respiration, lips, palate, laryngeal function, tongue, intelligibility and influencing factors (e.g. hearing, sight). The function of each articulator or speech production component is examined in a range of contexts. For example, the section on lips examines the lips at rest, when spread and sealed, in alternating movement and during speech. Intelligibility is examined for single words, sentences and in conversation. Normative data are reported for adults without dysarthria and for patients who have specific dysarthrias which are associated with confirmed medical diagnoses. The only normed and standardised test for AOS is the Apraxia Battery for Adults-2 (ABA-2; Dabul, 2000). This assessment takes approximately 20 minutes to administer and contains six subtests: diadochokinetic rate, increasing word length, limb apraxia and oral apraxia, latency time and utterance time for polysyllabic words, repeated trials test and an inventory of articulation characteristics of apraxia. The articulation characteristics in the inventory reflect the features described in section 4.4 including phonemic anticipatory errors (e.g. 'lelo' for 'yellow'), phonemic voicing errors (e.g. 'ben' for 'pen') and phonemic vowel errors (e.g. 'moan' for 'man'). Examination of areas such as limb apraxia is relevant to intervention – a speaker with AOS with limb apraxia may be unable to use certain forms of augmentative and alternative communication (AAC).

Although not included as standard, acoustic techniques can make an important contribution to the assessment of acquired speech disorders. Acoustic analyses can be used to confirm a range of perceived deviant speech dimensions in dysarthria including aberrant speech rate, consonant imprecision, breathy voice, voice tremor and reduced variability of pitch and loudness. Clinicians and researchers are able to characterise dysarthric speech according to acoustic parameters such as fundamental frequency measures, amplitude measures, noise-related measures, temporal measures, perturbation measures, formant measures, measures of articulatory capability and evaluations of manner of voicing (Murdoch et al., 2000). These parameters may be used to establish 'acoustic signatures' for different types of dysarthria which will prove beneficial in diagnosis. In this way, Rosen et al. (2006) used acoustic analysis to identify acoustic signatures of hypokinetic dysarthria associated with idiopathic PD. Intensity variation and spectral range consistently distinguished hypokinetic dysarthria from normal speech. Acoustic analysis also plays a role in the assessment of AOS. Seddoh et al. (1996) used acoustic analysis to investigate temporal parameters of speech in subjects with AOS. Shuster and Wambaugh (2000) used acoustic techniques to investigate speech errors (substitutions and distortions) in two individuals with AOS and aphasia. The specialist equipment and knowledge that are needed to undertake these types of investigations have tended to find acoustic techniques restricted to research studies and to a few major clinics and centres, rather than employed within assessment more generally.

Perceived speech defects in dysarthria and AOS may be the result of impairment in one or more speech production subsystems. However, perceptual techniques of assessment are generally powerless to locate deficits in any one particular speech subsystem. In an effort to understand the pathophysiological basis of disordered speech, clinicians and researchers have developed a range of instrumental techniques of assessment. These techniques include the use of nasometry to assess velopharyngeal function, EPG to assess tongue–palate contacts, electroglottography (EGG) to assess laryngeal function, and lip and tongue pressure transducers to assess articulatory function. McAuliffe et al. (2006) used EPG to examine the articulatory timing disturbance in subjects with PD. Although perceptual assessment confirmed impaired speech rate in the subjects in this study, EPG analysis revealed that segment durations of PD subjects were consistent with those of aged and young controls. The one exception was the duration of the release phase for /la/, which was significantly increased in PD subjects. Instrumental techniques have also been used in the assessment of AOS. Strauss and Klich (2001) examined the effects of word length on the timing of lip EMG activity for production of the vowel /u/ and the relationship of this activity to vowel duration in two speakers with AOS. Sugishita et al. (1987) used EPG to examine omission errors in the speech of two speakers with AOS. On account of the invasive nature of many instrumental techniques – an artificial palate, for example, must be worn in EPG – they tend not to be used routinely in assessment and are employed only in those cases where more extensive investigation of a client's speech disorder is required (e.g. in advance of surgical intervention).

Interventions for acquired speech disorders must be tailored to the communication needs, neurological and cognitive status and medical prognosis of each adult client. In a review of interventions for dysarthria due to non-progressive brain damage, Sellars et al. (2005) produce a comprehensive list of techniques that are in current use by speech and language therapists. These interventions include: (1) articulation, voice and prosody training, (2) behavioural interventions, (3) the use of sign language as a supplement or alternative to speech, (4) prosthetic devices, (5) assistive communication devices, (6) listener training programmes and (7) listener advice. Intervention may employ techniques in one of these areas to the exclusion of others. Wenke et al. (2010) used the Lee Silverman Voice Treatment (LSVT), an intervention more commonly associated with the treatment of vocal loudness in patients with dysarthric PD, to target articulation in 26 subjects with non-progressive dysarthria. LSVT produced significant increases in the vowel space area in these subjects and in intelligibility at six months post-treatment. More often than not, however, two or more of the above techniques are combined during intervention. For example, Ono et al. (2005) combined prosthetic and behavioural techniques when they used a palatal lift prosthesis and palatal augmentation prosthesis to treat velopharyngeal incompetence and articulation in a 71-year-old man who had sustained a stroke two years and five months earlier. Speech behavioural management of this patient involved self-monitoring and biofeedback training using the See-Scape (an instrument used to detect nasal emission of air during speech). These behavioural techniques helped promote an improvement in speech intelligibility to a functionally sufficient level following prosthetic intervention for velopharyngeal incompetence.

Only some of the techniques described by Sellars et al. (2005) are appropriate when dysarthria occurs in the presence of a progressive neurological disorder. In neurodegenerative diseases such as motor neurone disease, the progressive nature of dysarthria means that some type of AAC system will eventually have to be used to augment or replace speech. The changing neurological condition of patients with progressive disorders requires that clinicians stage dysarthria treatment in these clients. Yorkston and Beukelman (2000: 159) state that '[s]taging of intervention is the sequencing of management so that current problems are addressed and future problems anticipated. Staging is important in dysarthria intervention because many of the conditions associated with dysarthria are not stable'. AAC techniques are used in the latter stages of treatment of progressive dysarthria when natural speech is no longer a functional means of communication. Hirano et al. (2006) recorded the various means of communication used by 27 patients in the advanced stages of ALS. In 6.4 per cent of patients, ocular (eye) muscles only were used to communicate (e.g. looking up and down to indicate 'yes' and 'no', respectively). The remaining patients used ocular muscles in combination with lip-reading or vocal communication, written communication, a character sheet or computer-assisted communication. In the advanced stages of many neurodegenerative diseases, patients are often dependent on invasive mechanical ventilation. The clinician must also consider the communication needs of ventilator-dependent patients, many of whom are experiencing a range of distressing emotions at a time when they are least able to communicate with others. Staging of treatment is also important in PD, which has a slowly progressive course, and in TBI, which has a stable or recovering course (Yorkston and Beukelman, 2000).

Intervention for AOS emphasises slightly different considerations from those discussed above. Certainly, in cases of severe unintelligibility in speakers with AOS, AAC devices play a prominent role in therapy. But the focus of intervention in this clinical population is largely on spoken communication with articulation and prosody emphasised in equal measure. Wambaugh et al. (1998) treated sound errors in three speakers with chronic AOS and aphasia. The treatment approach adopted by these investigators combined the use of minimal contrast pairs with traditional sound production training techniques such as articulatory placement cueing and integral stimulation (the client is encouraged to watch the clinician and listen to his or her production of the target sound and then imitate it). A treatment technique that was first developed in the late 1970s for use with children but which has also been used to treat adults with AOS is Deborah Hayden's PROMPT technique. PROMPT (Prompts for Restructuring Oral Muscular Phonetic Targets) uses tactile cues that are 'designed to provide apractic patients with sensory input regarding place of articulatory contact, extent of mandibular opening, voice, tension, relative timing of segments, manner of articulation, and coarticulation' (Freed et al., 1997: 365). Prosodic interventions in adults with AOS target the rate, rhythm and stress of speech, either because these prosodic features are aberrant or because they may be used to achieve gains in other aspects of speech production. Wambaugh and Martinez (2000) used a rate and rhythm control intervention to treat consonant production in a speaker with AOS and aphasia. This subject was trained to produce multisyllabic words using metronomic rate control and hand-tapping. The focus on rhythm control in this study is also integral to melodic intonation therapy. Yorkston et al. (1999) argue that an intervention which targets contrastive stress can be most effective for speakers with mild to moderate AOS.

SUGGESTIONS FOR FURTHER READING:

Bressmann, T. (2014) 'Head and neck cancer and communication', in L. Cummings (ed.) *Cambridge Handbook of Communication Disorders* (Cambridge: Cambridge University Press), pp. 161–84.

McNeil, M.R. (ed.) (2009) *Clinical Management of Sensorimotor Speech Disorders* (New York: Thieme Medical Publishers, 2nd edn).

Murdoch, B.E. (2010) *Acquired Speech and Language Disorders: A Neuroanatomical and Functional Neurological Approach* (Chichester, West Sussex: John Wiley & Sons Ltd, 2nd edn).

EXERCISES

Exercise 4.1 Bressmann et al. (2009) studied articulation and speech acceptability in 22 patients who underwent partial glossectomy for the treatment of lateral or anterolateral carcinomas. Tumour sizes varied in these patients necessitating different degrees of surgery. Eleven patients had small defects which were closed using either primary wound healing or a local closure. A radial forearm flap or an anterolateral thigh flap was used to close larger defects in another 11 patients. For all patients, consonant distortions were recorded before and after surgery. The frequency of distortions is shown in the table below. Examine these figures and then answer the following questions:

(a) Six consonants display no post-surgical distortions in these patients. Why do you think this is the case?

(b) For 10 consonants, the frequency of pre-surgical and post-surgical distortions is similar. Why might the production of these consonants be distorted prior to surgery?

(c) For five consonants, the number of post-surgical distortions is considerably greater than the number of pre-surgical distortions. What places of articulation do these consonants have in common?

(d) Are any particular classes of sounds (e.g. plosives, fricatives) more adversely affected than others as a result of glossectomy in these patients?

(e) On the basis of the information provided, which of the words 'ditch', 'mummy' and 'hoof' is most likely to be produced with distorted consonants by these glossectomy patients?

Phoneme	Pre-surgery number of distortions	Post-surgery number of distortions
/d/	2	11
/k/	3	6
/r/	2	6
/s/	4	6
/ʧ/	1	5
/g/	5	4
/ʃ/	3	4
/dʒ/	2	3
/n/	3	3
/ŋ/	3	3
/t/	3	2
/ɵ/	1	2
/z/	2	2
/l/	0	1
/v/	1	1
/b/	0	0
/f/	0	0
/h/	0	0
/m/	0	0
/p/	0	0
/w/	0	0

Exercise 4.2 Consonant and vowel errors are common in the speech of adults with dysarthria. The following data are taken from Morgan Barry (1995c) who examined the speech produced by a 68-year-old man who had a diagnosis of moderately severe dysarthria of the spastic type following a left CVA. Characterise the type of speech sound errors produced by this patient.

feeling	[fɪən]	trade	[zeɪd]
get	[gɛ]	sun	[tsʌn]
started	[satɪ]	sheep	[dʒiːp]
Christian	[kɪzjən]	about	[baʊt]
expenses	[ɛzpɛnzɪz]	place	[beɪs]
good	[guːt]	market	[maʔ]
Ford's	[fɔʔz]	profit	[fɪɒfiʔ]
because	[pəɣəz]	actually	[æʧiː]

Exercise 4.3   La Pointe and Johns (1975) examined articulatory performance in 13 adults who developed apraxia of speech after sustaining cortical damage through CVA or trauma. The mean time since onset was 12.15 months (range = 1–35 months). The sequential nature of these subjects' articulatory errors was examined in detail. Three types of sequential error were identified: anticipatory, reiterative and metathesis. An error was classified as anticipatory if a phoneme was replaced by one that occurred later in the word. If a phoneme were replaced by one that occurred earlier in the word, the error was classified as reiterative. If two phonemes switched places within a word, the error was classified as metathesis. Several sequential errors produced by the subjects in this study are shown below (La Pointe and Johns used orthographic transcription to represent them). Examine these errors and classify them as (1) anticipatory, (2) reiterative or (3) metathesis:

(a)   sandwich: 'wansin – sanwich'
(b)   yellow: 'redul, ledul, (pause) lelo'
(c)   dress: 'dred'
(d)   grasshopper: 'grap – popper, let's see, – grass – hopper'
(e)   December: 'ees, ees, esender'
(f)   telephone: 'teflone – tefalone'
(g)   bicycle: 'b – bai – bai – s – s – sai – s – uh – bai – sikl'

ANSWERS TO EXERCISES

Exercise 4.1

(a)   Bilabial, labiodental and glottal places of articulation are not compromised by glossectomy.
(b)   Consonant distortion pre-surgery may indicate pre-existing speech disorders in the patients or may be the result of articulatory defects caused by the presence of a tongue carcinoma.

(c) Alveolar and velar places of articulation.
(d) No, plosives and fricatives are in the group of sounds with no post-surgical distortions and are also in the group of sounds with several post-surgical distortions.
(e) 'ditch'.

Exercise 4.2

feeling: deletion of /l/ in medial position
get: deletion of final consonant /t/
started: cluster reduction /st/→[s]; deletion of final consonant /d/
Christian: cluster reduction /kr/→[k]; voicing of /s/; spirantisation /ʧ/→[j]
expenses: cluster reduction /ks/→[z]; voicing of /s/
good: devoicing of final consonant /d/
Ford's: glottal replacement of /d/ (beyond what is expected dialectally)
because: devoicing of initial consonant /b/; spirantisation /k/→[ɣ]
trade: cluster reduction /tr/→[z]; spirantisation /t/→[z]
sun: affrication of fricative /s/→[ts]
sheep: affrication of fricative /ʃ/→[dʒ]
about: deletion of weak syllable /ə/
place: cluster reduction /pl/→[b]; voicing of /p/
market: replacement of syllable with glottal stop
profit: assimilation of /p/ to [f]; glottal stop expected dialectally
actually: simplification of syllable /æk/→[æ]; deletion of syllable; deletion of /l/

Exercise 4.3

(a) sandwich – metathesis
(b) yellow – anticipatory
(c) dress – reiterative
(d) grasshopper – anticipatory
(e) December – reiterative
(f) telephone – metathesis
(g) bicycle – anticipatory

Acquired Language Disorders

5

5.1 Acquired language disorders and their causes

For a significant number of adults, previously intact language skills can deteriorate or break down. This can occur suddenly as a result of a cerebrovascular accident (a CVA or stroke) or head injury, or gradually over a period of months or even years, as in the case of a patient with dementia. The language disorders that are caused by injury and disease can improve over time, particularly in the weeks and months immediately following the onset of a stroke or other medical episode. However, more often than not, return to the patient's pre-morbid language status is not possible. Indeed, in all but the mildest language impairments, affected individuals can experience significant psychological distress, reduction in occupational functioning and problems of social adjustment as a result of their altered language capabilities. These adverse psychosocial and occupational outcomes can be mitigated by effective assessment and treatment of language disorders by speech and language therapists. We will return to issues of clinical assessment and treatment in section 5.6. In this section, we describe the different events that can result in adults developing language disorders.

By far the largest single cause of language disorders in adults is stroke. A stroke occurs when there is disruption to the flow of blood in the brain. This disruption may be the result of a blood clot in one of the brain's blood vessels (an embolic stroke) or when one of the vessels in the brain ruptures and bleeds (a haemorrhagic stroke). In both cases, brain cells are starved of oxygenated blood and within seconds begin to die. When a stroke affects the language centres in the left hemisphere of the brain (the hemisphere that is dominant for language in most right-handed individuals), the resulting language disorder is called 'aphasia'. When a stroke occurs in the brain's right hemisphere, a different set of language problems can arise. We will examine aphasia in section 5.2 and right-hemisphere language disorder in section 5.3. Although language disorder is a common consequence of stroke, it by no means occurs in every person who sustains a CVA. Yavuzer et al. (2001) found aphasia in 70 patients (40 per cent) of 178 stroke patients who were admitted to a comprehensive rehabilitation programme for the first time between January 1998 and April 2000.

The brain's language centres may also be damaged as a result of a traumatic brain injury (TBI), brain tumours, infections (e.g. meningitis, encephalitis) and by neurodegenerative disorders like Alzheimer's disease. TBI is most often the result of road traffic accidents, but may also be caused by trips and falls (particularly in young children and elderly people), sports injuries (e.g. boxing), violent assaults (particularly in young men) and child abuse. In such injuries, the skull may be fractured by a missile or through impact with a stationary object (open head injury). Alternatively, the brain may be damaged while the skull remains intact (closed head injury). Unlike stroke, where there is usually a single, focal lesion, TBI can result in several different lesion sites in the brain. This results in a complicated clinical picture with language skills in clients with TBI often being impaired in the presence of cognitive deficits. It is for this reason that language impairments in TBI are often referred to as cognitive-communication disorders. The client with TBI poses a considerable assessment challenge for clinicians. These clients can often pass conventional language batteries. Yet, they present with bizarre communication skills that have been variously described as repetitive or overly talkative, confused and confabulatory and as exhibiting impoverished language content. We will examine the language disorder that occurs in TBI in section 5.4.

Language disorders are also commonly found in adults who develop brain tumours. These tumours are frequently localised resulting in focal lesions like those that occur in stroke. Wacker et al. (2002) used the Aachen Aphasia Test to determine the incidence of aphasic symptoms in patients with brain tumours. Aphasic disturbances were detected in 50 per cent of patients with left-sided tumours and 36 per cent of patients with right-sided tumours. There is also evidence that cranial irradiation during radiotherapy on patients with brain tumours may further contribute to the deterioration of language skills in these patients. Murdoch and Chenery (1990) describe the case of a 39-year-old woman who developed a latent aphasia and flaccid dysarthria 20 years after she received a course of radiotherapy following surgical removal of a pituitary fossa tumour. These authors relate her aphasia to a radiation-induced lesion involving the ventrolateral nucleus of the left thalamus. Cerebral infections such as encephalitis and meningitis can give rise to both temporary and long-term language disorders. Khan and Ramsay (2006) describe the case of a 59-year-old woman who developed encephalitis caused by herpes simplex virus type 1. This woman's main presenting symptom was mild aphasia, for which she required longer-term speech therapy. Van de Beek et al. (2004) studied all Dutch adults with community-acquired acute bacterial meningitis from October 1998 to April 2002. On admission, aphasia was present in 121 episodes of meningitis (23 per cent). At discharge, aphasia occurred in 11 episodes of meningitis (2 per cent).

Language can also deteriorate markedly in individuals with dementia. Alzheimer's disease is the most common cause of dementia. However, other, less common causes include problems with the blood supply to the brain (vascular dementia), abnormal protein deposits in the cerebral cortex (dementia with Lewy bodies), Pick's disease (frontotemporal dementia), HIV infection,

Creutzfeldt–Jakob disease and Korsakoff's syndrome (alcohol-related dementia). These different types of dementia have quite distinctive cognitive, behavioural and linguistic manifestations. For example, due to the predominance of frontal lobe pathology, frontotemporal dementia has more personality and behaviour involvement and fewer memory deficits at first than other forms of dementia. For temporal variants of frontotemporal dementia – progressive aphasia and semantic dementia – worse language performance relative to Alzheimer's disease is typically characteristic (Levy and Chelune, 2007). Traditionally, most studies of language impairment in the presence of dementia have involved patients with Alzheimer's disease. Increasingly, however, investigators are beginning to characterise language impairments in a range of other dementias. In section 5.5, we examine what is known about language disorder in Alzheimer's disease, as well as some other dementias.

5.2   Acquired aphasia

Aphasia is an acquired language disorder that results from damage to the language centres in the left hemisphere of the brain. Although a range of neurological problems and events can cause aphasia, the main causes of the disorder are CVAs or strokes. In Britain every year, approximately 11,400 new patients acquire aphasia after a stroke (Enderby and Philipp, 1986). Aphasia can compromise language at all levels including phonology, morphology, syntax, semantics and pragmatics. It affects language in all its input and output modalities. So as well as having problems producing and understanding spoken language, the adult with aphasia may struggle to produce and understand written language (acquired dysgraphia and dyslexia, respectively) or produce and comprehend signs (if the client with aphasia is a user of British Sign Language, for example). The disorder thus has far-reaching consequences for communication in the affected individual. Historically, a number of different terms have been used to characterise aphasia. Some of these labels reflect neurological criteria such as the site of lesion in the brain (e.g. Broca's aphasia, Wernicke's aphasia). Other labels reflect the fact that the production or comprehension of language can be chiefly affected (e.g. expressive or receptive aphasia). In this section, we follow the dominant classification system – the one used by the National Aphasia Association in the US – in which aphasia is broadly classified into two forms: fluent and non-fluent aphasia.

In fluent aphasia, there is a severe impairment in the comprehension of language in the presence of effortless, fluent speech. Utterances are well-articulated and the intonational and other suprasegmental features of normal speech are also present. This can give the client with fluent aphasia the appearance at least of being a reasonably competent communicator. However, language output is often very incoherent due to the extensive use of jargon by the client (hence, the term 'jargon aphasia' to describe this type of aphasia). Jargonistic output can take several forms. The client with fluent aphasia can link English words together to produce meaningless utterances (e.g. the jargon speaker who described a daughter's holiday as 'She's got a rainbow, you know, three monthly rainbow going to Alaska',

Marshall et al., 2001). Often, however, the client will create new words or 'neologisms'. Where these are used infrequently, the resulting utterance may still be understood by the listener (e.g. the jargon speaker, who wants to go for a walk in the park, utters 'We have to go to the pargoney', Robson et al., 2003). However, where neologisms dominate output, the result is completely meaningless language (e.g. the jargon speaker who described what he had done during the week as 'Oh I kegde treychoinge and cortlidge, oh erm partlie chulz, potiler crediss my children ringer', Robson et al., 2003). The client with fluent aphasia also displays poor monitoring and correction of incoherent language output. Other linguistic features of the disorder include echolalia (the client echoes back another speaker's utterance), circumlocution (the subject with aphasia is unable to produce a target word on account of lexical retrieval problems and proceeds to talk around it), and perseveration, where the speaker with aphasia continues to produce a linguistic form beyond what is appropriate. Finally, the client with fluent aphasia may also produce errors known as phonemic paraphasias (e.g. the use of *canerdillar* for 'caterpillar').

The client with non-fluent aphasia displays a quite different pattern of linguistic impairments. In this type of aphasia, comprehension is relatively intact. However, the client displays considerable struggle in producing utterances and is both aware of, and frustrated by, his or her expressive difficulties. On account of his or her restricted output, the client with non-fluent aphasia tends to speak in short intonation units with the result that the suprasegmental features of speech are disrupted. The syntactic structure of utterances is often considerably reduced and incomplete. For example, when asked to describe a picture in which a girl is handing a bouquet of flowers to her teacher, the client with non-fluent aphasia may struggle to produce 'Girl...flower...teacher'. Non-fluent output, which includes the retention of content words (e.g. nouns, verbs and adjectives) and the loss of function words (e.g. definite and indefinite articles, auxiliary verbs, prepositions), can give spoken language the appearance of a telegram (hence, the use of the term 'agrammatic aphasia' to describe this type of aphasia). When expressive problems are particularly acute, the client with non-fluent aphasia may use stereotypical forms (e.g. 'that's right', 'OK then', 'you know') to hold onto the floor during conversation and maintain the interaction. Finally, lexical-semantic disturbances in non-fluent aphasia may manifest themselves in errors known as semantic paraphasias. In these errors, the word uttered by the speaker with aphasia is often semantically related to the target lexeme (e.g. *watch* for 'clock'). For further discussion of the linguistic features of fluent and non-fluent aphasia, the reader is referred to section 5.4 in Cummings (2008) and section 3.2 in Cummings (2009).

KEY POINTS: Aphasia

- Acquired language disorder which is most often caused by cerebrovascular accidents (CVAs or strokes)
- Affects the production and comprehension of spoken, written and signed language

- Several aphasia syndromes, broadly classified into fluent and non-fluent types
- Fluent aphasia (includes Wernicke's aphasia) characterised by severe comprehension deficit and jargonistic verbal output
- Non-fluent aphasia (includes Broca's aphasia) characterised by relatively intact comprehension and agrammatic output (content words are retained and function words lost)
- Other linguistic deficits found in aphasia include word-finding difficulties, circumlocution, perseveration and echolalia

5.3   Right-hemisphere language disorder

The same injuries and diseases that cause damage to the brain's left hemisphere can also damage the right cerebral hemisphere. In at least some cases of right-hemisphere damage (RHD), the resulting language disorder is aphasia. Cases of crossed aphasia (aphasia following a right-hemisphere lesion in right-handed individuals) are relatively uncommon. The prevalence of crossed aphasia is below 3 per cent in the vast majority of estimates (Coppens et al., 2002) or between 0.4 per cent and 3.5 per cent of all aphasic syndromes (Dewarrat et al., 2009). However, when clinicians refer to right-hemisphere language disorder, they are referring to a set of linguistic deficits that differ significantly from those encountered in aphasia. Whereas structural language is impaired in the aphasias, the language disorder in RHD is characterised by deficits in pragmatics and discourse (Cummings, 2007a). In 1979, Myers published the first formal study of discourse-level communication disorders in adults with RHD. The paper arose out of the author's observation that stroke patients with RHD, who were receiving treatment for dysarthria and who had intact language skills, were nevertheless communicating inadequately. Specifically, these patients produced 'irrelevant and often excessive information' and seemed 'to miss the implication of [a] question and to respond in a most literal and concrete way' (Myers, 1979: 38). When attempting to respond to open-ended questions, these patients 'wended their way through a maze of disassociated detail, seemingly incapable of filtering out unnecessary information' (1979: 38). The components of a narrative, although available to these patients, could not be assembled. There was difficulty 'in extracting critical bits of information, in seeing the relationships among them, and in reaching conclusions or drawing inferences based on those relationships' (1979: 39). Although the detail provided by these patients was related to the general topic, its appearance seemed irrelevant because it had not been 'integrated into a whole' (1979: 39).

Although Myers did not use the term 'pragmatics' to capture these communicative impairments, it is clear that the features which she had identified were part of a pragmatic disorder in her patients with RHD. Today, that disorder is the focus of an increasing number of clinical studies (see Cummings (2007b), for critical discussion of clinical pragmatic studies). For example, the comprehension of non-literal language has been extensively investigated in the RHD population. Papagno et al. (2006) examined the comprehension of idioms in 15 subjects with RHD. Comprehension in these subjects was found to be severely impaired and was biased towards literal interpretation. Brundage (1996) examined the interpretation of proverbs in 10 subjects with RHD. Proverb familiarity and abstractness had a significant effect on interpretation. When explaining the meaning of proverbs high in abstractness, subjects with RHD tended to produce literal explanations. Cheang and Pell (2006) administered tasks tapping humour appreciation and pragmatic interpretation of non-literal language to 10 subjects with RHD. Although the ability to interpret humour from jokes was relatively intact in these subjects, they had problems understanding communicative intentions.

The following extract is taken from Abusamra et al. (2009: 77–8). It is a dialogue between an examiner (E) and a male patient (P) with RHD. The patient has been asked to explain the meaning of one of the metaphors from the MEC protocol (Joanette et al., 2004). P's utterances exhibit features which are typical of linguistic output in subjects with RHD. Specifically, the patient treats the metaphor in a literal way by describing conventional attributes of witches, attributes that are part of the literal, semantic meaning of the word 'witch' (e.g. 'tied down to religious sects'). At no point in the exchange does P show any appreciation of the metaphorical meaning of the expression in E's first utterance. Also, there is evidence of the type of 'egocentric' discourse that Lehman (2006) observed in patients with RHD (discussed later in this section). The patient persists in relating to the examiner situations which are within his personal experience and that are unrelated to the task at hand.

E: What does this phrase mean: My friend's mother-in-law is a witch?

P: Let's change also one word: My son-in-law's mother-in-law is a witch?

E: And so what does it mean?

P: I know she is a person who hasn't had a pleasant life, throughout her marriage. That... that she's about to be separated from her husband; I'm referring to the mother-in-law of my son-in-law (ha, ha, ha).

E: OK it's not important – it's the same.

P: Certainly! The mother-in-law of my son-in-law. The mother-in-law of my son-in-law is a witch!

E: What does being a witch mean?

P: Because the woman is separated, because all her life she has criticised her husband for the way he is; only seen in his defects, who has kept his daughter all her life under a glass bell and she's now a poor lady because she can't find the fiancé her mother would like.

E: So what does witch mean, then?

P: What does it specifically mean? It means being tied down to religious sects, to religions, to umbanda... who knows, there are so many.

E: So therefore, 'The mother-in-law of my son-in-law is a witch'. Does it mean the mother-in-law of my friend practices black magic? And the mother-in-law of my friend has many brooms and she is also a bad person and rude?

P: It's absolutely clear. My friend's mother-in-law has many brooms... no! My friend's mother-in-law practices black magic.

Many of the pragmatic deficits experienced by adults with RHD are related to cognitive deficits in this clinical population. One such deficit involves theory of mind (ToM) skills. Theory of mind describes the ability to attribute mental states to one's own mind and to the minds of others. To the extent that all pragmatic interpretation involves the attribution of communicative intentions to the mind of a conversational partner, it is unsurprising that ToM skills are related to pragmatic deficits in adults with RHD. McDonald (2000) relates problems comprehending sarcasm in patients with RHD to their difficulty processing information about the emotional state, intentions and beliefs of the speaker. Champagne-Lavau and Joanette (2009) examined pragmatic and ToM abilities in 15 subjects with RHD and 15 healthy control subjects. All subjects completed the metaphor comprehension subtest and the indirect requests comprehension task from a standardised communication protocol. Subjects with RHD performed worse than control subjects on the pragmatic tasks. Moreover, their ability to understand pragmatic aspects of language was closely associated with the ability to make inferences about the intentions of other people. Champagne-Lavau and Joanette (2009: 422) state that '[t]hese results confirm the hypothesis that pragmatic interpretation is a mind-reading exercise involving inferences concerning the speaker's mental state'.

Discourse and conversation deficits in the RHD population have also been widely studied. Lehman (2006) elicited discourse from eight subjects with RHD. Subjects with RHD produced discourse which was rated as more tangential and egocentric than that produced by healthy older controls. Extreme verbosity or paucity of speech also characterised the discourse of subjects with RHD. Marini et al. (2005) examined stories generated during two picture description tasks in 11 subjects with RHD, 11 subjects with left-hemisphere damage and 11 neurologically intact controls. The performance of subjects with RHD was poorer than that of controls in terms of information content and the coherent and cohesive aspects of narrative production. Hird and Kirsner (2003) examined the ability of subjects with RHD to take shared responsibility for the development of an intentional structure in conversation. These investigators found that speakers with RHD fail to use prosody to alert listeners to changes in discourse structure. Neither do they assume equal responsibility in conversation for the development and maintenance of discourse structure. The findings of these studies serve to confirm the early impression on the part of Myers of conversational and discourse deviance in subjects with RHD.

KEY POINTS: Right-hemisphere language disorder

- Right-hemisphere damage (RHD) is caused by the same injuries and diseases that can damage the left cerebral hemisphere
- Language disorder characterised by deficits in pragmatics and discourse; structural language is relatively intact
- Impaired comprehension of non-literal language (e.g. metaphor, idioms, proverbs); interpretation tends to be literal in nature

- Discourse and conversation may be tangential and egocentric; patients may exhibit extreme verbosity or paucity of speech; linguistic output may have low information content and problems with cohesion and coherence; poor use of prosody
- Pragmatic impairments in RHD are related to cognitive deficits (e.g. ToM deficits)

5.4   Language disorder in traumatic brain injury

Clients with traumatic brain injury (TBI) often present a complex clinical picture which reflects their underlying multifocal cerebral pathology. Clients with TBI can have problems with physical mobility, speech disorders (dysarthria and dyspraxia) and difficulty swallowing (dysphagia); they often experience sensory and perception deficits. In terms of language, these patients may have aphasia if there has been damage to the language centres in the left hemisphere of the brain. Gil et al. (1996) examined 351 patients with severe TBI and found aphasia in 11.1 per cent of these subjects. In this section, we will consider how language and communication may be disrupted in clients with TBI beyond the structural language impairments that are typical of aphasia. Indeed, it is the ability of these patients to pass language batteries that target the impairments of aphasia, and yet still exhibit subtle communication problems, which has served as an impetus to clinicians to develop alternative, discourse-based methods of assessment for use with this client group. These methods are better able to address the overriding difficulties with pragmatics and discourse that are experienced by clients with TBI (see section 5.6). As well as facing difficulties assessing the language and communication disturbances in clients with TBI, clinicians must also address a further challenge with this clinical population. The communication disorder in TBI has a substantial basis in cognitive deficits. Many of these deficits (e.g. executive function deficits) are related to frontal lobe pathology in clients with TBI. Clinicians must not only be aware of how these deficits impact upon communication, but also upon the ability of the client with TBI to participate in assessment and treatment. The cognitive sequelae of TBI will therefore also be considered in this section.

Specific pragmatic and discourse skills have been investigated in clients with TBI and have been found to be problematic. MacLennan et al. (2002) studied pragmatic impairments in 144 clients with TBI, who ranged in age from 18 to 71 years. Ratings on a pragmatic scale were based upon conversation, narrative discourse and procedural discourse. Pragmatic impairments were found in 86 per cent of patients. Cohesion, repair, elaboration, initiation and relevance were the five scales with the highest frequency of impairment. Turkstra et al. (1995) examined pragmatic communication skills in three brain-injured adolescents. The pragmatic deficits in these subjects included an inability to use an alternative strategy to make a request when a first attempt failed, difficulty producing indirect requests (polite, direct requests were used instead), difficulty giving the procedural steps to a listener on how to play a simple board game, problems with the use of hints and the negotiation of requests, and difficulty with a sarcasm task in which there were only a few contextual cues to aid the interpretation of verbally ambiguous conversational dyads. Douglas and Bracy (2006) examined 43 dyads, each consisting of an adult with severe TBI and a close relative, at a minimum of two years post-injury. The La Trobe Communication Questionnaire (Douglas et al., 2000) was administered to all adults with TBI and their relatives. These investigators found that 14 behaviours were particularly problematic in the adults with TBI and occurred significantly more frequently in clients with TBI than in matched controls. These behaviours involved violations in the quantity, relation and manner domains of Grice's cooperative principle.

Coelho et al. (2002) examined response appropriateness and topic initiation in the conversations of 32 subjects with closed head injury. These investigators found that subjects with head injury depended on their conversational partner (the examiner) to maintain the flow of the conversation and that they contributed information that did not facilitate the interaction. To compensate for these conversational impairments, the examiner asked more questions and introduced more topics than he did in conversations with subjects with no brain injury. Togher and Hand (1998) examined the use of politeness markers during the telephone interactions of five subjects with TBI with four different interlocutors (a bus service employee, the police, a therapist and the client's mother). These interlocutors varied in their contact with the clients with TBI and their relationships of power and status to these clients. Subjects with TBI used significantly fewer politeness markers per clause than control subjects in the therapist, bus and police interactions. Unlike controls, subjects with TBI were unable to vary the number of politeness markers used according to the tenor of the social relationship in each interaction. Jorgensen and Togher (2009) examined the production of narrative in 10 subjects with TBI. Subjects with TBI and 10 control subjects retold a story from a picture sequence. The resulting narratives were analysed for productivity, cohesion, story grammar, informational content and exchange structure. Jorgensen and Togher found a significant difference between subjects with TBI and control subjects on all narrative discourse measures. However, when subjects with TBI jointly produced narratives with a communication partner, there were no significant differences on discourse measures between subjects with TBI and control subjects.

The discourse difficulties experienced by clients with TBI are amply demonstrated in the following extract of narrative from Biddle et al. (1996: 462). The narrative has been produced by a 31-year-old man with TBI who has been asked to recount an occasion on which he got lost:

> (Long pause) About the only really good time I can remember getting lost was in West Virginia. Me and my brother had been walking into the woods one day and we found a pig in the woods. A pig. Pig got out of my uncle's... pig, uh... So we found a pig around. And then we found out that we did get lost. So we went walking through the woods for about two hours, until it got really dark. Then we found a house and went back home. But during the time that we were lost, we were really scared cause we didn't think we were going to make it back. And I got all upset and started crying like a little wimp. And I didn't think we were goin make it back. But we did. It was a little traumatic for me... cause I didn't think we were going to make it.

This narrative is typical of the linguistic output of clients with TBI in several respects. It is repetitive in parts particularly when the client relates the incident of finding the pig in the woods and recounting his belief that they would not be able to make it back home. The speaker with TBI starts utterances only to abandon them, e.g. 'Pig got out of my uncle's …'. The impression here, reinforced by the filler 'uh', is of a speaker who has lost his goal in speaking. The result is an incomplete information unit which places a burden on the listener, as he or she must attempt to fill in missing information in the narrative. An additional listener burden is created by missing information even within utterances that are completely expressed. When the speaker says 'Then we found a house and went back home', the listener must supply information in order to confer a temporal and logical order on the two events expressed in this utterance. For example, did the owner of the house allow the speaker and his brother to use the telephone to get someone to pick them up and drive them back home? Or did the speaker and his brother recognise the house and were able to use it as a point of reference for retracing their steps? The listener is left to fill in these necessary details which the speaker's narrative has failed to supply.

Pragmatic and discourse impairments in clients with TBI are increasingly being linked to cognitive deficits in these clients. These deficits consist largely in impairments of executive functions and ToM skills. In her study of pragmatics in closed head injury (CHI), McDonald (1992) relates the impaired pragmatic skills of subjects with CHI to their underlying cognitive deficits. Specifically, a subject with CHI who failed to adhere to Grice's maxim of manner in his instructions to a blindfolded listener on how to play a novel game exhibited frontal lobe cognitive deficits like rigidity, perseveration and poor planning and problem-solving skills. Also, two subjects with CHI who were unable to use indirect means (e.g. hints) of making requests exhibited considerable frontal lobe pathology. One subject was particularly concrete and perseverative. The other subject had fewer impaired abstraction skills but exhibited severe problems of impulse control. There is evidence that ToM deficits may account for the conversational and pragmatic difficulties experienced by speakers with TBI. Pragmatic interpretation is essentially dependent on ToM skills. Any act of pragmatic interpretation requires speakers and hearers to be able to attribute mental states, specifically communicative intentions, to the minds of their conversational partners. Such mental state attribution is the very essence of ToM. McDonald and Flanagan (2004) found that adults with TBI were able to recognise communicative intentions in the form of speaker beliefs in videotaped conversational exchanges only when this information was explicitly given. Second-order ToM judgements (i.e. inferences about someone's belief about another's belief) were related to the ability to understand conversational inference.

KEY POINTS: Language disorder in traumatic brain injury

- Complex clinical picture in TBI which is related to multi-focal cerebral pathology
- Aphasia can occur in clients with TBI; often structural language skills are relatively intact and most significant deficits are to be found in pragmatics and discourse

- Pragmatic deficits include difficulty adhering to conversational maxims, using indirect language (e.g. indirect requests, hints), judging politeness constraints and repairing conversational breakdown
- Discourse deficits include repetitiveness, missing information (low informational content), problems with cohesion and story grammar
- Pragmatic and discourse impairments are related to underlying cognitive deficits (e.g. executive function and ToM deficits)

5.5 Language disorder in dementia

Language disorder in the dementias is an often neglected aspect of the work of speech and language therapists. Reilly et al. (2010) remark that clinical academic training in dementia is not mandated in the UK, Australia or Canada. Neither is such training universally mandatory in the US for students who are pursuing graduate education in speech–language pathology. Discussion of language disorder in the dementias is largely conducted within research articles which are published in journals. Survey textbooks in communication disorders almost invariably neglect to mention the dementias and, if included, discussion rarely goes beyond the linguistic features of Alzheimer's disease. Shames and Anderson (2002), for example, devote just two paragraphs to the discussion of Alzheimer's disease and a single paragraph to primary progressive aphasia (a type of frontotemporal dementia). This situation is unacceptable in at least two respects. Firstly, it is estimated that by 2050, 13.2 million people in the US will have Alzheimer's disease (Hebert et al., 2003). This large figure is greater still when other forms of dementia are also considered. Clearly, this represents a considerable public health burden which speech and language therapists, along with other medical and health professionals, will have to address. Secondly, speech and language features are among the most reliable behavioural markers that clinicians can use to distinguish different types of dementia. In view of the diagnostic significance of these features, speech and language therapy is likely to play an increasingly important role in the management of dementia in years to come (Reilly et al., 2010). For these reasons, it is now timely to bring the discussion of language and communication problems in the dementias into the mainstream of clinical communication science.

The language decline in Alzheimer's disease has been extensively investigated. Clinical studies have shown that language subsystems are not uniformly impaired with deterioration in semantic and pragmatic knowledge occurring relatively early in the course of the disease and impairments in syntax and phonology occurring later in the condition. The disruption in semantic knowledge gives rise to naming and word-finding difficulties in clients with Alzheimer's disease, often within specific semantic categories and fields (Huff et al., 1986). Forbes-McKay and Venneri (2005) examined 30 patients with a clinical diagnosis of minimal to moderate probable Alzheimer's disease. A picture description task was used to assess spontaneous speech and writing skills. Over 70 per cent of patients with Alzheimer's disease performed below cut-off on scales that measured semantic processing skills. In a study of pragmatic skills in early Alzheimer's disease,

Feyereisen et al. (2007) studied the performance of 13 patients at a minimal or mild stage of the disease on a referential communication task. These investigators found that patients with Alzheimer's disease were less able to take previously shared information into account, used no definite referential expressions and were more idiosyncratic in their descriptions of the referent than healthy elderly adults. Lyons et al. (1994) examined the syntactic complexity of transcripts of interviews with 117 adults undergoing examination for Alzheimer's disease. Among the adults with mild dementia in this study, approximately 60 per cent of utterances were grammatically well-formed. This compared with 69 per cent of grammatically well-formed utterances produced by the adults with no dementia in the study. The reader is referred to Bayles et al. (1992), for discussion of linguistic abilities in different stages of Alzheimer's disease.

The non-Alzheimer's dementias have tended to be overlooked in the clinical communication science literature. Reilly et al. (2010) present an excellent overview of the clinical features of four such dementias – frontotemporal dementia, vascular dementia, Lewy body disease dementia and Parkinson's disease dementia. The language and communication features of progressive non-fluent aphasia (PNFA) and semantic dementia – two types of frontotemporal dementia – are well-characterised within this overview. Individuals with PNFA exhibit non-fluent speech with one or more of the following features: agrammatism, phonemic paraphasias and anomia. Stuttering, oral apraxia, impaired repetition, alexia, agraphia, early preservation of word meaning and late mutism are supportive diagnostic features. Specific linguistic findings in clients with PNFA include disproportionate impairment for the naming of verbs relative to nouns (Hillis et al., 2004) and grammatical processing impairment (Peelle et al., 2007). The progression to mutism in this type of dementia necessitates consideration of augmentative communication devices early in the course of the disease. Reilly et al. state that patients with semantic dementia produce fluent, empty speech which contains a preponderance of deictic expressions (e.g. I don't know ... It's that thing) and semantic paraphasias (e.g. 'cat' used for the target word 'Chihuahua'). A severe anomia is present. The ease with which these patients produce over-learned phrases can often make it difficult to discern any impairment in cursory conversation. Patients with semantic dementia exhibit surface dyslexia, i.e. they are unable to read irregular words (e.g. yacht) aloud. However, the ability to read orthographically regular words aloud is intact, as is single word repetition. Syntax and phonological processing are relatively preserved. Patients exhibit idiosyncratic word usage and press of speech (excessive speech produced at a rapid rate and which is difficult to interrupt).

It is estimated that between 15 and 20 per cent of patients in the advanced stages of HIV infection develop a progressive encephalopathy called AIDS dementia complex (ADC) or HIV dementia. ADC is not caused by opportunistic infections of the brain but is the result of the HIV virus itself (Portegies and Rosenberg, 1998). Cognition, motor function and behaviour are compromised in ADC. Aphasia, alexia and agraphia are typically absent. There may be few, if any, abnormalities on examination in mild ADC. However, in severe ADC, patients are mute, globally demented, paraparetic and incontinent of urine and faeces (Brew, 2007). McCabe et al. (2008) describe the language and communication skills of a 36-year-old male known as Warren who was diagnosed with ADC by an AIDS specialising neurologist. Neuropsychological testing revealed average working memory, psychomotor speed, visuo-construction and verbal fluency performance. However, Warren's attention in complex simultaneous processing tasks was significantly impaired. During a semi-structured interview conducted in his own home, Warren was observed to be verbose, unable to maintain topic, self-focused and unaware to a large extent of the needs of his listener. Although Warren displayed word-finding difficulties and produced circumlocutions, his language disorder was described as pragmatic in nature rather than a high-level aphasia. His pragmatic deficits are evident in the following exchange which is taken from the initial interview between Warren (W) and the researcher (R):

R: So you'd be 34 then?
W: I've been 34 for the last 3 years
R: ah, OK so you're actually?
W: Oh what happened was I added a year and a year at my birthday, didn't celebrate it so therefore I forgot about it. In September as a halfway between two ages I start saying what the next one is
R: Uh huh?
W: So I've added there as well and the years come along and I didn't remember doing either of the first two so I did it again when I was 32
R: Oh dear
W: Someone pointed out that I was 34 last year and 33 last year and I went 'no, I'm not I'm 34', I'm gonna get me a calculator and a new set of batteries that were still in the package so that guaranteed the calculator was working properly 'cause it kept telling me I was 33 and I could'a swore it was lying to me.
R: What year were you born in?
W: 64
R: 64
W: The odd thing was, was I was filling out doctors' forms and hospital forms and all sort of things, putting down the date of birth as xxth of xxxx of '64 and my age was 34 but a diversional therapist in a nursing home was the only person who actually noticed that there was something wrong with this picture. I thought 'well, it's fairly obvious I'm in it' so there's your problem. (McCabe et al., 2008: 208–9)

Warren's linguistic output displays problems with topic maintenance. On the one hand, he tends to perseverate on the topic of age. The result of this topic perseveration is that his language displays considerable informational redundancy. On the other hand, within each of his extended utterances, he can also veer off topic such as when he discusses points like the calculator and batteries and gives a detailed account of how he determines his age. The inclusion of these points and other unnecessary details finds his verbal output violating conversational maxims of relevance and quantity and confirms the initial clinical impression of verbosity. Of course, as he engages in each of these extended turns, he is also denying his interlocutor opportunities to take turns in the conversation. Indeed, the researcher is confined to taking minimal turns after her initial questions. Warren's language was judged to contain non-specific vocabulary. For example, it is difficult for the listener to determine the referents of several of the pronouns and adverbs that Warren uses (e.g. 'it's fairly obvious I'm in *it*'; 'So I've added *there* as well'). The effect of Warren's failure to manage reference in language is that the listener must work harder to make sense of his utterances. This suggests poor awareness on Warren's part of how referential difficulties in his own output are increasing the burden of comprehension for his listener. McCabe et al. attribute at least some of these pragmatic problems to Warren's reduced cognitive executive functioning.

KEY POINTS: Language disorder in dementia

- Alzheimer's disease is the most common cause of dementia; other dementias include frontotemporal dementia, vascular dementia, Lewy body disease dementia, Parkinson's disease dementia and HIV dementia (AIDS dementia complex)
- Speech and language features are reliable behavioural markers of different types of dementia and so have diagnostic significance
- In Alzheimer's disease, semantic and pragmatic subsystems are impaired before syntax and phonology
- Two types of frontotemporal dementia – semantic dementia and progressive non-fluent aphasia – are characterised by fluent and non-fluent speech, respectively
- In HIV dementia, pragmatic deficits are observed typically (but not always) in the absence of aphasia

---

5.6   Assessment and treatment

In order to plan effective intervention, language disorders must first be assessed by clinicians. Assessment methods can be broadly classified as formal or informal in nature. Formal assessment proceeds on the basis of published, standardised tests which are widely available in clinical settings. They can only be employed by speech and language therapists who are trained in how to administer them and interpret their results. Two of the best-known formal assessments in use with language disordered adults include the Boston Diagnostic Aphasia Examination (BDAE; Goodglass et al., 2001) and the Western Aphasia Battery-Revised (WAB-R; Kertesz, 2006). The BDAE evaluates perceptual modalities (e.g. auditory, visual and gestural), processing functions (e.g. comprehension, analysis, problem-solving) and response modalities (e.g. writing, articulation and manipulation). The third edition of the assessment includes extended tools that test syntax comprehension, locate category-specific difficulties in word comprehension and word production and assess grapho-phonemic processing. The Boston Naming Test, which examines visual confrontation naming abilities, has also been incorporated into the third edition. The standard form of the assessment takes 90 minutes to complete, although a short form which takes 30–45 minutes is also available. The WAB-R is a battery of eight subtests (32 short tasks). These tests examine content, fluency, auditory comprehension, repetition, naming, reading, writing and calculation. Two new supplementary tasks – reading and writing of irregular words and non-words – assist the clinician in distinguishing between surface, deep (phonological) and visual dyslexia. The full battery takes between 30 and 45 minutes to complete. However, a bedside version of the WAB-R can be carried out in 15 minutes.

The long-standing use of these formal assessments by clinicians attests to their clinical value (the BDAE and WAB were first published in 1972 and 1982, respectively). The BDAE, for example, has the benefits of being a standardised, valid, reliable assessment. Its standardisation permits clinicians to compare the performance of individual patients against a set of norms. As a valid assessment, the BDAE allows clinicians to discriminate accurately amongst aphasia types. The reliability of the BDAE consists in its good internal consistency in terms of what the items within the subtests are measuring. Formal assessments such as the BDAE permit clinicians to chart improvement in a patient's language skills over time, as the same test items are administered in the same way on all occasions of use. The undoubted benefits of these assessments, however, must be set against a number of important limitations. One such limitation concerns the ecological validity of formal assessments. While formal assessments may be able to measure a patient's ability to perform specific linguistic tasks, there is concern that these tasks do not reflect the 'real-life' communicative contexts in which clients must operate. So, the argument goes, knowing that a client cannot repeat sentences or name objects in pictures – two formal assessment tasks that adults with aphasia are regularly asked to perform – tells us little or nothing about how that client may communicate at home with his spouse and family, or communicate with his friends in a social setting. Only assessments that can give insight into how clients perform in these contexts have any ecological validity, it is argued. Concerns of this type are compounded by the fact that some clients (e.g. clients with TBI and pragmatic disorders) can perform well on formal language assessments, and yet exhibit significant communication problems. Coelho (2007: 123) addresses this issue when he remarks that:

> [E]xamining performance by means of [language] batteries may give the impression that communicative skills are intact. However, when individuals with disordered pragmatics are engaged in interactions, the listener has the impression that they are off target, disorganized, or tangential. Thus, the communicative behaviour of interest lies beyond the level of single words or sentences, which such individuals have little difficulty with, but rather involves longer units of language such as discourse.

The single-word and sentence testing formats used in formal language assessments are unable to target the language and communication skills that are most compromised in clients with pragmatic and discourse deficits. It is in an effort to assess these skills that clinicians have devised a range of informal assessments. These assessments examine language and communication skills in conversational and other everyday communicative contexts and are based on conversation- and discourse-analytic techniques. Some of these assessments are aimed at specific clinical groups. For example, the Conversation Analysis Profile for People with Aphasia (CAPPA; Whitworth et al., 1997) is specifically designed for use with adults with aphasia and their conversational partners. The CAPPA is based on the Conversation Analysis Profile for People with Cognitive Impairment (CAPPCI; Perkins et al., 1997) which is intended for use with clients who have generalised cognitive impairment (as in dementia or after head injury) and their key conversational partners. The CAPPA includes a structured interview that is conducted with the client with aphasia and his or her key conversational partner, an analysis of a 10-minute sample of conversation between the person with aphasia and his or her partner and a summary profile that brings together information obtained from the interview and conversation analysis. In the conversation analysis component of CAPPA, the three key areas of conversational management that are assessed are initiation and turn-taking, repair and topic management.

We have also seen in this chapter how analysis of narrative and procedural discourse can yield important information about a client's pragmatic language skills. The analysis of discourse can proceed on a number of levels. Coelho (2007) characterises these levels as microlinguistic, microstructural, macrostructural and superstructural. At the microlinguistic level, investigators are concerned to perform within-sentence analysis. Measures at the microlinguistic level include productivity (e.g. words per T-unit), grammatical complexity (e.g. subordinate clauses per T-unit) or tallies of propositions and content units. Microstructural or across-sentence analysis examines how well sentences are linked to each other within an extract of discourse. Sentences may be conjoined in a number of different ways, with the type of cohesive ties used varying, depending on the nature of the text and the ability and style of the speaker. Measures of local and global coherence are integral to a macrostructural analysis of discourse. Local coherence and global coherence describe the relationship of the meaning or content of an utterance to the preceding utterance and the general topic of discourse, respectively. A range of informational or content measures are also included in a macrostructural analysis of discourse. Such measures include content units, correct information units and propositions, as well as ratios that relate information units to time such as correct information units per minute. At the superstructural level, narratives may be analysed in terms of their story grammar. Story grammar describes 'the purported regularities in the internal structure of stories that guide an individual's comprehension and production of the logical relationships between characters and events (temporal and causal)' (Coelho, 2007: 125).

Assessments based on conversation and discourse analysis give clinicians considerable insight into the pragmatic functioning of clients. But this insight is achieved at a cost. The recording, transcription and analysis of even small amounts of conversation present a challenge to the busy clinician. Coelho (2007: 126) states that the transcription and analysis of a 15-minute sample of conversation may require three hours. This commitment of time is not possible within the working contexts of most clinicians. This fact alone has undoubtedly prevented the widespread clinical use of these assessment techniques. Regardless of the techniques employed during assessment, the findings of assessment must provide a rational basis for whatever treatment or intervention the clinician decides to pursue. Treatment may target specific language skills. For example, semantic-level deficits are routinely targeted in aphasia intervention. Drew and Thompson (1999) used a semantic-based treatment to train naming of nouns in two semantic categories. The subjects in this intervention were four subjects with Broca's aphasia who had severe naming deficits. Interventions may target spoken and/or written language in either input (comprehension) or output (expression) modes. In some cases, written language may be the target of therapy. In other cases, it may be the modality through which therapy is conducted when an auditory/verbal treatment has failed to produce any gain in language skills. The speaker with aphasia discussed in exercise 5.1 is a case in point. Hough (1993) used visual/written information and visual word and sentence comprehension tasks to treat an adult with Wernicke's aphasia. This client had failed to make linguistic or communicative gains in the eight months following a stroke. All auditory/verbal stimulus presentation was excluded from the intervention. After two months of treatment, improvement was observed in naming abilities and in a general ability to communicate in conversation.

Group therapy is now used extensively in the management of clients with aphasia. Its benefits in this clinical population are numerous. Group therapy more closely resembles everyday communication in both its number of participants and social dimensions than do individual sessions between a client and clinician. It provides an important opportunity for the generalisation of language skills to occur. Also, adults with aphasia derive much needed psychological support from engaging with other people who are experiencing similar communication problems. Clinicians have recognised the vital role that conversational partners can play in facilitating communication in adults with aphasia. This role is now addressed through the inclusion of training programmes for conversational partners in most interventions for aphasia. Kagan et al. (2001) evaluated an intervention called Supported Conversation for Adults with Aphasia (SCA). Twenty volunteers received SCA training and 20 control subjects merely interacted with clients with aphasia. On ratings of acknowledging competence and revealing competence in their partners with aphasia, trained volunteers scored significantly higher than untrained volunteers. Even though adults with aphasia did not receive training, there was nevertheless a positive change in ratings of social skills and message exchange skills in these clients as a result of their partners' training. Finally, where a language disorder is severe, an augmentative and alternative communication (AAC) system may be a client's only means of achieving functional communication. The choice of system is influenced by a range of factors, including residual language skills, the presence of cognitive deficits, visual and hearing impairments and the severity of any physical disability (e.g. hemiplegia). One such system is TalksBac which has been designed specifically for use with non-fluent adults with aphasia.

SUGGESTIONS FOR FURTHER READING

Bastiaanse, R. and Prins, R.S. (2014) 'Aphasia', in L. Cummings (ed.) *Cambridge Handbook of Communication Disorders* (Cambridge: Cambridge University Press), pp. 224–46.

McDonald, S., Togher, L. and Code, C. (eds) (1999) *Communication Disorders following Traumatic Brain Injury* (Hove, East Sussex: Psychology Press).

Murdoch, B.E. (2010) *Acquired Speech and Language Disorders: A Neuroanatomical and Functional Neurological Approach*, (Chichester, West Sussex: Wiley-Blackwell, 2nd edn), ch. 5 (right-hemisphere language disorder) and ch. 6 (language in the dementias).

EXERCISES

Exercise 5.1 Hough (1993) describes the case of a 66-year-old female who suffered two left-hemisphere strokes. This woman's language difficulties were documented over a 10-month period following the onset of these strokes. She received a diagnosis of Wernicke's aphasia which was characterised by neologistic jargon and a severe auditory comprehension deficit. Eight months post-stroke, no linguistic or communicative improvements had been observed. A new therapeutic regimen was then introduced. After just two months, the naming abilities of the patient improved as did her general ability to communicate in conversation. The table below contains the naming responses of this woman on items in the Boston Naming Test (BNT) and the Boston Diagnostic Aphasia Examination (BDAE) at different intervals post-stroke. These responses are characterised by neologistic and semantic jargon. Describe how this woman's naming errors change over time, particularly as a result of the introduction of a new treatment approach.

	At onset	**7 mths post-onset**	**8 mths post-onset**	**10 mths post-onset**
BNT: 'scissors' 'flower' 'pencil'	/ækwʌb/ /lɛdi/ /kwobɚ/	/fwɛno/ /wide/ /bɪvɪk/	/saɪbwɚ/ /fenhɑl/ /gɪfku/	/kʌtmæn/ /blumpat/ /pɛnres/
BDAE: 'drinking' 'cactus'	/pɛpo/ /kæbat/	/kɪbin/ /tukɪt/	/nodɪk/ /sʌtʌs/	/kʌpʌp/ /prɪkəl/

Exercise 5.2 A male patient with RHD studied by Abusamra et al. (2009: 75) produces the extract in (B) in response to a narrative text (A) from the MEC Protocol (Joanette et al., 2004). The patient's attempt to reconstruct this narrative is problematic in certain respects. Using your knowledge of language disorder in RHD, explain how this patient's narrative production is problematic.

Extract (A)

John is a farmer from the north. He has been busy for several days digging a well on his land. The work is almost over.

This morning John has arrived to finish his work and sees that during the night the well has collapsed and half of it is filled with earth. He's very upset about this. He thinks for some minutes and says to himself, 'I have an idea'. He leaves his shirt and cap on the edge of the well, hides the pick and pail, and climbs up a tree to hide himself.

Later, a neighbour passes by and approaches John to talk to him a little. When he sees his shirt and cap he thinks John is working at the bottom of the well. The fellow passes near by, bends down a little, and sees the well half-filled with dirt and starts to desperately cry out, 'Help! Help! Friends! Come immediately! John is buried under the well!...' The neighbors run towards the well and start digging to save poor John. When the neighbors stop taking away the earth, John comes down the tree, approaches them and says, 'Thanks a lot, you've been a great help'.

Extract (B)

There was a farmer who was digging a hole uh uh uh uh well he was digging a hole until at a certain depth... uh uh uh uh... er. who was digging a well eh eh eh so he was digging with a shovel and a pick... uh uh uh... objects that don't look like what we call shovel and pick I mean they have really something to do with the ground... not only uh uh uh... generally a wine... the farmer moves the it it it more with shovel than pick or at least like a pick. And so he went down to a certain depth and he was, was tired, it was night and so and the next day... he sees the well has collapsed I mean collapsed from a part of of of of You don't remind me any more...

Exercise 5.3   The following narrative was produced by a 41-year-old woman with TBI who was studied by Biddle et al. (1996: 461–2). The narrative production task required this client with TBI to recount an occasion on which she had got lost. Her linguistic output contains a number of features that are characteristic of the spoken discourse of clients with TBI. Describe these features using extracts of language from the narrative.

Well, I've gotten lost even coming here. It was probably the second time I came here. I, uh, went down, uh, 27, no 96, I think. And I came up... I remember they said 14 mile. I thought ended. Well, anyways, I just went around and around in circles. And uh... so I got lost there. And it doesn't seem... I do drive myself when I come here but I still get confused. I don't get lost but I get scared. I see Southfield Road and then I just... Southfield and Greenfield. And still, after coming since February, I'm still not sure whether for a few minutes, a few seconds there if I'm supposed to take Greenfield or Southfield, you know. And then I don't know Southfield, you know. And, uh... I did get lost the second time I came here.

Exercise 5.4   The following extracts of spontaneous speech are taken from Horner and Heyman (1981: 338). They are transcriptions of the descriptions given by two patients with Alzheimer's disease of the cookie theft picture from the Boston Diagnostic Aphasia Examination. Case 1 is a 55-year-old woman who presented with a memory disorder for two years prior to hospital admission. Her electroencephalogram (EEG) was borderline and her computerised tomography (CT or CAT) scan was abnormal. She had a full-scale IQ of 63. Case 2 is a 75-year-old woman who presented with Alzheimer's disease for 48 months. Both EEG and CT studies were abnormal. Her full scale IQ was 75. The spoken and written language skills of both subjects were judged to be markedly impaired. Examine each of the extracts and then identify examples of the following linguistic features:

(a) The use of a stereotyped utterance related to word-finding difficulties
(b) Perseveration on a verb phrase
(c) Production of a word that is semantically associated with the target word
(d) Use of a filler expression during word-finding difficulty
(e) Topic digression
(f) Use of non-specific vocabulary when unable to retrieve target word

Case 1

Right there is, gettin' up, this, right there, he gonna, get this, cookies, [cue] I don't know, [cue] well uh, the, this coming out, [cue] water is coming out, [cue] I don't know, [cue] she's, drying that uh, [cue] uh, plates [cue] this is a, girl, and this is a boy, [cue] I don't know, he's coming on out, this, this stool on, is coming out...

Case 2

Oh I see a little girl looking for something that she put on the top of the, the uh room, and here she's knocked over a, a t-table-chair, and up here, the boy sees a cookie, uh, jar and he can't, stay away from it, and over here, uh, she, continues to work with the children, and they like, here, and they like the things she's doing and here are the little aprons for the girls, they, it, helps give them a little pull when they've done something wrong...

ANSWERS TO EXERCISES

Exercise 5.1

In the months post-stroke, this woman's naming responses move from a pattern where neologistic jargon predominates to a pattern in which she is using semantic jargon (i.e. words that are semantically related to the target word). This transition occurs rapidly following the introduction of a new treatment approach which was necessitated by eight months of therapy in which little improvement had been achieved. So it is that at 10 months post-onset, the patient's productions of 'scissors', 'flower', 'pencil', 'drinking' and 'cactus' resemble the words 'cut', 'bloom', 'pen', 'cup' and 'prickle', respectively. Her production of 'pencil' could be a phonological error rather than semantic jargon.

Exercise 5.2

There are several features of linguistic output in clients with RHD in extract (B). This patient exhibits perseveration in his repetition of 'was digging a hole/well' at the beginning of the extract. In the middle of the extract, he strays from the topic by talking about the shovel and pick in a level of detail that is not warranted within the narrative.

However, towards the end of the extract, he does regain the topic. He is also on-topic at the very start of the extract. In his final utterance, the patient abandons the narrative altogether to challenge the examiner. Although we don't know the exact nature of this challenge – the patient may be berating the examiner for not reminding him about the events that took place in the story – it nonetheless stands as a somewhat inappropriate comment in the context of this narrative production task.

Exercise 5.3

The narrative produced by this woman contains the following features which are characteristic of spoken discourse in TBI:

(1) There is considerable repetition throughout the narrative. Greenfield and Southfield are mentioned repeatedly and the client tells the examiner at the beginning and end of the narrative that she got lost the second time she attempted to make the journey.

(2) Utterances are started and then abandoned, e.g. 'And I came up...'; 'And it does seem...'. These incomplete utterances place a substantial burden on the listener, who must try to decide if they are relevant to the narrative and, if they are, fill in the information that is missing. False starts of this type may reflect difficulty deciding what the components of the narrative should be and organising those components accordingly.

(3) There are numerous fillers ('uh') and other expressions ('you know') that may indicate word-finding difficulties on the part of the patient or, again, uncertainty as to what components to include within the narrative.

(4) Other difficulties include referential disturbances (e.g. we don't know the referent of 'they' in the utterance 'I remember they said 14 mile') and omission of grammatical parts (e.g. the subject of the verb 'ended' in the utterance 'I thought ended'). Referential disturbances create problems of cohesion in narrative discourse.

Exercise 5.4

(a) Case 1: repeated use of 'I don't know' particularly following attempt by interlocutor to cue target word

(b) Case 1: repetition of verb phrase 'coming out' on four occasions throughout extract

(c) Case 2: production of 'table' when the target lexeme is 'chair'

(d) Cases 1 and 2: use of the expression 'uh' leading up to production of a target word (Case 1: 'she's, drying that uh, [cue] uh, plates'; Case 2: 'the boy sees a cookie, uh, jar)

(e) Case 2: digresses from describing the aprons to saying that they may be pulled when the girls have done something wrong

(f) Case 1: extensive use of demonstrative pronouns ('this', 'that') when unable to produce a target word (e.g. 'he gonna, get this'; 'this coming out'; 'drying that')

Communication Disorders in Mental Illness

6

6.1 Psychiatry and communication disorders

Mental illness has not always been a prominent or well-funded part of the work of speech and language therapists. In the mid-1990s, Muir (1996: 524) describes how approximately 40 therapists were working in different branches of psychiatry in the UK. Muir continues '[i]f it were not bordering on the realms of fantasy to speculate on how one would wish to see a service, one might suggest that at least one full-time post would be the minimum required cover for a sectorised mental health unit' (1996: 526). Later figures show that Muir's aspirations for the development of speech and language therapy (SLT) provision to clients with mental health problems are still very far from being realised. A study conducted in 1999 of the provision of SLT services to children with speech and language needs in England and Wales found that 81 per cent of services made no provision to facilities for children with emotional and behavioural difficulties (Law et al., 2000). The mean number of schools/units/resource bases receiving support from an SLT service was 0.3 for those facilities catering for children with emotional and behavioural difficulties (the lowest of seven special educational needs categories). The study's authors report 'particular shortfalls' in service provision to these children. In a survey conducted between January and February 2009 of SLT service leads, managers and professional advisers in Scotland, the Royal College of Speech and Language Therapists report that although 80 per cent of mental health service users have communication support needs, there was only the equivalent of five full-time therapists providing service to these clients in the country (Royal College of Speech and Language Therapists, 2010). Clearly, there is still some way to go before SLT services to children and adults with mental health problems match those of other client groups and attain an acceptable level of provision.

While the provision of SLT services to clients with mental illness is still far from ideal, there is no dispute about the real need which exists for these services. The prevalence of communication impairment in both adult and child clients with mental illness is now well documented. Emerson and Enderby (1996) examined the prevalence of speech and language disorders in 138 adults (aged 21 to 94 years) who were receiving care from the mental health unit of a district health authority. Subjects presented with a range of psychiatric diagnoses including paranoid psychosis, schizophrenia, schizo-affective disorder, bipolar disorder, depression and anxiety. Of these subjects, 98 (71 per cent) were rated as moderately or severely impaired on one or more aspects of speech and language. The aspects most often impaired were comprehension (57 subjects), naming (37 subjects) and spontaneous speech (32 subjects). Walsh et al. (2007) studied 60 patients (aged 18 to 76 years) who were randomly selected from an acute psychiatric inpatient unit and associated community services. They found that over 80 per cent of patients demonstrated impairment in language and 60 per cent displayed problems in communication and discourse. Equally high rates of communication impairment have been found in child psychiatric populations. Cohen et al. (1998) reported that 63.6 per cent of children aged 7 to 14 years who presented as child psychiatric outpatients reached criteria for language impairment. Attention deficit hyperactivity disorder (ADHD) was the most common psychiatric disorder in these children, accounting for 46 per cent of subjects. Kotsopoulos and Boodoosingh (1987) examined the speech and language skills of 46 children who were referred consecutively to a day psychiatric programme. These investigators found that 33 children (71.7 per cent) presented with speech and/or language impairment that required therapy.

The psychiatric disorders that we will examine in this chapter often have communication impairments as part of their symptomatology. These impairments include disorganised speech and alogia (see section 6.2 below) in schizophrenia and the consistent failure to speak in certain social situations despite speaking in other situations in selective mutism. (These impairments are part of the diagnostic criteria for schizophrenia and selective mutism in the *Diagnostic and Statistical Manual of Mental Disorders* (DSM-5; American Psychiatric Association, 2013)). However, it is also worth remarking that there are high prevalence rates of mental illnesses such as depression and anxiety in children and adults with primary communication disorders. These mental illnesses may be a consequence of the communication disorder (e.g. the child with a stammer who develops anxiety in response to repeated communication failure) or may be caused by the same aetiological factors that give rise to the communication disorder (e.g. neurological damage may cause depression in the adult with aphasia). Kauhanen et al. (2000) found that 70 per cent and 62 per cent of the subjects with aphasia in their study of 106 stroke patients fulfilled the DSM-III-R criteria for depression at 3 and 12 months post-stroke, respectively. During the 12-month follow-up period, the prevalence of major depression increased from 11 per cent to 33 per cent. Blumgart et al. (2010) examined social anxiety disorder (social phobia) in 200 adults who stutter. These investigators recorded a spot prevalence of social phobia in these adults of at least 40 per cent.

Primary communication disorders in children may also predispose affected individuals to the development of mental health problems. These problems often become apparent many years after intervention from SLT has ceased and subjects are in adulthood. Clegg et al. (1999) reported that one third of the

20 boys who participated in the Language Development Project in the UK exhibited mental health problems such as depression and schizophrenia in later life (a control group consisting of the siblings of these boys displayed no psychiatric or behaviour problems). This project started in the 1960s when the boys were approximately 7 years old. All 20 participants were diagnosed with developmental language disorders and were in their mid-thirties when this assessment of their psychiatric functioning was undertaken. Conti-Ramsden and Botting (2008) found a marked higher rate of anxiety and depression symptoms in adolescents with SLI compared with adolescents with normal language development. However, these investigators conclude that these symptoms 'do not appear to be a direct result of impoverished communicative experiences' (2008: 516). Whatever is ultimately shown to be the cause of these mental illnesses, the reader will do well to remember that there is a significant number of communication disordered clients who experience psychiatric problems but which nonetheless fall outside of the issues addressed in this chapter.

6.2   Communication in schizophrenia

Schizophrenia is a severe mental illness. According to the American Psychiatric Association (2000), prevalences of the disorder among adults are in the range 0.5 per cent to 1.5 per cent (although a lower lifetime prevalence of 4.0 per 1,000 is reported by Saha et al. (2005) in a review of prevalence estimates from 188 studies). Annual incidences are in the range of 0.5 to 5.0 per 10,000 (American Psychiatric Association, 2000). The incidence of schizophrenia is significantly higher in males than in females and is also higher in migrants and those living in urban areas (McGrath, 2006). The mean age at onset is typically lower in males than in females. Gorwood et al. (1995) report a mean age at onset of 27.8 years and 31.5 years in the males and females in their study, respectively. Diagnosis of schizophrenia proceeds according to the presence of positive and negative symptoms which are described in DSM-5 (American Psychiatric Association, 2013). Positive symptoms include thought disorder (disorganised and illogical thought), delusions (the holding of false and bizarre beliefs) and hallucinations (perception of things that do not exist), the most common of which are auditory hallucinations (the client with schizophrenia hears voices). Negative symptoms involve the absence of normal behaviours. These symptoms include affective flattening (reduced or absent expression of affect as indicated, for example, by an unresponsive facial expression), alogia (poverty of speech), apathy, avolition (absence of initiative or motivation) and social withdrawal. A further characteristic is grossly disorganised or catatonic behaviour. An individual must exhibit two (or more) of these symptoms, each present for a significant portion of time during a one-month period.

The linguistic and communication features of schizophrenia are now well-characterised. It is widely acknowledged that clients with schizophrenia experience structural language problems along with significant impairments in pragmatic and discourse skills. Problems with phonology and morphology appear to be uncommon (Covington et al., 2005). However, Chaika (1990: 24) described morphemic disturbances in a patient with schizophrenia in the form of the loss of the inflectional and derivational morphemes –*ed* and –*ion*, respectively, in 'I am being help with the food and the medicate...'. Syntactic errors are common in schizophrenia. They include the use of incomplete phrases and sentences which lack clauses. Chaika (1990: 221) describes how one subject omitted the object of the preposition *for* in 'he was blamed for and I didn't think that was fair...'. Ribeiro (1994: 263) examined the language of a patient with schizophrenia who routinely omitted the direct object of the verb *have*, as in 'No, only if you have. Do you have?'. Thomas (1997: 40) described how a patient with schizophrenia responded to the question 'Why do you think people believe in God?' with 'Um, *because* making a do in life. Isn't none of that stuff about evolution guiding isn't true any more now...'. The clause introduced by the subordinating conjunction *because* must be followed by a main clause which is absent in this case. There is evidence of deficits in lexical semantics in schizophrenia. Bizarre lexical choices are common. Chaika (1990: 202) reported a subject with schizophrenia who used 'the cash register man handled the financial matters' to describe the ringing up of money for an ice-cream cone. Lexical retrieval problems are also evident. A patient with schizophrenia examined by Chaika (1982: 172) selected 'memory' instead of 'memorise' in the following output:

> I feel that I still do not have this I still not have the thought pattern and the mental process and the brain wave necessary to open up a page open up the old testament and start to memory it...

It is worth remarking that such an error may equally be analysed as morphemic in nature (the omission of the derivational morpheme –*ise*) or as syntactic in nature (the use of the noun *memory* as opposed to the verb *memorise*). Covington et al. (2005) make a similar point when they argue that what appear to be morphemic errors in schizophrenia might equally be related to disruptions of syntax or lexical retrieval. Neologisms (literally, 'new word') are common errors in schizophrenia. Chaika (1974) relates these errors to word-finding difficulties. Only some of these errors are suggestive of a target lexeme that the patient may have failed to retrieve. For example, Thomas (1997: 38) reported a patient who uttered 'I got so angry I picked up a dish and threw it at the geshinker', where *geshinker* has phonological similarities to the context-appropriate word 'sink'. The neologisms in italics in the following extract, discussed by Chaika (1982: 170), are altogether less suggestive of target lexemes that the patient has failed to retrieve:

> ... you have to have a *plausity* of amendments to go through for the children's code, and it's no mental disturbance of *puterience*, it is an *amorition* law.

Pragmatic and discourse deficits are commonplace in schizophrenia. In terms of pragmatics, subjects with schizophrenia have difficulties recovering the implicatures of utterances, understanding non-literal language such as metaphors, idioms and proverbs, establishing the illocutionary force of speech acts and appreciating humour and sarcasm (see section 3.4 in Cummings (2009), for detailed discussion). As well as these deficits in receptive pragmatics, speakers with schizophrenia routinely display expressive pragmatic deficits. For example, these patients often contribute utterances to conversation that violate one or more Gricean maxims. Thomas (1997: 41) discusses the following extract of schizophrenic language. Although we are not told what precedes it, it violates the maxims of both relation and quantity (the response contains irrelevant information and too much information) if treated as a response to a question about how the patient came to be living in San Francisco. It is also problematic in terms of linguistic politeness, another area that is of concern to pragmatics:

> Then I left San Francisco and moved to ... where did you get that tie? It looks like it's left over from the 1950s. I like the warm weather in San Diego. Is that a conch shell on your desk? Have you ever gone scuba diving?

Discourse deficits in schizophrenia include problems with cohesion and coherence. Cohesion describes that large class of linguistic devices (e.g. personal pronouns, conjunctions) that allows speakers to link utterances together in a meaningful way. Coherence describes that attribute of a text whereby it holds together and makes sense as a whole. Cohesive difficulties have been frequently observed in schizophrenia (e.g. Bartolucci and Fine (1987)). Chaika and Lambe (1989) examined cohesion in the narratives produced by normal subjects and subjects with schizophrenia and mania after they had been shown a videostory. Subjects with schizophrenia made extensive use of non-referential exophora (terms which lacked an antecedent or referent in the story), as indicated in italics in the extract below. Not a single instance of this same cohesive difficulty was observed in the narratives of normal subjects:

> ... and I didn't think *that* was fair the way the way *they* did *that* either, so that's why I'm kinda like asking could *we* just get together for one big party or something ezz it hey if it we'd all in which is in not *they've* been here, so why *you* jis now discovering it?... (Chaika and Lambe, 1989: 418)

A discourse can exhibit cohesion and yet be incoherent. Hoffman et al. (1982: 211) states that 'the experience of coherence is less dependent on the specificity of the noun phrase (NP) referents or use of conjunctions, but rather is more fundamentally linked to whether the specific statements composing the text are experienced by the listener as having some meaningful relationship with each other'. The following extract from Hoffman et al. (1982: 228) was produced by a 41-year-old male with chronic schizophrenia:

Interviewer: Tell me some of your thoughts about school.

Patient: I hate school. You wanna know why?///I threw a spitball/and she made me swallow it.///I like your outfit. I like your sweater, can I borrow it?

The incoherence of this extract consists in the fact that the speaker with schizophrenia departs from the original context that is framed by the question – as he speaks, the patient is unable to maintain and elaborate upon a single conceptual framework relating to school but instead brings in a second framework relating to the interviewer's attire. Yet, the extract is perfectly cohesive. The speaker is able to engage in anaphoric reference in the use of the pronoun 'it' to refer back to the spitball and the sweater (the listener could also supply a likely referent for 'she' (viz., teacher) from context). He is able to link clauses through the use of the coordinating conjunction 'and'. Finally, he is able to use a hyponym of 'outfit' (viz., 'sweater') to link his final utterance to the utterance immediately preceding it.

Two further features of schizophrenic language are perseveration and glossomania (also known as 'clanging'). Perseveration describes the repetition of a linguistic form beyond what is appropriate in the context. The form in question may be simple consonant–vowel combinations, a word, phrase or clause. Ribeiro (1994: 276–7) observed perseveration on the nonsense elements 'dedededededede' and 'cololololololololololo', as well as the repetition of 'It's the mother, it's the mother, it's the mother...' in a patient with schizophrenia. There is extensive perseveration in the following extract of language in schizophrenia from Chaika (1982: 171–2). Perseveration is not only evident on 'will I see Paradise will I not see Paradise' and 'should I answer should I not answer' at the beginning and end of the extract, but there is also considerable perseveration of 'pass by in the car in the house' in the middle of the extract and 'I could read their mind' at the start and in the middle:

> ... when I'm not sure if it's possible about the way I think **I could read people mind** about people's society attitude plot and spirit so I think **I could read their mind** as they drive by in the car sh- *will I see Paradise will I not see Paradise should I answer should I not answer* I not answer w- their thought of how I read think **I could read their mind** about when they <u>pass by in the car in the house</u> <u>pass by in the car in the house</u> <u>pass by in the car from my house</u> I just correct for them for having me feel better about myself not answer will I *should I answer should I not answer will I see Paradise will I not see Paradise*... (*italics*, **bold** and <u>underlining</u> added).

Glossomania occurs where a client with schizophrenia produces long sequences of utterances in which sound or meaning associations are developed. In the following extract from Cohen (1978: 29), the words *clay, gray, hay, hay-day* and *mayday* are phonologically similar, while meaning associations are developed in *mayday* and *help* (mayday is the international radiotelephone distress signal) and between the salmon pink colour of an object and the fish salmon:

> (Subject is asked the colour of an object. It is salmon pink)
> A fish swims. You call it a salmon. You cook it. You put it in a can. You open the can. You look at it in this colour.
> Looks like clay. Sounds like gray. Take you for a roll in the hay. Hay-day. Mayday. Help. I need help.

KEY POINTS: Schizophrenia

- serious mental illness that affects approximately 1 in every 100 people
- diagnosis based on positive and negative symptoms in DSM-5 (American Psychiatric Association, 2013)
- problems with phonology and morphology are relatively uncommon
- syntactic and lexical semantic deficits extensively reported
- receptive and expressive pragmatics are disordered
- deficits in discourse cohesion and coherence
- perseveration and glossomania evident in verbal output

6.3 Communication disorders in other mental illnesses

While schizophrenia has been extensively examined in the clinical communication literature, the same cannot be said of a range of other mental illnesses found in children and adults. As well as receiving limited SLT provision (see Law et al. (2000) in section 6.1), children with emotional and behavioural disorders have received little in the way of examination of their communication skills. These disorders include attention deficit hyperactivity disorder (ADHD), selective mutism and conduct disorder. It is increasingly being recognised that children with these psychiatric diagnoses present with significant communication disorders that require assessment and intervention. The communication impairments that attend bipolar disorder in adults will also be examined in this section. Like emotional and behavioural disorders, bipolar disorder has also been largely neglected in the clinical communication literature. This is despite the fact that there is now clear evidence that clients with bipolar disorder do experience impaired communication skills. We examine what the small body of literature in this area reveals about those skills.

6.3.1 Emotional and behavioural disorders

It has been known for some time that emotional and behavioural disorders (EBDs) and communication disorders quite often occur alongside each other in children. Cantwell and Baker (1980) reported a psychiatric diagnosis in 53 per cent of 200 children who attended a community speech and hearing clinic. The most common diagnosis was attention-deficit disorder which was followed by oppositional disorder and conduct disorder. Of the 107 children who received a psychiatric diagnosis, 51 were in the area of behaviour disorders. In a later study, Baker and Cantwell (1982) examined psychiatric disorders in three different groups of communication disordered children: purely speech-disordered children, speech-and-language-disordered children and purely language-disordered children. They found emotional disorders in 21 per cent of speech-disordered children, 30 per cent of speech-and-language disordered children and 53 per cent of language-disordered children. Behaviour disorders were also common in these children. Attention-deficit disorder affected 22 per cent of the speech-and-language-disordered children and 21 per cent of language-disordered children. Oppositional disorder occurred in 8 per cent of speech-and-language-disordered children and 16 per cent of language-disordered children. Conduct disorder affected 21 per cent of language-disordered children. Dyrborg and Goldschmidt (1996) examined 1,151 patients (0–17 years) consecutively admitted to a child psychiatric centre in a five-year period. This sample was found to have 116 patients (10 per cent) with language disorders. Dyrborg and Goldschmidt found that language disorders were most often comorbid with conduct disorders. With such clear evidence of the co-occurrence of EBDs and communication disorders, it is truly remarkable that more clinical communication research has not been undertaken in this area.

Attention deficit hyperactivity disorder affects between 3 per cent and 7 per cent of school-age children and occurs more frequently in males than females – male-to-female ratios can range from 2:1 to 9:1 (American Psychiatric Association, 2000). The disorder is diagnosed according to behavioural criteria. These criteria state that an individual must show six or more symptoms of inattention that have persisted for at least six months to a degree that is maladaptive and inconsistent with developmental level. In addition to these inattention symptoms, individuals must also show six or more symptoms of hyperactivity-impulsivity. Some hyperactive-impulsive or inattentive symptoms must be present before 7 years of age and impairment from these symptoms must be evident in two or more settings (e.g. at school and at home). Clinically significant impairment in social, academic or occupational functioning must be clearly demonstrated and the symptoms must not occur during pervasive developmental disorder, schizophrenia or other psychotic disorder. Neither should they be better accounted for by another mental disorder (e.g. mood disorder). There are three main subtypes of ADHD – a combined type, a predominantly inattentive type and a predominantly hyperactive-impulsive type. In individuals with ADHD there may be a history of multiple foster placements, child abuse or neglect, infections (e.g. encephalitis), neurotoxin exposure (e.g. lead poisoning), intellectual disability and drug exposure in utero (American Psychiatric Association, 2000).

In section 6.1, it was stated that a number of psychiatric disorders have communicative symptomatology as part of their clinical picture. This is particularly the case in ADHD where symptoms of inattention, hyperactivity and impulsivity relate directly to communication features. Diagnostic criteria include 'often does not seem to listen when spoken to directly' as one of the symptoms of inattention and 'often talks excessively' as a symptom of hyperactivity (American Psychiatric Association, 2000). Impulsivity symptoms are almost entirely characterised in terms of communication and include 'often blurts out answers before questions have been completed' and 'often interrupts or intrudes on others (e.g. butts into conversations)'. These communicative behaviours are amply demonstrated in the following exchange between an adult and an 8-year-old boy who has received a diagnosis of ADHD (Tannock, 2005: 45). The exchange occurs 20 minutes after the start of a psychoeducational assessment:

> Child: 'What are we gonna do next? Huh? What's in there? What's that?'
> (interferes by grabbing test materials)
> Adult: 'You'll see in a sec'
> (adult reaches into case for next set of test materials)
> – a few minutes later, child interrupts testing –
> Child: 'Where's the um ... the things ... um ... where's the um ... bugs?'
> (climbs on seat to peer into case)
> Adult: 'Pardon? What bugs? There are no bugs here. Now, tell me what –'
> – child interrupts again –
> Child: (loud unmodulated voice) '– The bugs. You said I'll see the bugs. I don't wanna do this. I wanna see the bugs ... the ... um ... secs ... the insecs!'

In this short exchange, the child interrupts the adult's conversational turn on two occasions and creates two further, non-verbal interruptions (he grabs test materials and climbs onto the seat). His verbal contributions consist largely of questions which are delivered in quick succession and do not wait for responses from the adult. Even when presented with a direct command ('Now, tell me what ...'), it is clear the child disregards the adult's instruction and continues to pursue a topic (the bugs) which the adult has indicated has no relevance to the exchange (the adult explicitly states 'There are no bugs here'). These conversational and pragmatic anomalies are compounded by structural language difficulties as well. The child exhibits some word-finding problems in his utterance in the middle of the exchange. He uses the non-specific term 'things' when he is unable to retrieve the target lexemes 'bugs' or 'insects'. The child's inattention may explain his misunderstanding of the adult's utterance 'You'll see in a sec(ond)'. The child appears to have heard the utterance 'You'll see an insect'. His inattention appears to have permitted a superficial phonological similarity between 'insect' and 'in a sec' to become the basis of a breakdown in comprehension.

Selective mutism – formerly known as 'elective mutism' – is a relatively uncommon disorder. It is generally agreed that the disorder has a prevalence ranging from 0.03 per cent to 0.2 per cent (Sharp et al., 2007). There is evidence that the disorder is more commonly found in girls than in boys. Female-to-male ratios are reported to range from 2.6:1 to 1.5:1 (Garcia et al., 2004). Diagnostic criteria require the individual with selective mutism to display a consistent failure to speak in certain social situations (e.g. at school) even though speaking occurs in other situations. The disturbance should last at least one month (not the first month of school) and should interfere with educational or occupational achievement or with social communication. The failure to speak must not be the result of a lack of knowledge of or comfort with the language required in a social situation. The disorder should not be better explained by a communication disorder (e.g. stuttering) and must not occur during a pervasive developmental disorder, schizophrenia or other psychotic disorder. Social anxiety or a phobia disposition, neurodevelopmental delay/disorder, family immigration and marital discord have all been associated with selective mutism (Elizur and Perednik, 2003).

The following case study from Johnson and Wintgens (2001) describes a girl named Isobel who received intervention from a speech and language therapist from the age of 8 years. The case demonstrates how a late referral to an experienced speech and language therapist can result in selective mutism becoming entrenched and taking longer to resolve as a consequence.

CASE STUDY: Selective mutism

Initial concerns about Isobel's lack of verbal communication were first raised from the age of 3 years. During her first term at playgroup, Isobel did not speak at all. Before starting nursery school at the age of 4 years, Isobel said she was not going to talk at nursery. When she was 6 years old, Isobel was referred to an educational psychologist. No direct intervention took place and her mutism persisted unaltered. At 7 years of age, Isobel was referred to an art therapist. Although she attended weekly individual sessions for a period of six months, and enjoyed the art work, she did not speak to the therapist and no improvement was observed in her mutism. Isobel was nearly 8 years old when she was first referred to a speech and language therapist. The therapist worked in a child mental health department and had some experience of selective mutism.

During an initial SLT assessment with Isobel and her parents, it emerged that Isobel spoke easily to her closest family members at home, but did not speak to teachers and peers or even to her own parents while in the school building. She engaged in limited speaking to close friends and family members when outside. Isobel had grommets inserted bilaterally and had intermittent hearing loss. However, she did not have developmental speech and language problems. Her own parents described how they had been quiet and shy as children.

At 8 years of age, SLT with Isobel was initiated. She received 10 sessions in the clinic every two to three weeks. Therapy took the form of a structured programme that moved through stages of confident speaking. It also monitored in-school work with her mother which aimed to bring about speaking with her mother and then small groups of children in the school's library. Isobel was recorded reading. These recordings were used to let her classmates gradually hear her voice. When Isobel was 9 years old, a sliding-in technique was used as a means of introducing the teacher in simple structured talking activities. Two or three times a week for 10 minutes, Isobel participated in an in-school programme during which the teacher extended confident speaking on a one-to-one basis. New locations and people were also introduced. Progress was reviewed through SLT appointments which were held every four, six, then eight weeks. These reviews were used to set community talking targets. Between these appointments, occasional telephone reviews took place. At 10 years of age, a talking circle was used in school to extend Isobel's range of classmates and talking content.

At 10.5 years of age, Isobel had a considerably enhanced verbal repertoire. She was able to speak to the friends of her parents, answer the telephone and speak with ease to anyone in her community. She was able to speak to the teacher at his desk, to other teachers and children in school and within groups composed of 10 to 15 of her classmates. However, she was still unable to speak in front of the whole class and could not answer the register. In order to increase her confidence in social communication skills, she was going to attend drama classes.

WEBSITE: Selective mutism

View the video file *Help Me to Speak-Selective Mutism* (broadcast on Channel 4 in the UK on 10 April 2006). This programme charts the experience of a 5-year-old girl called Madeleine who has selective mutism. Madeleine is seen receiving treatment from speech and language therapist Maggie Johnson. This programme is a RDF Television Production for Channel 4. The permission of both RDF Television and Channel 4 to use this material is gratefully acknowledged.

For a diagnosis of conduct disorder to be made in accordance with DSM-IV-TR criteria, an individual must exhibit 'a repetitive and persistent pattern of behaviour in which the basic rights of others or major age-appropriate societal norms or rules are violated' (Biederman et al., 2007: 98). Such an individual must exhibit three or more of the following criteria in the past 12 months, with at least one criterion present in the last six months: aggression to people and animals; destruction of property; deceitfulness or theft; serious violations of rules. The behaviour disturbance in conduct disorder must cause clinically significant impairment in social, academic or occupational functioning. Criteria for antisocial personality disorder must not be met if the individual is 18 years or older. There are three subtypes of conduct disorder – a childhood-onset type (onset of at least one criterion prior to 10 years of age), adolescent-onset type (absence of criteria prior to 10 years) and unspecified onset (age at onset unknown). In general population studies, the prevalence of conduct disorder varies from less than 1 per cent to more than 10 per cent (American Psychiatric Association, 2000). Eme (2007) reports that boys are about two to four times more likely than girls to develop a form of conduct disorder and 10 to 15 times more likely than girls to develop the life-course-persistent type.

Although children and adolescents with conduct disorder are known to have communication problems, few studies have systematically examined communication skills in this clinical population. Olvera et al. (2005) examined language functioning in 34 incarcerated juvenile offenders who met criteria for conduct disorder. Additionally, eight of these offenders had comorbid bipolar disorder. Relative to controls, impairments in verbal memory–language functioning were found in all subjects with conduct disorder regardless of their bipolar disorder status. Gilmour et al. (2004) used the Children's Communication Checklist to investigate pragmatic abilities in 142 children who were referred for clinical investigation. Of these children, 55 had a predominant diagnosis of conduct disorder, 87 had an autism spectrum condition and 60 displayed typical development. Pragmatic language impairments and other behavioural features similar to those found in autism were observed in two thirds of the children with conduct disorder. Other language skills discussed in relation to conduct disorder include reading. Although reading deficits are frequently reported in children with conduct disorder, the exact nature of this relationship is unclear. In an effort to address the role of reading in conduct disorder, Bennett et al. (2003) examined the relation between reading achievement at school entry and conduct problems 30 months later in a sample of kindergarten and grade-1 children. These investigators found that an eight point increase in reading scores resulted in a 23 per cent decrease in the risk of conduct problems 30 months later. Bennett et al. concluded that reading problems may contribute to the early onset of conduct disorder.

6.3.2　Bipolar disorder

Bipolar disorder (formerly, 'manic depression') is a psychiatric disorder in which the patient's mood alters between manic episodes (characterised by euphoria, restlessness, poor judgement and risk-taking behaviour), depressive episodes (characterised by depression, anxiety and hopelessness), and episodes of normal mood (known as 'euthymia'). There are four types of bipolar disorder – bipolar I, bipolar II, rapid cycling and cyclothymia – which vary in accordance with the number and duration of manic and depressive episodes. Prevalence figures vary between studies. In a New Zealand study, Wells et al. (2010) reported that the lifetime prevalence of bipolar disorder (types I + II) is 1.7 per cent. Kozloff et al. (2010) recorded a lifetime prevalence of 3.0 per cent in 15–24-year-olds in a Canadian sample. Reviewing data from the Cross-National Collaboration on major depression and bipolar disorder, Grant and Weissman (2007) found that there were no consistent sex differences in bipolar disorder.

There is now considerable evidence that individuals with bipolar disorder experience significant language and communication disturbances. In a study that analysed the speech output of clients with schizophrenia, bipolar disorder and depression, Lott et al. (2002) found illogicality in 62.1 per cent of clients with bipolar disorder, the highest figure of all three psychiatric diagnoses. Poverty of speech was present in 6.9 per cent of patients with bipolar disorder (patients who display poverty of speech have a decreased amount of speech). In a study of the prevalence of speech and language problems amongst patients receiving care from a mental health unit, Emerson and Enderby (1996) recorded language comprehension problems in 33 per cent of their patients with bipolar disorder. Difficulties with spontaneous speech, picture description, naming and fluency were observed in 25 per cent, 25 per cent, 16 per cent and 8 per cent of clients with bipolar disorder, respectively. Radanovic et al. (2008) examined the performance in language tests of 33 euthymic elderly patients with bipolar disorder but no dementia. When compared with healthy controls, these patients exhibited a mild but significant impairment in language-related ability scores. McClure et al. (2005) found that paediatric outpatients with bipolar disorder performed more poorly than healthy comparison subjects on the pragmatic judgement subtest of the Comprehensive Assessment of Spoken

Language. Finally, Sigurdsson et al. (1999) found that adolescents who developed early-onset bipolar disorder were significantly more likely to have experienced delayed language than a group of control subjects with depression but without psychotic features.

Episodes of depression and mania in bipolar disorder are characterised by quite distinct linguistic features. In the case of depression, Fine (2006) lists these features as the use of negative sentences, lack of normal intonation and choice of topic (referring typically to death, suicide or hopelessness). Negative words – not (n't), no, never, neither, nothing, nor, nowhere – can be seen to predominate in the verbal output of the depressed patient. The following extract from an interview with a speaker with depression contains a number of negative markers which signal the individual's depressed mood:

I: was she willing to take care of the baby?
S: I would<u>n't</u> let her … <u>no</u> … you know … I just did<u>n't</u> feel like that um if I could<u>n't</u> take care of her. I did<u>n't</u> want anybody else to
I: right
S: plus I did<u>n't</u> want to run into her … if I saw her I would keep her
I: right
S: I do<u>n't</u> know … I do<u>n't</u> know why she turned against me to tell you the truth … in fact that's one of the reasons … she does<u>n't</u> like A (name), my husband (Fine, 2006: 240; underlining added)

The speaker may also signal depressed mood and a diminished interest or pleasure in activities through certain lexical choices. Fine (2006) states that there may be reduced use of verbs that report affection (e.g. like, want, enjoy), use of adjectives that report a negative subjective state (e.g. bored, uninterested, fed up, tired of) and use of negative expressions that contain intensifiers such as 'very' and 'really' (e.g. 'not very much', 'not especially'). The depressed speaker may exhibit psychomotor retardation in slowed speech and thinking. In speech, this may be evidenced by a reduction in the amount of talk produced by the speaker, reduced variety of the content of talk or reduced variation in intonation (Fine, 2006). A reduced amount of talk can occur both within clauses and across clauses. Within clauses, a depressed speaker may fail to describe the kinds and types of objects (e.g. *'prisoner of war* camps') but may tend to describe the qualities or attributes of things (e.g. *'truthful nasty* jokes'). There may be little expansion of information across clauses so that answers to questions are short and undeveloped. This can be seen in the following interview with a depressed speaker:

I: so we were talking about you and your present condition and that kind of thing
S: right
I: is there any way you are … all the time would you say I mean that's worse now and … other things are going on but would you say that by-and-large you always were a rather self-conscious person
S: … yes I am

> I: do you know where it comes from ... do you think that as a child you had experiences that made you ah ... become self-conscious and kind of ashamed of some things about yourself
>
> S: ... hmm ... it could be (Fine, 2006: 245)

Reduced variety of the content of talk is evident in the choice of content words made by the depressed speaker. According to Fine (2006), the speaker may use a restricted set of nouns encoding things, people and places (uninterrupted talk about the lake, etc.), of verbs encoding events (repeated talk about sleeping, eating, etc.) and of adverbs encoding the time and place of events (repeated talk about yesterday, here, etc.). Content words may also reflect feelings of worth-lessness or excessive or inappropriate guilt (e.g. 'I'm *afraid* to say something to somebody that *might hurt their feelings*'). A diminished ability to think or concentrate may be evident in subjective claims made by the depressed speaker (e.g. 'I can't think of the answer'), but is also apparent through the use of verbs of mitigation which reduce the speaker's commitment to the truth of a claim. These verbs, which include modal verbs, are particularly evident in the follow-ing extract from Fine (2006: 248). The recurring use of the expression 'you know' is an indication that the speaker is insecure about how his message is being understood and is seeking reassurance from the listener:

> I looked at my bosses ... I looked at ... people I <u>could</u> talk to you know people that <u>seem</u> friendly ... you know ... for a little bit of guidance well ... at the time it didn't work out too well ... you know ... I <u>would</u> take their advice and some-times it <u>would</u> backfire you know so ... (underlining added)

Indecisiveness is further conveyed by a level tone at the end of clauses which makes it unclear whether the speaker knows the truth of the statement.

Manic episodes are also characterised by certain language features. Fine (2006) lists the main clinical categories of manic mood expressed in language as euphoria, enthusiasm for interaction, inflated self-esteem, irritability, manic speech, flight of ideas and distractibility. The elevated mood of euphoria is conveyed by linguis-tic and paralinguistic means. Linguistically, the speaker may make frequent use of positive attributes of people, places and things (e.g. the play was *wonderful*, the *fantastic* trip), while paralinguistic features include increased laughter, smiling and accelerated speech rate. Fine (2006) states that enthusiasm for interaction is evident in atypically high rates of initiating exchanges across contexts and topics. The initiating utterances are most often in the form of questions, statements and imperatives that open up interactions and require the interlocutor to respond. In a study of 140 inpatients, Grossman and Harrow (1996) found that patients with mania and bipolar disorder displayed significantly more interactive behaviour than either patients with schizophrenia or no psychosis. An example of interactiveness occurred in this study when a patient responded to the question 'Why does a train have an engine?' with the following questions and comments:

> That's an easy one. Do you know the answer to it? So it can run, of course. Do you like your job? I like the sweater you are wearing (Grossman and Harrow, 1996: 247).

Inflated self-esteem or grandiosity in mania is often manifested in the assumption of roles by the speaker beyond what would be expected. The speaker may assume the role of an expert, for example, as evidenced by the use of technical language that the speaker does not understand and which is used out of context. Irritability in mania can take the form of unexpected, short, angry exchanges. These occur with greater than normal frequency and involve responses by the manic speaker that are confrontational in that they express disagreement or non-compliance. They may be evident when the manic speaker's wishes are denied, as in the following exchange from Fine (2006: 254):

A: I want a sandwich with mustard (request for goods and services)
B: sorry we don't have any left (confronting response that denies request)
A: what's wrong with you (irritable follow-up to denial)

Manic speech is manifested in the delivery of speech, which is pressured, loud and difficult to interrupt, and in atypical features such as joking, punning, amusing irrelevancies and theatrical speech. Speech which is pressured contains fewer and shortened pauses and has rapid delivery. Other speakers may not be able to take their turn even to answer a question. Increased loudness on syllables may actually distort the meaning of the speaker's utterances. Joking, punning and amusing irrelevancies are typically out of context, but can nevertheless have a positive social dimension even to the extent of creating comical effect. During theatrical speech, the speaker with mania can assume a role that is out of context in the interaction. This assumed role finds the speaker altering voice quality, changing facial expressions and body movements and engaging in mimicry (Fine, 2006).

Flight of ideas in mania can be characterised in the following terms:

[T]he patient's thinking leaps from topic to topic with changes of direction determined by such features as puns, rhymes, alliterations, chance distractions from environment – a tap dripping, a door shutting, a dog barking. Although the precise direction of the affected person's communication may be lost, the shifting direction of thought and the connection between successive topics can usually be understood by an observer. Some manic individuals describe the feeling of thoughts racing through their minds... (Clare, 1993: 2)

Clare's account touches on a feature of flight of ideas that distinguishes it from the derailments that occur in schizophrenia: the shifts in topic in flight of ideas can usually be followed. First et al. (2002: 52) state that '[t]heoretically, at least, one can discern how the patient got from one topic to the next in flight of ideas, whereas the derailments in the speech of patients with schizophrenia are much less understandable'. Clare's account also highlights a cause of the topic changes that occur in flight of ideas – the heightened distractibility on the part of the manic speaker from external stimuli. The speaker may directly refer to these external stimuli in speech through the use of deictic expressions (e.g. *that* dripping tap), thus revealing his distractibility. When a speaker's distractibility causes him to change topic, referential disturbances may occur. For example, where the pronoun 'it' referred to 'a party' when the topic was the speaker's birthday party, 'it' may be used to refer to the speaker's car when the topic changes to automobile repairs. Distractibility will then be observed not only in changes of vocabulary as the speaker moves from one topic to another, but also in referential disturbances.

6.4   Gender dysphoria

Gender dysphoria is a little known aspect of the work of speech and language therapists and is one of the least investigated areas within clinical communication research. In DSM-5, for a person to be diagnosed with gender dysphoria, there must be a marked difference between the individual's experienced or expressed gender and the gender that others would assign to him or her. This must continue for at least six months. The condition must cause clinically significant distress or impairment in social, occupational or other important areas of functioning (American Psychiatric Association, 2013). Gender dysphoria is *not* a mental illness. Rather, it is discussed in this chapter solely on account of its diagnosis by psychiatrists and the role of psychiatrists as the lead physicians in the management of the client with gender dysphoria. Prevalence studies suggest that gender dysphoria is a relatively uncommon condition. Wilson et al. (1999) reported a prevalence of 8.18 per 100,000 amongst patients aged over 15 years in Scotland. The male-to-female sex ratio was 4:1. In a study conducted in The Netherlands, Bakker et al. (1993) recorded a prevalence of 1 per 11,900 for male-to-female (MTF) transsexualism and 1 per 30,400 for female-to-male (FTM) transsexualism in a population aged 15 years and above. The male-to-female sex ratio was 2.5:1. Little is known about the aetiology of gender dysphoria. However, neurobiological, ecological and hormonal factors have all been advanced as possible causes (Snaith, 1998).

Management of the client with gender dysphoria involves surgery, pharmacotherapy and SLT. Surgical procedures include bilateral orchidectomy and vaginoplasty for the MTF transsexual and bilateral mastectomy, hysterectomy, oophorectomy and phalloplasty for the FTM transsexual. Androgens are administered to biological females, while biological males receive oestrogens, progesterone and testosterone-blocking agents. SLT will attempt to effect voice and communicative changes in clients with gender dysphoria. Voice therapy will focus on the pitch, resonance, intonation, rate and intensity of the speaking voice. However, therapists will also consider features such as articulation, language and pragmatics as these can also play a significant role in listener perceptions of the gender of the speaker (see Freidenberg (2002), for an overview of work in these areas). Long-term changes in fundamental frequency can be achieved through voice therapy, although they do not always result in alterations in listener perceptions of gender (see Case Study 2 below). Dacakis (2000) examined fundamental frequency increases in 10 MTF transsexuals at the start of voice therapy, at discharge and at long-term follow-up. These clients had received between 10 and 90 speech therapy sessions and were on average 4.3 years post-discharge from therapy (range 1 to 8.9 years). The mean fundamental frequencies at the start of therapy, at discharge and at follow-up were 125.5 Hz, 168.1 Hz and 146.5 Hz, respectively. These values were significantly different. Dacakis found a significant correlation between the number of treatment sessions and the maintenance of fundamental frequency increases.

In cases where voice therapy is unable to achieve desired pitch changes, a range of surgical procedures may be used. Phonosurgery is more often pursued by the MTF transsexual than by the FTM transsexual. This is because removal of the testes and oestrogen therapy in the MTF transsexual may achieve only minor changes in pitch (Rosanowski and Eysholdt, 1999). Currently, a popular technique is cricothyroid approximation (see section 7.4 in Chapter 7). In this technique, the cricoid and thyroid cartilages are approximated and held in position by sutures. This has the effect of stretching the vocal folds with the result that the fundamental frequency of the voice is raised. Pickuth et al. (2000) examined 29 transsexual patients who underwent cricothyroid approximation. On average, cricothyroid distance was reduced by 6mm (range 2–10mm). The greatest elevation in vocal pitch was achieved in patients who had the largest reduction of cricothyroid distance. Brown et al. (2000) examined the effects of cricothyroid approximation surgery in 14 MTF transsexuals. Mean and modal frequency were recorded before and two weeks after surgery. There was a significant increase in modal frequency but not in mean frequency. The mean increase in modal frequency was 31.57 Hz. Modal pitch correlated significantly with listener perception of the voice as female.

WEBSITE: Cricothyroid approximation

Listen to the pre- and post-surgical voices of speakers who have undergone cricothyroid approximation. These recordings have been reproduced with the kind permission of James P. Thomas, MD and are from voicedoctor.net.

In demonstration of the management of transsexual clients, two case studies are presented below. The first case describes a FTM transsexual who received androgen therapy and was followed longitudinally by Van Borsel et al. (2000). The second case describes a MTF transsexual who received hormone and voice therapy and was examined longitudinally by Mount and Salmon (1988).

CASE STUDY 1: Subject A (FTM transsexual)

Subject **A** is a female-to-male transsexual who was aged 22 years and 4 months at the start of the investigation. Before the start of the study, **A** (a non-smoker) had attempted smoking temporarily in an effort to lower his voice. However, he refrained from further smoking as this had caused him to develop a sore throat. Before hormone therapy commenced, **A** was consistently mistaken for a female on the telephone. To start with, **A** received testosterone undecanoate 40mg twice a day which increased after 2 months to four times a day. **A** enjoyed singing and practised for approximately one hour a day.

Data on **A** were collected on eight occasions for 17 months. When possible, data were collected at intervals of 2 months – research suggested that virilisation of the female voice due to androgynous hormones first becomes evident from 6 to 12 weeks to several months. Two voice therapy sessions took place before androgenic hormones were administered. **A**'s phonational frequency range (lowest and highest pitch level) was determined at each session. A high-quality recording of sustained vowel production (/a/) and **A**'s reading aloud of a standard paragraph was also undertaken. Further acoustic analysis of fundamental frequency, jitter and shimmer was based on this latter recording.

Before androgen therapy commenced, **A** could phonate at a pitch level >800 Hz. The highest pitch level he could produce after 2.5 months of therapy had decreased to ~660 Hz. His maximum pitch from 4 months post-therapy onwards was in the range 440–525 Hz. Before hormone therapy was initiated, the lowest level he could attain was ~165–175 Hz. This level decreased gradually to ~105 Hz as a result of receiving androgens. During a session 4 months and 10 days after androgen therapy started, it first became apparent that **A**'s fundamental frequency had declined steeply. In the last session, 13 months and 4 days after hormone treatment started, fundamental frequencies of 128 Hz (sustained vowel production) and 155 Hz (reading of paragraph) were recorded. Male and female voices also differ in vocal jitter and shimmer, with male voices displaying significantly more vocal shimmer and a smaller vocal jitter than the female voice. However, shimmer did not increase or jitter decrease in **A** as a result of androgen therapy.

CASE STUDY 2: Subject B (MTF transsexual)

Subject **B** is a 63-year-old male-to-female transsexual. **B** commenced hormone treatment a year before gender reassignment surgery was conducted. She attended a speech clinic for assessment six months after surgery. **B** reported a low-pitched voice which was not perceived as female, particularly on the telephone. Her speaking voice during conversation and production of sustained vowels was low pitched and appropriate for a bass male speaker. During sustained production of /i, a, u/, **B**'s average fundamental frequency was 110 Hz. **B**'s fundamental frequency at the lowest and highest pitch levels ranged from 110 to 340 Hz.

Voice therapy goals were (1) to train **B** to use successively higher pitch levels while avoiding vocal abuse, and (2) to modify tongue carriage as a means of achieving higher resonance within the vocal tract. The use of a breathy vocal attack and appropriate inflection patterns at higher pitch levels were secondary goals of voice therapy. Words that contained high front vowels and anterior consonants were used in order to increase fundamental frequency and alter resonance characteristics. Words beginning with /h/ were used to establish easy onset of phonation and the use of a breathy voice quality. Phrases and sentences were constructed from these words and used to encourage different types of intonation patterns. To begin with, **B** listened to the clinician's production and, using Visi-pitch display, attempted to match the pitch contours. In increments of 10 Hz, frequency was raised until **B** could maintain a consistently good vocal quality at an average fundamental frequency of 210 Hz. Other tasks targeted inflection, resonance and a breathy vocal attack. Role-play situations that emphasised functional conversations were used in the final months of therapy. **B** was required to engage in conversations in person and over the telephone with people who were unknown to her. In order to assess the appropriateness of vocal behaviours, these conversations were recorded. Telephone work continued until the number of feminine references to **B** (use of 'Ma'am', for example) predominated.

Treatment extended over 11 months and included 88 one-hour sessions. After 4 months of therapy, **B** was able to achieve a fundamental frequency that was comparable to that of females. However, **B** was not perceived as female on the telephone until six months later. At this time, the altered resonant frequencies of the vocal tract combined with her feminine fundamental frequency was sufficient to elicit female perception. At 5 years post-treatment, **B** maintained female vocal characteristics and continued to be perceived as a female on the telephone.

KEY POINTS: Gender dysphoria

- Condition in which the individual experiences persistent discomfort with his or her natal sex and the gender role of that sex
- Relatively uncommon condition affecting more males than females
- Management involves surgery, hormone treatment and speech and language therapy (SLT)
- Speech and language therapists assess and treat vocal attributes (e.g. fundamental frequency) and other aspects of communication
- Alteration of fundamental frequency of the voice is possible but is not always associated with changes in listener perception of the gender of the speaker
- Phonosurgery (e.g. cricothyroid approximation) is pursued when voice therapy is unable to achieve desired pitch changes (most common in MTF transsexuals)

SUGGESTIONS FOR FURTHER READING

Bryan, K. (2014) 'Psychiatric disorders and communication', in L. Cummings (ed.) *Cambridge Handbook of Communication Disorders* (Cambridge: Cambridge University Press), pp. 300–17.

Cummings, L. (2009) *Clinical Pragmatics* (Cambridge: Cambridge University Press), ss. 2.4 (emotional and behavioural disorders) and 3.4 (schizophrenia).

France, J. and Kramer, S. (eds) (2001) *Communication and Mental Illness: Theoretical and Practical Approaches* (London: Jessica Kingsley).

EXERCISES

Exercise 6.1

The monologue presented in this exercise (comprising four sets) is a transcription of an audio recording of a 37-year-old woman with schizophrenia studied by Chaika (1974). The language used by this patient reveals certain deficits but also a number of intact skills. Read the transcription and then select one example of each of the features listed below.

Part (A): Linguistic deficits

(a) Production of sentences according to the semantic features of previously uttered words rather than topic of discourse.
(b) The presence of unexpected topic shifts.
(c) Production of sentences according to the phonological features of previously uttered words rather than topic of discourse.
(d) Use of the same word with subtle shifts in meaning.
(e) Verbal output is such that it is difficult for the listener to track the referent of pronouns.

Part (B): Linguistic skills

(a) The use of pronominalisation as a cohesive device.
(b) Deletion of a repeated subject after initial use to indicate that initial and subsequent utterances are related.
(c) Sophisticated verb use including (i) infinitive form, (ii) imperative form, (iii) auxiliary verbs, (iv) simple present tense, (v) simple past tense, (vi) future tense, (vii) present perfect, (viii) present progressive, (ix) present perfect progressive, (x) negated auxiliary verbs.
(d) The use of quantified expressions involving 'some' (existential quantifier) and 'all' (universal quantifier).
(e) The use of coordinating and subordinating conjunctions to link clauses.

   Set 1:

   a. Good mornin' everybody!
   b. (lower pitch, doubtfully) I don't know what that is. (laughs)
   c. [ðɪ sɔəndan sɔ tʰɜ̌č fɔ ǰuəri]
   d. (loudly, very surprised) Oh! it's that thorazine. I forgot I had it.
   e. That's Lulubelle.
   f. This one's Jean. J-E-A-N.
   g. I'll write that down.
   h. Speeds up the metabolism.
   i. Makes your life shorter.
   j. Makes your heart bong.
   k. Tranquilises you if you've got the metabolism I have.
   l. I have distemper just like cats do, 'cause that's what we all are, felines. (pause)
   m. Siamese cat balls. They stand out.

n. I had a cat, a manx, still around somewhere.
o. You'll know him when you see him.
p. His name is GI Joe; he's black and white. (no sentence break in intonation)
q. I had a little goldfish too, like a clown. (pause)
r. Happy Hallowe'en down. (pause)
s. [dʌdn̩] (pause)
t. He sill had [fʊč] with [tʰekraimz] I'll be willing to betcha.
u. Nobody takes my word for what I wanna do. Not even God.
v. I believe I'll try anyhow.
w. (declaiming) I believe in the spirit of the mountains.
x. Right now I'm thinking Pike's Peak for a rehaul of the Korean thing.
y. This time I'll marry E---P---, or 'bout H---G---?
z. Or Frank Sinatra, he's already set. (Modified from Chaika, 1974: 260–1)

Set 2:

Preceded by 20 second pause
a. My mother's name was Bill. (pause)
b. (low pitch, as in an aside, but with marked rising question intonation)…and coo?
c. St Valentine's Day is the official startin' of the breedin' season of the birds.
d. All buzzards can coo.
e. I like to see it pronounced buzzards rightly.
f. They work hard.
g. So do parakeets. (Chaika, 1974: 260)

Set 3:

a. This is a holy smoke (Dr: that's a cigarette you're holding)
b. It's a holy one. (pause)
c. It goes in one hole and out the other and that makes it holy. (Chaika, 1974: 260)

Set 4:

Preceded by 45 second pause
a. In a month I've been upstairs, they've been taking my brains out a piece at a time or all together.
b. Federal case doesn't mean communication.
c. Steal from Mrs. Gotrocks, she can afford it.
d. I've got something (inaudible).
e. Did that show up on the X-rays?
f. You'll see it tonight.
g. I've been drinking phosphate.
h. You'll see it in the dark (inaudible)
i. Glows.
j. We all glow as we're glowworms. (Chaika, 1974: 260)

Exercise 6.2

Emotional and behavioural disorders in children have received relatively little attention in clinical communication research. In section 6.3.1, we examined three such
disorders: attention deficit hyperactivity disorder (ADHD), selective mutism and

conduct disorder. The following scenarios capture the communication and behavioural impairments that occur in these disorders. For each scenario, indicate if it relates to ADHD, selective mutism or conduct disorder:

(a) Harry is 5 years old and attends weekly SLT with his mother. Observation of his communication skills in clinic reveals that he engages in frequent topic shifts during conversation.

(b) Sally is a physically well 6-year-old child. Her case history reveals consistent failure to speak in school even though she speaks to close family members at home.

(c) John is 8 years old and is attending SLT because of significant receptive and expressive language problems. He has a history of disruptive behaviour in class and has recently been excluded from school because of an attack on another child.

(d) Molly is 7 years old and is attending SLT for the first time. During the taking of a case history, parental reports indicate that she is highly distractible, does not listen to others or keep her mind on conversations.

(e) During formal language testing of a 6-year-old boy called Tom, a speech and language therapist observes significant deterioration of behaviour when he is asked to carry out syntactically complex instructions. The session is terminated when he starts to throw test equipment.

(f) Susan is 6 years old and lives with her father following her parents' divorce. Her problems, which include long periods of no verbal communication even with some family members, commenced shortly after her parents separated.

(g) Mark is 5 years old and has just started primary school. His teacher reports that he talks excessively, blurts out answers before questions have been completed and fails to listen to her instructions to him.

(h) Sam is 9 years old. His teacher reports poor classroom and playground behaviour which seems to be triggered when other children attempt to engage in playful teasing of him. An assessment of his communication skills reveals receptive difficulties, particularly in the comprehension of pragmatic aspects of language.

(i) Pippa is 6 years old and has recently been referred to SLT. Her mother reports that she makes comments out of turn, initiates conversations at inappropriate times and interrupts others excessively.

(j) Fran is a reticent 5-year-old who is being assessed by a speech and language therapist in her own home. During play, the therapist observes no expressive language but notes that she is able to act on complex verbal instructions. She also attends well to the task at hand and is cooperative throughout the session.

Exercise 6.3

The following utterances have been taken from interviews and tape recordings of subjects with mania studied by Durbin and Martin (1977: 213–15). These investigators were specifically interested in examining the use of anaphora and ellipsis by speakers with mania. One of these linguistic devices was found to be disrupted while the other was relatively intact. For each of the utterances below, you should state whether the speaker has used anaphora or ellipsis appropriately or inappropriately and describe the expressions that are the basis of anaphora and ellipsis. Finally, you should indicate which linguistic device is most disrupted on the basis of the presented data.

(a) The folks up in Missoula have been pushing a lot of paperwork and sending it around.

(b) Sounds like a trippy deal; I'd like to be in on it.

(c) I saw a man using a toy to take to his daughter which the rich people in suburbia had thrown away.

(d) I saw one of the patients to the right of me in bed and I thought she was dead and I got up and they flashed in her face and said she's OK.

(e) I don't think I'm the one who is crazy.

(f) He built the University Club. What's he doing with the old one?

(g) In respect to them being problems, they have already been solved, however, the solution of them is a problem, the passing them on is a problem and that is why I am here and actually, some of these solutions were acquired in my coming here and that's part of the reason I was here, and, the perfecting of them came through here and the only problem now is the one we are solving now.

(h) I've been making contact with them [public libraries] for everything I wanted to know that I couldn't find within myself or that I could find thereabouts.

(i) The only problem is the one we're solving now, is the passing them onto a recorder.

(j) We just came from the meeting downstairs where we discussed most of this.

ANSWERS TO EXERCISES

Exercise 6.1

Part (A): Linguistic deficits

(a) Set 2: The use of the name *Bill* triggers *coo* ('Bill and coo' is an expression meaning to kiss and whisper amorously among lovers). The romantic connotations of this expression then trigger *St Valentine's Day* which is a day when people celebrate their love for each other. The idea of love then triggers reproduction in *the breedin' season of the birds*. The use of 'birds' here could also be triggered by Bill which is an anatomical part of a bird. The introduction of birds then triggers *buzzards* and *parakeets*, both of which are hyponyms of bird. The buzzards *can coo* which takes us back to the same expression used non-literally in 'bill and coo'.

(b) Set 1: In (d), the speaker begins to talk about the drug thorazine. She then leaves that topic in (e) and (f) where she begins to introduce people who are presumably other patients. In (h) to (k), she returns to the drug thorazine and describes its effects upon the body.

(c) Set 1: In (q), the speaker says *like a clown*. The word 'clown' then triggers 'down' in the next utterance (r) *Happy Hallowe'en down*.

(d) Set 1: In (v), 'believe' is used with the meaning of *to think* (this is confirmed through the use of 'thinking' in the utterance in (x)). In (w), 'believe' is used to mean *to have faith in something*.

(e) Set 4: The referent of *something* in (d) is unclear. This lack of clarity extends into (e) and (f), as it is not possible to identify the referents of *that* and *it* in these utterances, respectively. The word *phosphate* is introduced in (g). But it is not possible to tell if the *it* in (h) refers to phosphate or to the same thing that is being referred to by *it* in (f) – possibly the latter, given the similarity of the utterances in (f) and (h).

Part (B): Linguistic skills

(a) Set 1: In (d), the use of the pronoun *it* to refer back to *thorazine*, thus linking the two utterances together.

(b) Set 1: The drug *thorazine* is first mentioned in (d). It then becomes the implicit subject of the verbs *speeds* (h), *makes* (i and j) and *tranquilises* (k), thus linking these utterances together.

(c)   (i)   infinitive form – I like *to* see; set 2 (e)

    (ii) imperative form – *Steal* from Mrs. Gotrocks; set 4 (c)

   (iii) auxiliary verbs – I've got something, set 4 (d); All buzzards *can* coo, set 2 (d); You'll see it tonight, set 4 (f)

   (iv) simple present tense – They *work* hard, set 2 (f); It *goes* in one hole, set 3 (c); I *believe* in the spirit of the mountains, set 1 (w)

    (v) simple past tense – I *had* a little goldfish too, set 1 (q); I *forgot* I had it, set 1 (d)

   (vi) future tense – You'll know him, set 1 (o); I'll marry, set 1 (y)

  (vii) present perfect – I've *been* upstairs, set 4 (a)

 (viii) present progressive – I'm *thinking*, set 1 (x)

   (ix) present perfect progressive – they've *been taking* my brains out, set 4 (a)

    (x) negated auxiliary verbs – Federal case *doesn't* mean communication, set 4 (b); I *don't* know what that is, set 1 (b)

(d) (Universal) *All* buzzards can coo, set 2 (d); (existential) I've got *something*, set 4 (d); (universal) *Nobody* takes my word, set 1 (u)

(e) (Coordinating) It goes in one hole *and* out the other *and* that makes it holy, set 3 (c) (subordinating) Tranquilises you *if* you've got the metabolism I have, set 1 (k)

Exercise 6.2

(a) ADHD

(b) selective mutism

(c) conduct disorder

(d) ADHD

(e) conduct disorder

(f) selective mutism

(g) ADHD

(h) conduct disorder

(i) ADHD

(j) selective mutism

Exercise 6.3

(a) anaphora is used appropriately: the pronoun 'it' refers to 'paperwork'

(b) anaphora is used appropriately: the pronoun 'it' refers to 'deal'

(c) ellipsis is used inappropriately: the speaker has deleted the obligatory instrument 'as a gift'

(d) anaphora is used appropriately: the pronoun 'she' refers to 'one of the patients'; the referent of 'they' – hospital personnel – is easily recoverable from the context; the possessive 'her' refers to the face of the identified patient

(e) anaphora is used appropriately: the relative pronoun 'who' relates the relative clause to 'the one'

(f) the speaker may be using either anaphora or ellipsis inappropriately: he has either deleted the adjective 'new' from the first utterance (inappropriate ellipsis), or he is using 'one' to refer to something other than 'University Club' without any indication of what the referent might be (inappropriate anaphora)

(g) anaphora is used appropriately: the first instance of the pronoun 'them' refers forward to 'problems' (cataphoric reference); all subsequent uses of the pronouns 'they' and 'them' refer backwards to the antecedent 'problems'; towards the end of the utterance, the speaker employs an anaphoric device called substitution in using 'one' to refer backwards to 'problem'

(h) ellipsis is used inappropriately: the speaker deletes the negative from the clause 'I could find thereabouts'; for the negative to be legitimately deleted, the disjunction 'or' would need to be replaced by the conjunction 'and'

(i) ellipsis is used inappropriately: the speaker has inappropriately deleted 'the only problem' in the second clause; intact use of anaphora in that the referent of 'them' (i.e. problems) is recoverable from the context and the referent of 'one' is 'problem' (linguistic substitution)

(j) anaphora is used appropriately: the second clause 'we discussed most of this' refers backwards to 'the meeting downstairs' through the use of 'where'

On the basis of the data presented, anaphoric devices are largely intact in the subjects with mania in Durbin and Martin's study. However, the use of ellipsis is impaired, as evidenced in the frequent use of inappropriate deletions. Durbin and Martin (1977: 217) state that '[i]t may be that such deletion errors play an important part in the long-reported flight of ideas and other abnormalities manifest in the speech of manics'.

Disorders of Voice

7

7.1 The classification of voice disorders

The production of voice is a complex process that demands the proper physiological integration of intact anatomical structures. The anatomical structures in question are the cartilages and muscles of the laryngeal apparatus. These structures cannot serve their function of producing voice if they are not receiving innervation from a network of laryngeal nerves. If any of these parts of the voice production mechanism are compromised, a voice disorder (dysphonia) will result. Some voice disorders may have a minimal effect on the perceptual attributes of the speaking voice and cause little in the way of adverse impact on an individual's quality of life. Other voice disorders may manifest as perceptually very deviant and present a considerable challenge to an individual's ability to function in social, occupational and interpersonal contexts. Regardless of how they manifest perceptually or their impact on an individual's quality of life, all voice disorders must be extensively investigated in order to eliminate the presence of serious disease as a cause of the disorder. In this chapter, we will examine the main aspects of such an investigation. This examination will include the knowledge that clinicians must have of the aetiology and epidemiology of voice disorders. We will also discuss the assessment and treatment of at least some of the voice disorders that we consider in this chapter. At appropriate junctures, readers will be directed towards audio and visual resources that allow them to develop an appreciation of the deviant perceptual attributes of disordered voices. These same resources will enable the reader to view a range of laryngeal anomalies during laryngological examination. The reader is strongly advised to make extensive use of both types of resource.

Typically, voice disorders are classified according to their underlying aetiology. Where there is a clear medical cause for a voice disorder, the disorder is described as organic in nature. If an extensive examination of a speaker's laryngeal mechanism has been performed by an otorhinolaryngologist (ENT consultant in the UK) and no medical cause for a voice disorder can be found, it is classified as a functional disorder. Psychological factors are often attributed with causing the latter type of voice disorder, hence the use of the term 'psychogenic' to describe this class of voice disorders. Organic voice disorders can be further classified according to whether they are caused by a structural anomaly, a neurological disorder, an infectious disease or by trauma. Benign and malignant growths on the vocal folds (cords) of the larynx present a structural barrier to normal voice production. One or more of the nerves supplying innervation to the muscles of the larynx may be damaged in a cerebrovascular accident (CVA) or stroke leading to vocal fold paralysis. Also, a speaker may develop a neurological disorder such as Parkinson's disease and multiple sclerosis, and develop a voice disorder as a result. Bacterial, viral and fungal infections can compromise the structure and function of the laryngeal mechanism. While viral laryngitis is a relatively common cause of voice disorder, less common infections of the larynx include tuberculosis, syphilis and cytomegalovirus. Finally, the larynx can sustain trauma in a road traffic accident. The nerves that innervate the larynx may also be damaged during different types of surgery. For example, the recurrent laryngeal nerve may be damaged during thoracic surgery. These traumatic events must not be overlooked in the aetiology of voice disorders.

It should be emphasised that it is not uncommon to find more than one of these problems involved in the aetiology of a voice disorder. Organic and functional factors frequently interact to produce a voice disorder. For example, the patient with Parkinson's disease has a voice disorder of neurological aetiology. However, if this patient attempts to compensate for his reduced vocal loudness by forcefully adducing the vocal folds (hyperadduction), his neurological voice disorder will also assume functional (behavioural) elements. If forced adduction becomes an established phonatory pattern for this patient, he risks developing vocal nodules, at which point there is also a structural component to his voice disorder. The school-age child who screams repeatedly in the playground may develop benign lesions on his vocal folds. His resulting voice disorder may appear to have just structural and functional components. However, upon taking a case history in the voice clinic, the laryngologist may discover that this child has also experienced numerous upper respiratory tract infections and repeated episodes of hoarseness. Seen in this light, the child's poor vocal patterns may be a compensatory reaction to his infection-related hoarseness. In this case, there are structural, infectious and functional components at work in the child's voice disorder. It will be for the examining clinician to judge the significance of any one of these factors in a particular case based upon a complete history of the client and thorough examination of the anatomy and physiology of the laryngeal mechanism.

Several studies have examined the epidemiology of voice disorders. Duff et al. (2004) examined the presence of voice disorders in 2,445 African-American and European-American preschool children aged between 2 and 6 years. Voice disorders were found in 95 children (3.9 per cent of the sample). There were no significant differences for age, gender or race. Carding et al. (2006) examined the prevalence of dysphonia in a cohort of 7,389 children who were 8 years of age. The prevalence rate of dysphonia in these children, as recorded by research speech and language therapists, was 6 per cent. Older siblings and male sex were significant risk factors for dysphonia. Roy et al. (2005) conducted a telephone questionnaire on a random sample of 1,326 adults in Iowa and Utah. These investigators obtained a lifetime prevalence rate of voice disorder of 29.9 per cent and a prevalence rate of current voice disorder of 6.6 per cent. Factors that contributed to increased odds of reporting a chronic voice disorder included female sex, age (40–59 years), voice use patterns and demands, oesophageal reflux, chemical exposures and frequent colds and sinus infections. Alcohol and tobacco use did not independently increase the odds of reporting a chronic voice disorder. This is surprising given what is known about the link between serious laryngeal disease and alcohol and tobacco use (see section 7.5).

Certain occupational and clinical populations experience an increased prevalence of voice disorder and laryngeal pathology. Roy et al. (2004) found that the prevalence of current voice problems in a sample of 1,243 teachers was 11 per cent. This figure is significantly greater than a prevalence of 6.2 per cent in a sample of 1,288 non-teachers examined in the same study. Sliwinska-Kowalska et al. (2006) examined the prevalence of voice problems in 425 female Polish teachers aged 23–61 years. Overall lifetime vocal symptoms were more common in teachers than in a control group of 83 female non-teachers (69 per cent versus 36 per cent). In a study of 882 patients with dysphonia who consulted an ENT department, Van Houtte et al. (2010) found that professional voice users accounted for 41 per cent of the workforce population, with teachers forming the main subgroup. Functional dysphonia was present in 41 per cent of professional voice users, while vocal fold nodules and pharyngolaryngeal reflux were found in 15 per cent and 11 per cent of this group, respectively. Speyer et al. (2008) examined the prevalence of dysphonia in 166 subjects with rheumatoid arthritis and 148 healthy controls. The subjects with rheumatoid arthritis had a statistically significant higher prevalence and relative risk of dysphonia (12 per cent to 27 per cent, depending on the questionnaire used) than the control subjects (3 per cent to 8 per cent). Phonatory disturbances have also been found in certain syndromes including infants and children with Down syndrome (Pryce, 1994) and cri-du-chat syndrome. Moreira et al. (2008) describe the case of a 10-year-old girl with cri-du-chat syndrome (literally, 'cry of the cat'). Although her vocal pronunciation displayed a disturbance of fundamental frequency, laryngoscopic examination revealed no abnormal anatomical findings.

WEBSITE: Cri-du-chat syndrome

Listen to the audio files of a baby boy and girl with cri-du-chat syndrome. The cry of these babies is quite distinctive and is noticeably aberrant. These files are reproduced with the kind permission of the Cri Du Chat Support Group of Australia.

7.2 Organic voice disorders

In this section, we examine the laryngeal pathology that is associated with a number of organic voice disorders. These voice disorders result from growths and other processes that degrade the structures of the larynx or from damage to any part of the network of nerves that supply innervation to the muscles of the larynx. Their aetiologies are thus structural and neurological in nature. We will also consider the perceptual attributes of the deviant voice that attends these laryngeal anomalies. In sections 7.4 and 7.5, we discuss how clinicians assess and treat this group of voice disorders.

7.2.1   Structural aetiology

Vocal nodules and polyps are among the most common growths to affect the larynx. These structures develop at the middle of the vocal folds and are benign in nature (i.e. they do not invade laryngeal tissues or tissues beyond the larynx). Nodules are similar to calluses in texture and tend to develop on both vocal folds. Polyps tend to be larger than nodules. According to Wallis et al. (2004), a biopsy larger than 0.3 cm is likely to be a polyp while nodules tend to be less than 0.3 cm. Polyps are fluid-filled structures which may have their own blood supply. They can be found on one or both vocal folds. Nodules and polyps are associated with inflammation that is caused by stress or irritation (Wallis et al., 2004). They are thus commonly found in patients who are placing excessive demands on their speaking voice (e.g. teachers) or who are engaged in patterns of vocal abuse and misuse. Akif Kiliç et al. (2004) studied 617 children aged 7 to 16 years and found that 30.3 per cent had some form of vocal nodule or polyp.

WEBSITE: Vocal nodules and polyps

View the two sets of images of vocal nodules and polyps on the website. In one of the nodule images, a small capillary has ruptured producing a haemorrhagic nodule. These images have been reproduced with the kind permission of The New York Eye and Ear Infirmary Voice and Swallowing Institute (www.nyee.edu/vsi) and Bechara Y. Ghorayeb, MD (www.houstonoto.com/PicturesLarynx.html).

Cysts are a further benign lesion to affect the larynx. There are two types of cyst: epidermic and mucous-retention cysts. They differ in their histology (cell and tissue type) and aetiology. An epidermic cyst has caseous content and is covered by a stratified squamous and keratinised epithelium that makes it resistant to manipulation. It may be secondary to vocal abuse (Martins et al., 2011). A mucous-retention cyst has mucous content and is covered by a cylindrical ciliated epithelium. It arises from the obstruction of the glandular ducts which may be caused by voice overuse, laryngitis that is secondary to gastroesophageal reflux or upper-airway infections (Martins et al., 2011). In a study of 37 patients with vocal fold cysts, Milutinović and Vasiljević (1992) found that 65 per cent of patients had epidermoid cysts and 35 per cent had retention cysts. Cysts were most frequently located in the area of the junction of the anterior and middle thirds of the free edge of the vocal fold. The presence of a cyst causes the vocal fold to bulge or protrude. By repeatedly making contact with the other vocal fold, the protruding fold can cause a reactive lesion to develop in it. When the protruding vocal fold creates an indentation in the reactive lesion, the vocal folds assume a 'cup and saucer' appearance.

WEBSITE: Vocal cysts

View the two sets of images of vocal cysts on the website. These images have been reproduced with the kind permission of Bechara Y. Ghorayeb, MD (www.houstonoto.com/ PicturesLarynx.html) and The New York Eye and Ear Infirmary Voice and Swallowing Institute (www.nyee.edu.vsi). Pay particular attention to image 9 from NYEE. This shows a large cyst on one vocal fold which has caused irritation of the mucosa of the other vocal fold.

Reinke's oedema (also referred to as 'polypoid degeneration' and 'polypoid corditis') involves 'expansion of Reinke's space by an inflammatory gelatinous amorphous material that extends from the anterior commissure to the vocal process' (Rosen and Simpson, 2008: 113). On inspiration, the swollen vocal folds prolapse inferiorly giving the vocal folds a 'saddle bag' appearance (Rosen and Simpson, 2008). Goswami and Patra (2003) studied 92 cases of Reinke's oedema. Lesions were more commonly found unilaterally (74 per cent) than bilaterally (26 per cent), in men (57 per cent), in smokers (83 per cent) and in patients with vocal abuse or misuse (80 per cent) and chronic respiratory tract infection (43 per cent). In a study of 110 patients with benign vocal mucosal lesions, Chung et al. (2009) found a significantly higher prevalence of pathological laryngopharyngeal reflux in patients with Reinke's oedema than in control patients (90 per cent and 65 per cent, respectively). Granulomas are a benign inflammatory lesion of the vocal folds. They are most often located over the vocal process of the arytenoid cartilage. It is common to find a corresponding ulcer on the contralateral side (Storck et al., 2009). Factors which have been linked to the development of granulomas include endotracheal intubation, gastroesophageal reflux, external laryngeal trauma and phonotrauma (Martins et al., 2009). Granulomas tend to recur following surgical excision. Recurrence rates can approach 92 per cent (Carroll et al., 2010). In a study of 53 patients with 54 granulomas, Wang et al. (2009) found that 44 granulomas (81 per cent) achieved complete remission within a mean period of 30.6 weeks in the absence of specific treatments.

WEBSITE: Reinke's oedema and granulomas

View images of Reinke's oedema and granulomas on the website. These images have been reproduced with the kind permission of Bechara Y. Ghorayeb, MD (www. houstonoto.com/PicturesLarynx.html) and The New York Eye and Ear Infirmary

Voice and Swallowing Institute (www.nyee.edu.vsi). The case of Reinke's oedema has been caused by smoking. A case of granuloma related to intubation is shown. Pay particular attention to image 13 from NYEE, which shows how a granuloma has caused a reactive lesion on the opposite vocal process.

Laryngeal papillomas are relatively rare benign growths of the larynx that are caused by the human papilloma virus (HPV) types 6 and 11. Campisi et al. (2010) studied the incidence and prevalence of juvenile onset recurrent respiratory papillomatosis in Canada between 1994 and 2007. The national incidence was 0.24 per 100,000 children aged 14 years and younger, while the prevalence was 1.11 per 100,000 children. Papillomas grow quickly and can compromise the airway. They also recur, necessitating repeated surgical interventions. In a study of 34 cases of recurrent respiratory papillomatosis (29 adult onset, 5 juvenile onset), Van Nieuwenhuizen et al. (2010) reported that the median number of surgical procedures was five (range 1 to 17). Laryngeal papillomas may cause stridor (high-pitched sound during inspiration), dyspnoea (laboured respiration) and hoarseness (Andratschke et al., 2008).

WEBSITE: Laryngeal papillomas

View the images of laryngeal papillomas on the website. These images have been reproduced with the kind permission of Bechara Y. Ghorayeb, MD (www.houstonoto.com/PicturesLarynx.html). The papillomas in these images are found on the true and false vocal folds and affect one or both folds.

Sometimes, the structures of the larynx are compromised by something other than a growth. Vocal folds may bleed or haemorrhage causing tiny, visible capillaries (varices or capillary ectasias) or larger perfusions of blood into the tissue of the folds. In singers, varices and ectasias result from the impact of phonotraumatic shearing stresses and/or collision forces upon the microcirculation in the superficial lamina propria, the layer immediately below the epithelium of the vocal fold (Zeitels et al., 2006). Apart from phonotrauma, other risk factors for vocal fold haemorrhage include laryngeal trauma, aspirin, non-steroidal anti-inflammatories and hormonal imbalances (Neely and Rosen, 2000). In a study of 42 patients who presented with a total of 87 varices and ectasias, Hochman et al. (1999) found 67 (77 per cent) of these microvascular lesions on the superior surface of the vocal fold and 20 (23 per cent) on the medial surface of the fold. The area of the fold that sustains the greatest aerodynamically induced shearing stresses during phonation contained 83 per cent of all varices and ectasias. Some microvascular lesions are asymptomatic, while others cause dysphonia by disrupting the normal vibratory pattern, closure or mass of the folds (Postma et al., 1998).

WEBSITE: Vocal fold haemorrhage

View the image of a submucosal haemorrhage of the vocal fold on the website. This image has been reproduced with the kind permission of Bechara Y. Ghorayeb, MD (www.houstonoto.com/PicturesLarynx.html). The haemorrhage in this case has been caused by traumatic endotracheal intubation.

Sulcus vocalis is a linear depression or groove in the vocal fold mucosa. It runs parallel to the free border of the fold and is usually bilateral and symmetrical (Martins et al., 2007). There are three types of sulcus configuration. Sulcus type I is the physiologic type and is superficial. Sulcus type IIa is sulcus vergeture. The deepness of the groove is variable and may involve deeper layers of the lamina propria. Sulcus type IIb is the pouch type or true sulcus and takes the form of an open cyst (Giovanni et al., 2007). Lim et al. (2009) studied 146 patients with bilateral sulcus configuration of the vocal folds. These patients were categorised according to sulcus type, with 21.9 per cent type I (physiologic), 41.8 per cent type II (vergeture) and 36.3 per cent type III (pouch). The aetiology of this condition is unknown. However, studies of sulcus vocalis in monozygotic twins (Cakir et al., 2010) and close relatives (Martins et al., 2007) suggest a genetic aetiology for the disorder. The glottic dysfunction in sulcus is complex, consisting of both glottal leakage (causing breathy voice) and stiffness of the free edge of the folds (causing rough voice) (Giovanni et al., 2007).

WEBSITE: Sulcus vocalis

View the images of sulcus on the website. These images have been reproduced with the kind permission of The New York Eye and Ear Infirmary Voice and Swallowing Institute (www.nyee.edu/vsi). There is incomplete glottal closure during phonation due to poor mucosal wave vibration.

A further structural anomaly of the larynx to affect voice production is vocal fold bowing. This is often the result of degenerative, age-related changes in the larynx in a condition known as 'presbylarynx' ('old larynx'). Alternatively, vocal fold bowing may result from inadequate innervation of the vocal folds, in which case the resulting voice disorder has a neurogenic aetiology (see section 7.2.2). In presbylarynx, the vocal folds close at the front and back but fail to adduct in the middle. This leads to a rapid loss of air through the glottis during phonation with consequent reduction of phonation time. Takano et al. (2010) studied 72 patients with age-related vocal fold atrophy. The mean age of these patients was 71 years. Men and women accounted for 65 per cent and 35 per cent of these patients, respectively. The mean airflow rate was higher in these patients with presbylarynx than in normal elderly people in the study. Also, maximal phonation time correlated negatively with age (with increasing age, maximal phonation time decreased). As well as vocal fold bowing, other glottic characteristics of presbylarynx include prominence of the vocal processes and a spindle-shaped glottic chink. Pontes et al. (2005) found a strong correlation among these characteristics in 210 patients aged over 60 years who sought otorhinolaryngologic treatment. In a later study, Pontes et al. (2006) found significant differences in vocal fold bowing, prominence of the vocal process and glottic proportion in the larynx of young adults (20–45 years) and the larynx of elderly subjects (65–85 years).

WEBSITE: Presbylarynx

Listen to the audio file of a speaker with presbylarynx. This file has been reproduced with the kind permission of Dr Richard Stasney of the Texas Voice Center (www. texasvoicecenter.com). The voice is hoarse, weak and breathy.

7.2.2 Neurological aetiology

Vocal fold paralysis and paresis (VFPP) is a significant cause of neurogenic voice disorder. In VFPP, the vocal folds do not adduct, abduct or elongate normally as a result of damage to one or more of the nerves that innervate them. VFPP may be unilateral or bilateral and may involve the recurrent laryngeal nerve (RLN), superior laryngeal nerve, or both (Rubin and Sataloff, 2007). Bilateral VFPP compromises the airway and necessitates a tracheotomy. Surgical procedures are a common cause of RLN damage. Paniello et al. (2008) conducted laryngeal examinations of 47 patients who had undergone anterior cervical spine procedures. Thirteen examinations (26 per cent) produced abnormal laryngeal findings which included VFPP in 11 cases (22 per cent). Sancho et al. (2008) examined the role of inferior (recurrent) laryngeal nerve damage in vocal cord dysfunction in 188 patients who underwent total thyroidectomy or lobectomy. These investigators found vocal cord dysfunction in 10.9 per cent of patients. Paresis and paralysis were found in 4.3 per cent and 6.6 per cent of patients, respectively (see Echternach et al. (2009) who found evidence that laryngeal dysfunction after thyroidectomy is caused primarily by intubation and only to a lesser extent by RLN damage). Apart from surgical damage to the laryngeal nerves, there may be no known cause for VFPP ('idiopathic' VFPP) or a congenital malformation may compromise one of the nerves. Oestreicher-Kedem et al. (2008) studied six children who had vocal fold paralysis as a result of RLN damage related to a congenital tracheoesophageal fistula (a malformation in which there is communication between the trachea and oesophagus). Paralysis was bilateral in five children, and unilateral in one child. Five children required a tracheotomy.

Vocal fold paresis can be difficult to diagnose due to preservation of fold mobility (Sulica and Blitzer, 2007). Typically, paresis presents with symptoms of glottic insufficiency. Simpson et al. (2009) studied 195 patients with an initial diagnosis of paresis or paralysis. Using strobovideolaryngoscopy, these investigators found vocal fold bowing in 70 per cent of patients, incomplete closure in 62 per cent and increased vibratory amplitude in 38 per cent. Vocal symptoms include a weak, breathy voice as air is rapidly lost through the glottis. The patient may also experience fatigue as he or she is forced to take repeated breaths during speech to compensate for the loss of air. There is evidence that some cases of VFPP can resolve over time. Sancho et al. (2008) found that all paretic cords and all but one paralytic cord recovered fully after an average of 61 days in the post-thyroidectomy patients in their study. In a review of 717 cases of unilateral idiopathic vocal fold paralysis, Sulica (2008) found complete recovery of motion in 36 +/−22 per cent of individuals. Complete recovery of voice occurred in 52 +/−17 per cent of cases.

WEBSITE: Vocal fold paralysis and paresis

Listen to the audio files of unilateral and bilateral vocal fold paralysis. These files have been reproduced with the kind permission of Dr Richard Stasney of the Texas Voice Center (www.texasvoicecenter.com). The speaker with unilateral paralysis has a weak, breathy voice. The speaker with bilateral paralysis achieves greater phonation, but has stridor on inspiration, as the paralysed folds are impeding inhaled air.

A further neurogenic voice disorder is spasmodic dysphonia (SD). There are three types of SD: adductor type, abductor type and a mixed adductor-abductor type. In adductor SD, the vocal folds spasm shut abruptly at irregular intervals during phonation. The vocal folds fail to maintain normal contact during phonation in abductor SD. The adductor type is most common. In a study of 1,300 patients with spasmodic dysphonia, Blitzer (2010) identified adductor SD in 82 per cent of patients. The disorder is more commonly seen in women – women accounted for 63 per cent of the subjects in Blitzer's study. Adductor SD is characterised by a strained, strangled voice. There is effortful phonation and words are frequently cut off or are difficult to start (Siemons-Lühring et al., 2009). Vocal tremor is found in up to one third of patients who present with adductor SD (Kendall and Leonard, 2011). The symptoms of adductor SD are similar to those of muscle tension dysphonia (see section 7.3.2). This can create diagnostic confusion and can lead to inappropriate management (Houtz et al., 2010).

WEBSITE: Spasmodic dysphonia

Listen to the audio files of adductor SD and abductor SD. These files have been reproduced with the kind permission of Dr Richard Stasney of the Texas Voice Center (www.texasvoicecenter.com) and the National Spasmodic Dysphonia Association (www.dysphonia.org). The speaker with adductor SD has a strained, strangled voice with breaks in phonation at regular intervals. The speaker with abductor SD has a pattern of phonation that is marked by frequent interruptions of air.

Dysphonia is a significant clinical feature of many neurological disorders including Parkinson's disease, multiple sclerosis and myasthenia gravis. Sewall et al. (2006) report that nearly one third of patients with idiopathic Parkinson's disease report dysphonia to be their most debilitating deficit. Dysphonia can be the first presenting sign of Parkinson's disease (Merati et al., 2005). Dogan et al. (2007) conducted a stroboscopic examination of 27 female patients with multiple sclerosis. These investigators found that 16 patients (59 per cent) had a 'posterior chink' as their glottic closure pattern. Several acoustic and perceptual anomalies of voice in multiple sclerosis were also identified. Montero-Odasso (2006) describes the presence of fluctuating dysphonia as the first symptom of late-onset myasthenia gravis in an elderly man. Fairley and Hughes (1992) report a case of myasthenia gravis in a 46-year-old man who presented with acute stridor and bilateral abductor paralysis of the vocal folds. These clinical populations should not be overlooked as a significant source of neurogenic voice disorders.

WEBSITE: Dysphonia in neurological disorders

Listen to the audio files of voice samples taken from clients who have Parkinson's disease, multiple sclerosis and myasthenia gravis. These files have been reproduced with the kind permission of Dr Richard Stasney of the Texas Voice Center (www/texasvoicecenter.com). These voices have quite different perceptual characteristics. Try to identify these characteristics.

7.2.3   Other aetiologies

Organic aetiologies that are not structural or neurological in nature can also compromise the structure and function of the larynx. For example, laryngeal and vocal anomalies can be related to endocrine disorders, medications, laryngopharyngeal reflux (LPR) disease, and a range of infectious diseases. Hormones have a direct impact on laryngeal health. Premenstrual and menopausal voice syndromes are now well-documented (Abitbol et al., 1999). Hormone-related voice changes can be observed in hypo- and hyperthyroidism. Altman et al. (2003: 1931) state that 'alterations in the voice may occur even in cases of mild thyroid failure, suggesting that the larynx is a target tissue for thyroid hormone'. Barreto et al. (2009) obtained higher values for roughness, breathiness, strain and fundamental frequency of voice in subjects with isolated growth hormone deficiency.

Prescribed and non-prescribed medications are a significant cause of laryngeal and vocal anomalies. Gallivan et al. (2007) documented a number of abnormalities in 38 patients with voice complaints related to the use of inhaled corticosteroids to treat asthma. Strobovideolaryngoscopy revealed abnormal mucosal wave symmetry/periodicity, phase closure, glottic closure, mucosal wave amplitude/magnitude, supraglottic hyperactivity, mucosal quality and glottic plane in these subjects. Baker (1999) examined four women who experienced vocal symptoms following the treatment of conditions with medications containing virilising agents. Objective acoustic analysis of the voices of these women revealed a constellation of features that are typically observed in the pubescent male. Morris et al. (2011) examined the effects of initiating oral contraceptive use on acoustic measurements of the voice in a 23-year-old woman. Changes in glottal characteristics – measures of closed quotient and glottal width – were observed in this subject following the commencement of oral contraceptive use. Ray et al. (2008) reported the case of a 47-year-old professional body builder who experienced severe laryngitis following abuse of anabolic steroids over a two-year period. Such was the extent of structural changes in his larynx as a result of chronic steroid abuse that a tracheotomy was performed to secure his airway.

Bacterial, viral, fungal and parasitic infections can compromise the larynx. The infectious agents in acute laryngitis are most often viral in nature, but may sometimes be bacterial. Uncommon bacterial infections of the larynx, at least in developed countries, are tuberculosis (Nalini and Vinayak, 2006; Ozudogru et al., 2005), syphilis (Lacy et al., 1994), and anthrax (Leblebicioglu et al., 2006). Marelli et al. (1992) report a case of cytomegalovirus infection of the larynx in a patient with AIDS. Fungal infections of the larynx include an encapsulated yeast called *Cryptococcus neoformans* (McGregor et al., 2003) and *Histoplasma capsulatum*, the agent that causes histoplasmosis (Subramaniam et al., 2005). Finally, Fontes Rezende et al. (2006) describe involvement of the larynx in a parasitic infection *Trypanosoma cruzi* (Chagas' disease).

In people with gastroesophageal reflux (GER), gastric contents leak through the sphincter at the top of the stomach and work their way back along the oesophagus. When these contents spill into the larynx, their acidic nature damages the mucosal lining of the laryngeal structures. GER and LPR disease is increasingly being linked to the development of laryngeal disease and dysphonia. Belafsky et al. (2008) studied 20 patients who met diagnostic criteria for oesophagopharyngeal reflux (regurgitation of gastric contents from the proximal oesophagus into the laryngopharynx). The most common symptoms in these patients were cough (40 per cent), dysphonia (25 per cent) and chronic throat clearing (25 per cent). Cohen and Garrett (2008) examined patients who had a primary diagnosis of hoarseness with a view to establishing the prevalence of proton pump inhibitor (PPI) use in these patients (PPI is a treatment for GER). Among these patients, 56.1 per cent had previously tried PPIs or were currently on PPI treatment, a higher than expected prevalence if GER were not contributing to the hoarseness of these patients. Makhadoom et al. (2007) studied 30 patients who attended ENT and phoniatric outpatient clinics. Almost 80 per cent of the laryngeal and voice disorders seen in these patients were related to GER disease. GER disease with hiatus hernia accounted for the largest group of patients with reflux disease (63.3 per cent).

Clearly, reflux conditions are a further significant component in the complex organic aetiology of voice disorders.

WEBSITE: Laryngopharyngeal reflux

View the image of the larynx in the presence of LPR disease on the website. This image has been reproduced with the kind permission of The New York Eye and Ear Infirmary Voice and Swallowing Institute (www.nyee.edu.vsi). There is inflammation, indicated by redness and swelling, at the back of the larynx. The vocal fold mucosa is irritated and there are copious thick secretions on the folds.

KEY POINTS: Organic voice disorders

- Group of voice disorders in which there is a medical aetiology to account for dysphonia
- Aetiology may be structural, neurological, infectious, traumatic or hormonal in nature; also medications and laryngopharyngeal reflux can cause voice disorder
- Structural anomalies of the larynx include vocal nodules and polyps, cysts, laryngeal carcinomas, Reinke's oedema, granulomas, laryngeal papillomas, vocal fold haemorrhages, sulcus vocalis and presbylarynx
- Neurogenic voice disorders include vocal fold paralysis and paresis, spasmodic dysphonia and dysphonia in the presence of neurological disorders such as Parkinson's disease, multiple sclerosis and myasthenia gravis
- A range of symptoms can accompany organic voice disorders including hoarseness, breathiness, a strained-strangled voice, stridor, vocal fatigue and pain

---

7.3   Functional voice disorders

When an extensive laryngological examination reveals no lesion or other medical anomaly as a cause of a voice disorder, the disorder is classified as functional in nature. Within the group of functional voice disorders are those which have a psychological aetiology (so-called 'psychogenic' voice disorders) and disorders which have arisen through repeated abuse and misuse of the laryngeal mechanism (so-called 'hyperfunctional' voice disorders). This classification is somewhat problematic, however. Many cases of vocal abuse and misuse lead to the development of lesions such as vocal nodules, thus introducing an organic element into many functional voice disorders. It is becoming increasingly clear that functional voice disorders are a very significant cause of dysphonia in patients. Angelillo et al. (2008) examined voice disorders in 312 children between 2 and 16 years of age. These investigators found functional dysphonia in 92 per cent of their sample. Van Houtte et al. (2010) studied 882 patients between the ages of 4 and 90 years who attended an ENT department on account of dysphonia. Functional problems were the most common cause of dysphonia in these patients, accounting for 30 per cent of voice disorders. This section will address the presenting features of some functional voice disorders.

7.3.1 Psychogenic voice disorders

Baker (2003: 308) defines psychogenic dysphonia as a loss of voice the nature and severity of which is not accounted for by structural or neurological pathology and where 'loss of volitional control over phonation seems to be related to psychological processes such as anxiety, depression, conversion reaction, or personality disorder'. Baker states further that such dysphonias 'develop post-viral infection with laryngitis, and generally in close proximity to emotionally or psychologically taxing experiences'. These claims are broadly supported by the findings of a study conducted by Andersson and Schalén (1998) who investigated possible aetiological factors in 30 patients with psychogenic voice disorders. Fifteen patients (50 per cent) reported previous symptoms related to the respiratory tract such as asthma, allergic rhinitis, chronic bronchitis, or frequent respiratory tract infections. Problematic life events occurred in different combinations or singly in 97 per cent of patients. The most frequently reported events related to family and work. However, it was not possible to identify a specific life event which was linked to the onset of voice disorder in 93.3 per cent of patients. Psychogenic voice disorders are more commonly found in women than in men. Schalén and Andersson (1992) studied 40 consecutive patients with psychogenic voice disorder, 35 (87 per cent) of whom were female.

In conversion aphonia, the patient experiences a loss of voice in response to a traumatic event or some other psychological stressor. There is full movement of the vocal folds which can adduct normally during vegetative phonation (e.g. coughing) but which fall short of the adduction required to achieve voicing (Rammage et al., 2001). A range of sharp or high-pitched whispers are possible in the aphonic patient, indicating that the internal laryngeal muscles are in a state of hypercontraction (Aronson and Bless, 2009). Onset, which is often associated with exhaustion or fatigue, can be sudden – within seconds or minutes – or over a period of hours. Colds or flu and associated laryngitis can serve as a trigger for conversion aphonia. Even when the upper respiratory tract infection resolves, dysphonia remains and worsens to become aphonia (Aronson and Bless, 2009). Conversion aphonia is more commonly found in females than males. According to Aronson and Bless (2009), approximately 80 per cent of patients with conversion aphonia are female. Baker (1998) described the case of a 57-year-old woman who developed conversion aphonia some three years after the death of her husband. This woman, known as CR, had nursed her husband through a protracted illness of 10 years' duration. Upon initial presentation, she reported experiencing a severe upper respiratory tract infection which had left her feeling lethargic and run down. Otolaryngological examination revealed a normal larynx. CR displayed strong vocal fold apposition and normal voice on coughing. However, during attempts to phonate there was incomplete adduction of the vocal folds and a high-pitched, breathy falsetto voice. CR's therapist assessed her aphonia to be a true conversion reaction which served 'the defensive and expressive purpose of a delayed grieving response' (Baker, 1998: 529).

Puberphonia (also known as 'mutational, functional or persistent falsetto') is a relatively rare disorder that occurs predominantly in males. Some clinicians recognise a form of puberphonia, called 'juvenile resonance disorder', in post-pubescent females (Verdolini et al., 2006). In males, puberphonia presents as the persistence of a high-pitched voice beyond the point when voice mutation occurs. Laryngeal structures are normal. Verdolini et al. (2006) state that in North American males with the disorder, the fundamental frequency of the voice is often above 200 Hz. The voice may be characterised by observable downward pitch breaks. During these breaks, the natural lower pitch level of the voice is revealed. This may be closer to 110–125 Hz. A number of factors have been attributed with causing the disorder, most of which relate to emotional stress stemming from psychosocial changes that occur during puberty. However, Stemple et al. (2009) state that the condition is more likely to result from attempts to stabilise unstable pitch and quality characteristics that are present in the male pubescent voice. Gallena (2007) described the case of a 15-year-old boy called Travis who presented with an inappropriately elevated pitch and a breathy, rough voice quality secondary to puberphonia. Travis had a speaking fundamental frequency for /a/ of 218 Hz, which is in excess of that expected for his gender. His volitional phonation range was from 139–502 Hz. An optimal pitch, estimated at 110–120 Hz, was achieved through throat clearing and hard glottal attack initiation of vowel sounds. Frequent pitch breaks and periods of diplophonia were heard (diplophonia is the simultaneous presence of two separate tones in the voice, heard as different in pitch). Travis's high-pitched voice was a source of criticism and teasing from his classmates. Otolaryngological examination revealed normal vocal fold motion and small bilateral contact ulcers.

WEBSITE: Puberphonia

Listen to the puberphonia audio files on the website. The files contain voice samples from two speakers recorded before and after a course of voice therapy. The first file is from an examination conducted by Dr Apurva Thekdi of the Texas Voice Center. They have been reproduced with the kind permission of Dr Richard Stasney of the Texas Voice Center (www.texasvoicecenter.com).

7.3.2 Hyperfunctional voice disorders

In hyperfunctional voice disorders (also known as 'muscle tension dysphonia' – MTD), the vocal folds are adducted with excessive force on account of several factors. The client may be experiencing general laryngeal muscle tension in response to the stress of life (e.g. depression or anxiety, excess vocal loading related to occupational and recreational demands). Alternatively, the client may engage in forceful adduction of the folds on account of personality traits or as a compensatory strategy in the presence of an underlying laryngeal pathology

(Aronson and Bless, 2009). The behavioural patterns, psychological factors and organic components involved in these voice disorders make for a large and aetiologically complex group of dysphonias. This is evident in a study of muscle tension dysphonia conducted by Altman et al. (2005). These investigators performed a retrospective chart review of all patients over a 30-month period who attended the Voice, Speech and Language Service and Swallowing Center at their institution. Among the 150 patients identified, significant factors believed to play a role in the development of muscle tension dysphonia included gastroesophageal reflux (49 per cent of patients), high stress levels (18 per cent), excessive amounts of voice use (63 per cent) and excessive loudness demands on voice use (63 per cent). In 82 per cent of patients, an otolaryngological examination was performed. This revealed lesions, significant vocal fold oedema or paralysis/paresis in 52.3 per cent of patients. This diverse range of aetiologies has led some clinicians to distinguish between primary and secondary forms of muscle tension dysphonia. In primary MTD, dysphonia occurs in the absence of concurrent organic vocal fold pathology, while in secondary MTD such pathology is present (Van Houtte et al., 2011).

Perceptual and laryngeal features have been extensively documented in muscle tension dysphonia. Lee and Son (2005) examined eight male children with MTD. All children had markedly strained and breathy voices. In five children, pitch breaks and/or inadequately high or low speaking fundamental frequencies were observed. Anteroposterior contraction, false vocal fold approximation, incomplete glottal closure and decreased vibration of the true vocal folds were revealed by laryngoscopic evaluation. Nguyen et al. (2009) examined 47 Northern Vietnamese female primary school teachers with MTD. Photolaryngoscopy was used to assess laryngeal features. A glottal gap was the major laryngeal characteristic of MTD in these subjects. The glottal shapes observed in these subjects included incomplete closure (44.7 per cent of subjects), a posterior gap (29.8 per cent), an hourglass-shaped gap (12.8 per cent) and a spindle-shaped gap (8.5 per cent). Only 4.3 per cent of subjects had complete glottal closure. There is a measurable increase in the tension of the (para) laryngeal musculature in MTD. In a study of 11 patients with MTD, Hocevar-Boltezar et al. (1998) found a sixfold to eightfold increase of electromyographic activity in the perioral and supralaryngeal muscles before and during phonation. Altered tension of the extrinsic laryngeal musculature in MTD results in an elevated position of the larynx in the neck (Van Houtte et al., 2011).

WEBSITE: Muscle tension dysphonia

Listen to and watch the audio and video files of muscle tension dysphonia on the website. These files have been reproduced with the kind permission of Dr Richard Stasney of the Texas Voice Center (www.texasvoicecenter.com). Laryngeal appearance in MTD can also be seen in an image which has been reproduced with the kind permission of The New York Eye and Ear Infirmary Voice and Swallowing Institute (www.nyee.edu.vsi). The vocal tract above the true vocal folds is constricted, making voice production difficult.

KEY POINTS: Functional voice disorders

- When a laryngological examination reveals no medical (organic) cause for a voice disorder, functional dysphonia is diagnosed
- Includes dysphonias which have a psychological basis (psychogenic voice disorders) and dysphonias that arise on account of behavioural factors (hyperfunctional voice disorders)
- Psychogenic voice disorders may be related to anxiety and depression, a conversion reaction or a personality disorder; include conversion aphonia and puberphonia (mutational falsetto)
- Hyperfunctional voice disorders (or muscle tension dysphonias) are caused by forceful adduction of the vocal folds related to general laryngeal tension, personality traits or a compensatory strategy in the presence of an organic vocal fold pathology
- Muscle tension dysphonias can be either primary (absence of vocal fold pathology) or secondary (presence of vocal fold pathology)

7.4   Assessment and treatment

Voice disorders are assessed by means of instrumental, acoustic and perceptual techniques. The otolaryngologist uses instruments to observe the larynx, either directly or indirectly, and examine its function during phonation. The longest-established method of indirectly viewing the interior of the larynx is mirror laryngoscopy. In this procedure, the otolaryngologist places a laryngeal mirror against the patient's elevated soft palate as he or she says 'ee' at a relatively high pitch. The patient's tongue is wrapped in gauze and held by the examiner. A mirror worn on the examiner's head reflects light from an external source on to the laryngeal mirror, which then reflects it into the pharynx and larynx. This procedure is not tolerated by all patients. For these patients, fibreoptic laryngoscopy may be a more appropriate technique. In this procedure, a flexible endoscope is passed transnasally into a position above the larynx. Phonation during connected speech can be observed using this technique (this is not possible during mirror laryngoscopy). A technique that has become 'the definitive tool in differential diagnoses of laryngeal pathology' is videostrobolaryngoscopy (Mathieson, 2001: 433). In this procedure, intermittent flashes of light, which are delivered by means of a rigid or flexible endoscope, have the effect of simulating slow motion of the vocal folds. This enables the otolaryngologist to examine different stages of the vibratory cycle. Videostrobolaryngoscopy allows even minute lesions and their effect on the mucosal wave to be examined.

WEBSITE: Laryngoscopy

Watch the demonstration on the website of how a laryngoscopy is performed. This recording has been reproduced with the kind permission of James P. Thomas, MD and is taken from voicedoctor.net.

Acoustic assessments of voice provide objective data that can be compared with normative values and used as a baseline for treatment. Commercially available techniques of acoustic assessment include the Kay Computerised Speech Lab: Multi-Dimensional Voice Program (MDVP; Kay Elemetrics, 1993), VisiSpeech and Kay Visi-Pitch. MDVP is a software tool for quantitative acoustic assessment of voice quality. It can calculate more than 22 acoustic parameters on a single vocalisation, including fundamental frequency, jitter, shimmer and turbulence. The number and range of these parameters reflect the fact that one or two voicing parameters are often not adequate to describe an aberration in a patient's voice. For example, a patient may have a breathy voice and yet jitter values may be within normal limits. The use of acoustic assessments requires considerable expertise on the part of clinicians and therapists. They must understand, for example, how particular acoustic findings relate to perceptual speech features. Also, the technology used in acoustic analysis is expensive. The least expensive way to obtain MDVP is as part of Multi-Speech or Sona-Speech and this costs US$2,500 to US$3,000, including local hardware (personal communication, KayPENTAX, 17 July 2006). Notwithstanding the cost of this technology, the important contribution of acoustic analysis to an overall voice assessment means that these techniques are now a standard feature of all specialist voice clinics.

Data that describe various acoustic parameters of the voice are still no substitute for how a voice sounds to a listener. A perceptual evaluation of the voice is thus a central component of the assessment process. Typically, perceptual evaluation is achieved by means of scales. One of the most widely used scales in the UK and internationally is the GRBAS scale of the Japan Society of Logopaedics and Phoniatrics (Hirano, 1981). This perceptual rating system contains five parameters: G (overall grade of hoarseness), R (roughness), B (breathiness), A (asthenic) and S (strained quality). Each parameter is given a rating on a four-point scale between 0 and 3, where '0' indicates non-hoarse or normal, '1' slight, '2' moderate and '3' severe. The GRBAS scale is not fully comprehensive – it does not include parameters for vocal pitch, for example (Freeman and Fawcus, 2000). Nevertheless, this scale is a reliable method of perceptual assessment that has been shown to correlate with voice-related quality of life (Jones et al., 2006; Karnell et al., 2007). The perceptual scheme that is most often used by British speech and language therapists is Laver et al.'s (1981) Vocal Profile Analysis Scheme (Shewell, 1998). The scheme assesses supralaryngeal features, tension features, phonation type and prosodic features within a series of specific subcategories. For example, prosodic features include pitch (mean, range, variability), tremor and loudness (mean, range, variability).

Voice disorders should be treated by a multidisciplinary team consisting of the laryngologist, speech and language therapist, gastroenterologist, psychologist (counsellor or psychotherapist), psychiatrist, radiologist and occupational health worker. Voice treatments include surgery, radiotherapy, drugs and voice therapy, which are typically undertaken in combination rather than in isolation. Surgical techniques are increasingly being used to treat a range of pathologies that cause voice disorders. Bioplastique injection and lipo-augmentation of the vocal folds, as well as medialisation thyroplasty using a titanium implant, are among the preferred treatment methods for unilateral vocal fold paralysis (Bihari et al., 2006). Varices and ectasias can be successfully treated using pulsed angiolytic lasers (Zeitels et al., 2006). Knott et al. (2006) used endoscopic carbon dioxide laser resection in conjunction with cryoablation – the application of extreme cold to destroy cancer cells – to treat patients with early-stage glottic cancer (see section 7.5). Autologous transplantation of fascia into the vocal fold has been used to treat sulcus vocalis (Tsunoda et al., 2005). Surgical procedures are increasingly being used to help the transsexual client attain the voice of his or her newly-assigned sex (see section 6.4 in Chapter 6). Cricothyroid approximation may be undertaken to raise the fundamental frequency of clients who are unable to achieve desired pitch changes through non-surgical means (McNeil, 2006). Other surgical techniques that are used to raise the pitch of the male-to-female transsexual voice are anterior commissure advancement, scarification, injection of triamcinolone into the vocal folds and endolaryngeal shortening of the vocal folds (Gross, 1999).

WEBSITE: Cricothyroid approximation

Listen to the 15-minute lecture on cricothyroid approximation on the website. This recording has been reproduced with the kind permission of James P. Thomas, MD and is taken from voicedoctor.net.

Radiotherapy and drugs are also used extensively in the treatment of voice disorders. Freeman and Fawcus (2000) state that radiotherapy tends to be the primary form of treatment in Britain for laryngeal tumours at stages T1 and T2. (In a T1 glottic carcinoma, the tumour is limited to the vocal folds, which have normal mobility. A T2 tumour extends to the subglottic and/or supraglottic region with impairment of vocal fold mobility.) As well as treating the pathologies (carcinomas) that cause voice disorders, radiotherapy can also have some undesirable consequences both for anatomy and the voice. Preoperative radiotherapy has been linked to the development of post-laryngectomy pharyngocutaneous fistula, while post-operative radiotherapy has been shown to correlate with laryngeal stenosis (Paydarfar and Birkmeyer, 2006; Wu et al., 2005). Van Gogh et al. (2005) studied 177 patients after radiotherapy or laser surgery for early glottic cancer. Voice impairment was reported by 44 per cent of the patients who received radiotherapy (only 29 per cent of patients receiving laser surgery reported voice impairment). Drugs may also be used to treat voice disorders and the medical conditions that cause voice disorders. It is now widely accepted that botulinum toxin is an effective treatment for adductor spasmodic dysphonia (Woodson et al., 2006). Voice disorders that are caused by gastroesophageal reflux may be treated by proton pump inhibitors, while the antiviral drug cidofovir has been found to be efficacious in treating recurrent respiratory papillomatosis (Issing et al., 2004; Lee and Rosen, 2004).

Voice therapy is integral to the treatment of dysphonia and can include the use of specific voice production techniques, the provision of counselling and relaxation methods, and advice on voice care. Schindler et al. (2008) used direct voice techniques to treat 40 patients with unilateral vocal fold paralysis of different aetiologies. The aim of voice therapy was to improve glottal closure and avoid undesirable compensatory behaviours (e.g. tongue backing to aid glottal closure). Glaze (1996) used three 'direct vocal function exercises' – easy onset of voice plus resonant tone, the accent method of phonation and physiological exercises – in a programme of therapy with children who had hyperfunctional voice disorders. Where psychological factors play a role in the aetiology of a voice disorder, therapists integrate counselling or psychotherapeutic techniques within voice therapy. Andersson and Schalén (1998) reported on the treatment of 30 patients with psychogenic voice disorder related to family- and work-based interpersonal conflicts. Treatment consisted of traditional vocal exercises. In addition, one of the researchers, who was trained in psychosomatic disorders and behavioural techniques, used interactive therapeutic discourse with the aim of mapping the patterns of the patients' social networks and focusing on conflicts. Finally, the voice therapist has an important role to play in educating clients in a range of issues relating to voice care. This may include advice on improved patterns of voice use in the case of patients with hyperfunctional voice disorders. It will also include information on various aspects of vocal hygiene such as the effects of alcohol, tobacco smoke, dehydration, allergens and gastric reflux on the laryngeal mucosa.

7.5 Communication after laryngectomy

Laryngeal cancer is a significant cause of communication disability in the adults who develop this disease. In 2006, there were just over 1,800 new cases of laryngeal cancer diagnosed in the UK. There were 743 deaths from laryngeal cancer in the UK in 2007, the large majority of which (80.3 per cent) were in men. Laryngeal cancer is rarely diagnosed in people under 40 years, but the incidence rises steeply after this age and peaks in people aged 75–84 years. Most cases (72 per cent) occur in people over 60 years of age. Survival rates vary with the stage of tumour at diagnosis. Cancer Research UK reports that in 2006, there were just over 1,800 new cases. Approximately 67 per cent of all individuals diagnosed with laryngeal cancer live for at least five years and 61 per cent live for at least 10 years. A number of factors have been linked to the development of laryngeal cancer including smoking and drinking, gastrooesophageal reflux disease, immunosuppression (in HIV/ AIDS and transplant recipients), infection with human papilloma virus 16 and helicobacter pylori, and a history of head and neck cancer in first-degree relatives.

WEBSITE: Laryngeal cancer

View the images of laryngeal cancer on the website. These images have been reproduced with the kind permission of Bechara Y. Ghorayeb, MD (www.houstonoto.com/

PicturesLarynx.html). One of these images shows an extensive squamous cell carcinoma that involves subglottic, glottic and supraglottic regions. It necessitated a tracheotomy prior to laryngoscopy. There is also an image of chronic laryngitis that is related to heavy smoking (80 cigarettes daily). The whitish mucosa is leukoplakia, a smoking-related condition that is precancerous.

If an advanced laryngeal tumour is diagnosed, a total laryngectomy is performed. During surgery, the patient's trachea is directed onto the neck to create a stoma. The patient permanently breathes through this stoma, as there is no longer a connection between the lungs and the oral and nasal cavities. Voice production can be achieved through the use of an artificial larynx, oesophageal voice or a voice prosthesis (speaking valve). An artificial (or electronic) larynx is held against the neck and vibrates the air in the oral cavity. This vibrated air is then shaped into speech sounds by the movement of the articulators as normal. The resulting voice lacks intonation and has a certain robotic quality. Also, immediately after surgery and radiotherapy, neck tissues may be too tender for the pressure of this device. In oesophageal voice production, the patient can be taught how to take air down into the oesophagus and bring it up again under voluntary control. The exiting air causes the sphincter at the top of the oesophagus (the cricopharyngeus muscle) to vibrate. Excellent speaking voices can be achieved through this method of communication, although in some cases the voice is rather deep and has a 'wet' quality. Nowadays, most patients are being offered the opportunity to have a voice prosthesis fitted during the laryngectomy operation. Although different valves are available (e.g. Provox, Blom-Singer), they all operate by shunting air from the trachea into the oesophagus where it is used to produce oesophageal voice. Some valves require the laryngectomee client to block the stoma with the thumb, while an adjustable tracheostoma valve may be used with other prostheses permitting hands-free operation. Because a pulmonary airstream is involved (as opposed to air being gulped back into the oesophagus as in standard oesophageal voice), the laryngectomee client can maintain a longer flow of speech and achieve greater volume using a voice prosthesis. Figure 7.1 presents anatomical structures after laryngectomy and methods of post-laryngectomy voice production.

WEBSITE: Laryngectomy

Watch the two video files on laryngectomy. These files explain the significant anatomical changes that occur as a result of laryngectomy. You will also have the chance to listen to several speakers who have undergone laryngectomy. All three main methods of communication are demonstrated. These video files have been reproduced with minor modifications with the kind permission of the National Association of Laryngectomee Clubs (www.laryngectomy.org.uk).

(A)

(B)

(C)

(D)

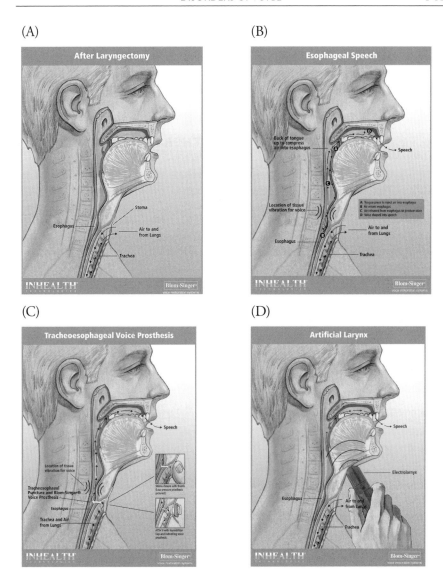

Figure 7.1 Diagrams showing (A) anatomical structures after laryngectomy and various methods of post-laryngectomy voice production: (B) oesophageal voice, (C) tracheoesophageal voice prosthesis and (D) artificial larynx. (Images courtesy of InHealth Technologies)

KEY POINTS: Laryngectomy

- Surgical removal of the larynx either in part (partial laryngectomy) or in whole (total laryngectomy)
- Performed in order to treat laryngeal cancer (more common in individuals with history of heavy smoking and alcohol consumption)

- Three methods of communication after laryngectomy: (1) artificial larynx, (2) oesophageal voice (OV), and (3) voice prosthesis (speaking valve)
- Artficial larynx vibrates air in oral cavity; oesophageal sphincter vibrated in OV; valve directs pulmonary air for vibration in cricopharyngeal segment

SUGGESTIONS FOR FURTHER READING

Aronson, A.E. and Bless, D.M. (2009) *Clinical Voice Disorders* (New York: Thieme Medical Publishers).

Mathieson, L. (2001) *Greene and Mathieson's The Voice and Its Disorders* (London: Whurr Publishers).

Stemple, J.C., Glaze, L.E. and Klaben, B.G. (2009) *Clinical Voice Pathology: Theory and Management* (San Diego, CA: Plural Publishing, 4th edn).

EXERCISES

Exercise 7.1   Using your knowledge of organic voice disorders, identify the laryngeal pathology that is involved in each of the cases described below. In one case, the pathology is structural in nature; in the other case, it is neurological. As well as identifying the laryngeal pathology, state what features were significant in your choice of disorder.

Case A

NB, a 61-year-old Caucasian female, complained of irregular speech breaks without hoarseness or aphonia. Symptoms started about two years ago. The patient underwent assessment by means of stroboscopy, clinical neurological examination and voice lab. She presented signs of tense voice, vocal tiredness, breathy voice, laryngeal pain, loss of voice extension and lack of frequency control. Stroboscopy revealed mild bilateral vocal tremor which was more intense in the left vocal fold. There were no structural lesions on the vocal folds and no oedema. NB had good lamina propria expansion bilaterally without glottal gaps. She was treated with the injection of Botulin toxin (Botox) in the left thyroarytenoid muscle. Her voice was somewhat breathy in the first week and after that it became stable (Santos et al., 2006: 426).

Case B

NAR, a 44-year-old female, complained of hoarseness, vocal tiredness and weak voice since childhood. She did not smoke and did not complain of reflux. Her voice sounded high, blowy, with vocal effort and reduction in phonation time. Laryngological examination revealed a spindle-like cleft. The patient refused to undergo surgery. Her case history revealed that she had three brothers with dysphonia. These brothers were aged 22, 29 and 42. Two reported hoarseness and weak voice since childhood. The third brother reported mild hoarseness during vocal abuse. All three brothers denied smoking and experienced vocal symptoms similar to NAR. One brother had undergone phonosurgery in the form of a fat graft (Martins et al., 2007: 573).

Exercise 7.2   Using your knowledge of functional voice disorders, identify the specific type of dysphonia that is involved in each of the cases described below. In one case, the dysphonia is psychogenic in nature; in the other case, it is hyperfunctional. As well as identifying the voice disorder, state what features were significant in your choice of disorder.

Case A

Judith, a 53-year-old professional woman, first experienced hoarseness and voice loss two months prior to her voice evaluation. She reported a sudden onset to her voice problems, intermittent pitch breaks and frequent coughing. It was difficult for Judith to project her voice or sing. She described a feeling of fullness in her throat and of food sticking in her throat. Both professionally and personally, her life was being adversely affected by her voice problems. Judith reported having an anxiety disorder and occasionally had panic attacks. She does not smoke or drink alcohol. During the week she works long hours and she volunteers with several organisations at the weekend.

A diagnosis of laryngopharyngeal reflux was made following flexible nasendoscopy. Reflux symptoms are reported to have improved since Judith started taking medication some three weeks before her voice evaluation. Laryngeal findings included oedema and erythema (redness) of the arytenoid cartilages and cartilaginous portion of the vocal folds along with tissue hypertrophy of the posterior glottis. There was no evidence of contact ulcers or granulomas. Medial compression of the vocal folds with a large posterior glottal chink was revealed by stroboscopy. There were thick mucous strands across the vocal folds and the mucosal wave was reduced.

Judith's voice evaluation revealed anomalies in pitch, quality, and respiration. Her speaking fundamental frequency in contextual speech (174 Hz) was low for her age and gender. Judith's fundamental frequency pitch range (133–348 Hz) was not within normal limits. A frequency perturbation of 2.85 for /a/ correlated perceptually to vocal hoarseness. She displayed moderate to severe breathiness, mild to moderate roughness and moderate strain. Breaks in phonation and hard glottal attack upon initiation of phonation were heard. The maximum phonation duration for sustained /a/ was 9 seconds, which is not within normal limits for Judith's age and gender. Judith displayed a number of vocal abuse behaviours including coughing, talking excessively, throat clearing and singing (Gallena, 2007: 24–5).

Case B

AB, a 23-year-old female student, experienced viral laryngitis with subsequent loss of voice and a whispery dysphonia for three weeks. She underwent otolaryngological examination which revealed muscle tension dysphonia, anteroposterior constriction and normal vocal fold movement on coughing. There was no other laryngeal pathology. AB was told that her dysphonia was related to laryngitis and protective tension of the laryngeal muscles. She was referred to speech pathology to work on correct use of the voice.

A full psychosocial interview was conducted at AB's first speech pathology session, which she attended with her mother. Normal phonation was readily elicited during coughing and facilitating exercises and this was quickly consolidated into comfortable conversational speech. Psychogenic dysphonia was explained to AB and her mother with the therapist discussing physical, functional and psychosocial or emotional influences on the voice as part of her explanation. AB explored these potential factors with the therapist and her mother and felt that her ongoing studies and work pressure were the only factors that might be of significance in the development of her voice disorder. However, AB still believed these could not fully account for her voice problems and wondered whether there might be an alternative explanation. Although AB left the session happy with the outcome, the therapist felt that the problem had not been fully resolved.

At her second session a week later, which she attended on her own, AB appeared relaxed and chatted at ease about her studies and work. It was towards the end of the session when AB quietly asked the therapist if an event some four months earlier could have given rise to her voice problems. She recounted how she had been brutally raped by a young man on her course, who had taken her to his family home. She tried to scream during the assault, but was unable to make anyone in the house hear her. AB did not report the assault for fear of academic and career repercussions. The man responsible for the attack had been assigned to AB's immediate work environment at the beginning of the week in which AB had developed viral laryngitis and subsequent dysphonia (Baker, 2003: 311–12).

Exercise 7.3   Listen to the audio file 'communication after laryngectomy'. You will hear the voices of six people (five men and one woman) who have undergone laryngectomy. Two of the speakers are using an artificial larynx to communicate. A further two speakers are communicating using oesophageal voice. There are also two speakers who are communicating using a speaking valve. Your task is to:

(a)   Identify the method of communication for each of the six speakers.
(b)   Identify the speaker whose tongue nerve was severed during laryngectomy. A clue to help you is that this person struggles to say the word 'communication'.
(c)   State which speech sound in 'communication' is particularly problematic for the speaker you identify in part (b).

(The audio file used in this exercise is reproduced with the kind permission of the National Association of Laryngectomee Clubs (www.laryngectomy.org.uk). It has been minimally altered for the purpose of this exercise.)

ANSWERS TO EXERCISES

Exercise 7.1

Case A: NB has adductor spasmodic dysphonia

Features: irregular speech breaks (intermittent phonation); vocal symptoms (tense voice; vocal tiredness reflecting intense vocal effort); vocal tremor; absence of structural lesions and oedema; treatment (intramuscular injection of Botulin toxin)

Case B: NAR has sulcus vocalis

Features: onset of voice problem in childhood; presence of dysphonia in biological relatives; absence of other risk factors (smoking and reflux); spindle-like cleft (unable to achieve full glottal closure); vocal symptoms (suggestive of inadequate glottal closure); treatment (use of fat graft in phonosurgery)

Exercise 7.2

Case A: Judith has muscle tension dysphonia secondary to laryngopharyngeal reflux (LPR)

Features: primary disorder of LPR indicated by reported symptoms (sensation of fullness in throat and food sticking in throat; frequent coughing) and laryngeal findings (thick mucous strands on folds, oedema, erythema and hypertrophy at back of larynx); secondary disorder of muscle tension dysphonia suggested by vocal abuse behaviours, vocal features (breaks in phonation; low speaking fundamental frequency; breathiness and roughness) and laryngeal findings (medial compression of vocal folds; large posterior glottal chink).

Case B: AB has a psychogenic voice disorder caused by a conversion reaction

Features: viral laryngitis followed by dysphonia; no other laryngeal pathology; normal phonation during coughing; able to produce whispered voice; traumatic event (rape) that led to a conflict over speaking out. AB's dysphonia served the purpose of avoiding awareness of emotional conflict and stress which would have been intolerable if directly countenanced.

Exercise 7.3

(a) Bert and John (artificial larynx); Don and Stan (oesophageal voice); Joan and Derek (speaking valve)
(b) John
(c) voiceless velar plosive /k/

Disorders of Fluency

8

8.1 Fluency disorders

Successful speech production depends as much on the fluency with which speech is produced as it does on the accurate articulation of speech sounds. Speech is never produced without some degree of hesitation, pausing and repetition. These breaks in the flow of speech serve several important functions including securing time in which to perform linguistic processing, providing an opportunity for self-correction and inhaling air in order to produce the next utterance. These so-called 'normal non-fluencies' are quite unlike the anomalies that occur in fluency disorders. In fluency disorders, breaks in the flow of speech are performing none of these essential functions and serve only to compromise the speaker's effectiveness as a communicator. The impact of fluency disorders can be considerable, limiting everything from personal relationships and social interaction to opportunities for employment and even one's quality of life. In an effort to mitigate these adverse consequences, speech and language therapists devote considerable clinical time and energy to the assessment and treatment of fluency disorders. In this chapter, we will examine how clinicians assess and treat these disorders. We will also address what is known about the causes of fluency disorders. We will see that in the case of at least one prominent fluency disorder, stuttering or stammering, knowledge of a clearly identifiable aetiology remains as elusive as ever. We will also consider what is known about the epidemiology of these disorders. Like many communication disorders, the incidence and prevalence of fluency disorders have not been extensively investigated. Nevertheless, it is important to consider the studies that have been undertaken in this area, particularly in terms of what they might be able to tell us about the aetiology of these disorders.

Most of this chapter will be devoted to the discussion of stuttering. This fluency disorder has a developmental and an acquired form. The developmental form is the most prominent type of stuttering both in terms of general public awareness of the disorder and clinical research into the condition. In developmental stuttering, there is a failure to acquire normal speech fluency during the developmental period. This fluency disorder is found in children and adults, the latter with onset in the developmental period. The reasons for the failure to acquire normal speech fluency are still unclear, although causal explanations of stuttering have tended to coalesce around genetic, psychological and neurological factors. Acquired stuttering has its onset in adulthood. In individuals with this disorder, previously normal skills of speech fluency are disrupted by brain injury or disease. The aetiology of this disorder is thus clearly neurological in nature. Another, less well-known fluency disorder is cluttering. This disorder is frequently misdiagnosed as stuttering by clinicians. Cluttering has received relatively little attention in the clinical communication science literature. It is unsurprising, therefore, that little is known about the epidemiology and aetiology of this fluency disorder. However, the features of cluttering are beginning to be systematically investigated by researchers. They reveal a quite different impairment of speech fluency from that which occurs in stuttering. The epidemiology, aetiology and clinical features of all three fluency disorders will be examined in this chapter. Examples of dysfluent speech will be used to demonstrate the features of these disorders. The chapter will also address how clinicians assess and treat fluency disorders.

8.2   Developmental stuttering

In a stark assessment of our current state of knowledge of stuttering, Wingate (2002: 11) remarks that 'the three most thoroughly supportable and significant facts about stuttering, of which anyone involved in the field should be clearly aware, [are] namely: (1) its cause is unknown, (2) its essential nature is not understood, and (3) there is no known cure'. Whilst acknowledging that there is much that we do not know about stuttering, particularly in regard to the aetiology of the disorder, studies are nonetheless improving our understanding of this fluency disorder. The general population prevalence of developmental stuttering is typically taken to be 1 per cent. However, prevalence figures can vary considerably depending on the population studied. Van Borsel et al. (2006) studied 21,027 school pupils aged 6–20 years in Flanders, Belgium, and obtained a prevalence figure for stuttering of 0.58 per cent. Ardila et al. (1994) examined 1,879 Spanish-speaking university students and obtained a prevalence rate of self-reported stuttering of 2 per cent. As might be expected, prevalence rates also vary with the age of the population studied. Craig et al. (2002) reported that prevalence rates of stuttering in the state of New South Wales in Australia were highest in younger children (1.4–1.44) and lowest in adolescence (0.53). This reflects the fact that many cases of developmental stuttering resolve spontaneously. The incidence of stuttering has also been investigated. Månsson (2000) studied the entire population of children born within a two-year period on the Danish island of Bornholm. The incidence of stuttering in this population reached 5.19 per cent. In children aged 2–5 years and 6–10 years studied by Craig et al. (2002), the incidence of stuttering was 2.8 per cent and 3.4 per cent, respectively.

Several other features of the epidemiology of stuttering are noteworthy. The disorder is consistently reported to affect males more often than females. Craig et al. (2002) obtained a male-to-female ratio in the adolescents in their study of 4:1. Higher prevalence rates for stuttering have also been reported in a number of special populations including pupils attending a special school, adults with Down syndrome and adults with learning disabilities (Devenny and Silverman, 1990; Stansfield, 1990; Van Borsel et al., 2006). To the extent that what distinguishes these populations is some degree of neurological impairment, there is perhaps a clue to the aetiology of developmental stuttering in these increased prevalence figures. A genetic aetiology is another active area of investigation. Van Beijsterveldt et al. (2010) examined the heritability of stuttering in over 10,500 5-year-old Dutch twin pairs. Genetic analyses revealed that stuttering was moderately heritable with a heritability estimate for probable stuttering of 42 per cent obtained. Felsenfeld et al. (2000) screened a large population-based twin sample from the Australian Twin Registry for stuttering. These investigators found that approximately 70 per cent of the variance in liability to stuttering was found to be attributable to additive genetic effects, with non-shared environmental effects accounting for the remaining variance. Studies have found an increased rate of stuttering in the biological relatives of stutterers. Viswanath et al. (2000) found that the biological relatives of stutterers have an approximately tenfold higher risk of stuttering than that in the general population. It appears increasingly likely that genetic factors play a prominent role in the distal aetiology of stuttering.

The age of onset of stuttering, remission or recovery rates and prognostic indicators in relation to stuttering have all been the focus of recent research work. Månsson (2000) established the age at onset for 12 children who were identified as stuttering at the start of a study on the Danish island of Bornholm and at follow-up two years later. The mean age at which onset occurred was 33 months, with an age range at onset from 24 to 42 months. In a study of 1,619 2-year-old Australian children, Reilly et al. (2009) obtained a median age of onset of 29.9 months, with a range of 12.0 to 36.9 months. Onset can occur gradually or suddenly. Reilly et al. (2009) reported that onset occurred suddenly over 1 to 3 days in 49.6 per cent of 137 children confirmed to have stuttering in their study. Gradual onset (over one week) and sudden onset (1 to 7 days) occurred in 67 per cent and 33 per cent, respectively, of the children studied by Månsson (2000). Consistently high rates of remission or recovery have been reported. Yairi and Ambrose (1999) followed 147 preschool children who stuttered for several years after the onset of stuttering. These investigators obtained stuttering recovery and persistency rates of 74 per cent and 26 per cent, respectively. Only 15 of 51 children originally identified as exhibiting stuttering by Månsson were still stuttering two years after their first screening. This resulted in recovery and persistency rates of 71.4 per cent and 28.4 per cent, respectively. A range of factors has been investigated with a view to establishing their value as prognostic indicators for stuttering. These factors can be used by clinicians to determine which children are likely to become persistent stutterers or recover from stuttering. Yairi et al. (1996) found that language indexes, non-verbal performance, phonological skills, genetics and dysfluency characteristics may all contribute to the prediction of persistent (chronic) stuttering.

The speech features of stuttering have been extensively characterised. As Wingate (2002: 9) describes these features, they consist in 'iterative and/or perseverative speech elements involving word/syllable-initial position'. The 'speech elements' that are involved in iterations are single speech sounds or two speech sounds. For example, in attempting to say 'spoke', the person who stutters may engage in iteration of /s/ or /sp/. A vowel sound, typically a schwa, may also be involved in the iteration, e.g. /spə/ for 'spoke'. The 'speech elements' that are involved in perseverations or protractions are always single speech sounds. The protracted sound may be unreleased, as in /s:::/ for 'soap'. Both iterations and protractions may be silent or audible. Several studies have examined the iterations and protractions of stuttering. Natke et al. (2006) examined dysfluencies in 24 German-speaking preschool children who stutter. Several stuttering dysfluencies – namely, prolongations, blocks and part- and one-syllable word repetitions – were significantly more frequent in these preschoolers (mean = 9.2 per cent) than in a control group of 24 children who did not stutter (mean = 1.2 per cent). Children who stutter also produced significantly more iterations (mean = 1.28 iterations) than non-stuttering children (mean = 1.09 iterations). Zebrowski (1991) examined the duration of within-word dysfluencies in 10 children who had been stuttering for one year or less and in 10 non-stuttering children. No significant group differences were found in the duration of acoustically measured sound/syllable repetitions and sound prolongations. Zebrowski (1991: 483) concluded that these results 'support findings from previous perceptual work that type and frequency of speech dysfluency, not duration, are the principal characteristics listeners use in distinguishing these two talker groups'.

How iterations and perseverations are manifested in the speech of people who stutter can be seen by examining the blocks that are produced by these speakers. Sheehan (1974) undertook a phonetic transcription of 25 blocks that were produced consecutively by an adult who stutters, 22 of which are transcribed in Table 8.1.

Perseverations are particularly common in the data in Table 8.1 and occur both on single consonants word initially (e.g. 'nineteen', 'Shanahan', 'seventeen') and on consonants that are part of clusters (e.g. 'fracture'). Less often, perseverations occur in the middle of words (e.g. 'hospitalisation'). Occasionally, perseverations involve irrelevant sounds (e.g. 'concussions'). Repetitions or iterations are also widespread and involve single consonants or consonant and vowel (syllable) combinations (e.g. 'therapy'). Word repetition is also commonplace (e.g. 'one', 'at', 'to'), although Sheehan argues that these productions are likely to be better explained as syllable repetitions. Iterations are sometimes combined with perseverations such as in 'nineteen' [n:ʌ.nʌ:naɪntin]. The schwa vowel was so frequently stressed by this individual who stutters that its accented equivalent [ʌ] is used in the transcriptions in Table 8.1. Some uses of this vowel appear to function as starters which trigger the production of the target form (e.g. the second utterance of 'nineteen'). Other uses appear to mark time until a relevant speech attempt is made or interrupt perseverations or repetitions once the relevant sound has begun (e.g. 'Rushville'). The schwa vowel is used in these contexts, even though it is often superseded by a different vowel (e.g. 'Percy'), because it is the most easily and readily articulated of the vowels. Its ease of articulation probably

Table 8.1 Iterations and perseverations in the speech of an adult who stutters

today	[tu..tudeɪ]	at	[æt.æt.æ.æt]
January	[dʒɪ.dʒɪ..dʒæ.dʒænjuɛrɪ]	fracture	[f::rækʧʊr]
nineteen	[n::aɪntɪn]	concussions	[s::kənkʌʃənz]
Shanahan	[ʃ::::ænəhæn]	hospitalisation	[haspɪtɪlɪz::eɪʃən]
Percy	[pʌ..pɜsɪ]	month	[mʌ.mʌnθ]
Rushville	[ɣ::ʌ.əʃvɪl]	United	[jʌ.junaɪtɪd]
seventeen	[s::ɛvɪntɪn]	therapy	[θʌ.θʌ..θɛrəpi]
my	[mʌ.:maɪ]	to	[tu..tu]
city	[s::ɪtɪ]	correct	[kʌ .kərɛkt]
thirty-five	[θ.θɜ..θɜtɪfaɪv]	long	[l:.loŋ]
nineteen	[n:ʌ.nʌ:naɪntɪn]	one	[wʌn.wʌn]

Based on: Sheehan (1974).

also explains its preponderance in syllable repetitions (e.g. 'therapy'). Some of these productions involve a gradual build-up to the target form. This can be seen in 'thirty-five' where a single consonant sound is followed by the first syllable of 'thirty' (a consonant and vowel) and then finally the full target form.

WEBSITE: Developmental stuttering

Watch the video clips of children and adults who stutter on the website. Using these clips, try to identify the various speech features of stuttering described above. These clips have been provided courtesy of the Stuttering Foundation (www.StutteringHelp. org), the National Stammering Association and Alex Murphy (Director of *Let Me Finish*).

As well as speech features, stuttering is also characterised by verbal and non-verbal behaviours known as 'secondary' or 'accessory' features. In a review of these behaviours in the literature, Wingate (2002) identifies 29 accessory features, the most prominent of which are eye blinking and closing, lip tremor, grimace and the use of certain words and phrases. Notwithstanding widespread discussion of these features in the stuttering literature, Wingate cautions that these behaviours are neither common nor well understood. He remarks: 'In some cases of stuttering one may also observe, in addition to the cardinal features [iterations and perseverations], certain subsidiary acts, aptly designated accessory features, that vary in respect to their character, frequency of occurrence, and their essential nature. Although these actions may appear in the vicinity of stutters, their relationship to stutters is, in general, unclear' (Wingate, 2002: 59). For Vanryckeghem et al. (2004), secondary behaviours are a means of coping with the anticipation and/or presence of speech disruption. These investigators examined the behaviours employed secondary to the anticipation or occurrence of speech disruption by 42 adults who stutter. The top 10 behaviours used by these adults included substitution of one word for another, pausing, avoidance of eye contact, silent rehearsal and looking away. The total number of these behaviours used by adults who stutter ranged from a low of 6 to a high of 59 different behaviours. The mean number of behaviours was 20.79. Vanryckeghem et al. (2004: 246) concluded that '[t]hough these responses are secondary to stuttering, rather than a constituent element of it, the frequency with which they occur, their often aberrant and attention getting nature and the fact that they can interfere with communication all point to the need for a better understanding of their nature and use'.

WEBSITE: Accessory features

View the video file *Help Me to Speak – Stammering* (broadcast on Channel 4 in the UK on 3 April 2006). This programme charts the experiences of three children who stutter. They are 11, 16 and 18 years of age. Observe these speakers and record the different types of accessory features that accompany their stuttering. This programme is a RDF Television Production for Channel 4. The permission of both RDF Television and Channel 4 to use this material is gratefully acknowledged.

KEY POINTS: Developmental stuttering

- Developmental stuttering occurs when there is a failure to acquire normal speech fluency in the developmental period; affects children and adults
- General population prevalence of 1 per cent although higher prevalences occur in special populations (e.g. children with learning disabilities); more common in males than females
- Aetiology unknown although genetic, neurological and psychological factors feature in causal explanations of disorder
- Main speech characteristics (Wingate's so-called 'cardinal features') are iterations or repetitions and perseverations
- Accessory or secondary features are also reported; these verbal and non-verbal behaviours may not be as common as first thought and their role in stuttering is somewhat uncertain

8.3 Acquired stuttering

Acquired stuttering is usually the result of a stroke (cerebrovascular accident – CVA) or head injury. Other neurological diseases, such as progressive supranuclear palsy (a form of parkinsonism), are less commonly associated with the disorder (Sakai et al., 2002). Unlike the aetiology of developmental stuttering, acquired stuttering is clearly neurological in nature (hence, the use of the term 'neurogenic stuttering'). Because studies of acquired stuttering usually involve the examination of individual cases, it is not possible to establish the incidence and prevalence of this particular fluency disorder. Clinical studies reveal that several neuroanatomical areas may play a role in acquired stuttering. Doi et al. (2003) examined a 60-year-old man who acquired stuttering after a brainstem infarction (stroke). These investigators claimed that the midbrain and upper pons could be lesion sites responsible for acquired stuttering. Balasubramanian et al. (2003) examined a 57-year-old male who developed neurogenic stuttering following an ischaemic lesion to the orbital surface of the right frontal lobe and pons. Van Borsel et al. (2003) described the case of a 38-year-old male who presented with neurogenic stuttering subsequent to an ischaemic lesion of the left thalamus. Helm-Estabrooks and Hotz (1998) reported the case of a 30-year-old woman who developed stuttering following a head injury sustained in a road traffic accident. One week after this accident, MRI revealed a right frontal/parietal lesion. While these studies very clearly point to the role of brain lesions in the aetiology of acquired stuttering, they fail to locate this fluency disorder in damage to a specific neuroanatomical site. Further research will determine whether this involvement of many sites simply reflects the role of several neuroanatomical areas in the control of speech fluency.

The speech and accessory features of acquired stuttering, both in general and in relation to specific aetiological groups, are increasingly being investigated. Tani and Sakai (2010) reported the case of a 45-year-old male patient who developed neurogenic stuttering after cerebellar infarction. Analysis of this patient's speech samples revealed very frequent syllable repetition and part-word repetition. Almost all this patient's stuttering occurred on word initial sounds, with stuttering on word medial and final sounds much less frequent. Observed secondary behaviours included eye closing and grimacing. Theys et al. (2008) examined the speech features and secondary behaviours of 58 Dutch-speaking patients with neurogenic stuttering following various neurological injuries. The most common aetiological group was stroke (29 patients) followed by traumatic brain injury (TBI) (11 patients) and neurodegenerative diseases (9 patients). The type and localisation of dysfluencies were similar across these aetiological groups. Sound and syllable repetitions were more common in each of these groups than repetitions of words or parts of sentences. Sound prolongations were less common in each group than sound repetitions. In all groups, dysfluencies were found most often on initial sounds followed by medial and then final sounds. In the TBI and neurodegenerative diseases groups, dysfluencies occurred equally on function and content words. Only in the stroke group were there slightly more dysfluencies on content words than function words. Secondary behaviours occurred in 55 per cent, 64 per cent and 44 per cent of patients with stroke, TBI and neurodegenerative disease, respectively. The three secondary behaviours that were observed across all groups were facial grimaces, limb movements and avoidance behaviours.

Mower and Younts (2001) describe a case of neurogenic stuttering in the presence of a neurodegenerative disease, namely, multiple sclerosis (MS). The patient, a 36-year-old man known as S.S., was hospitalised for the treatment of MS. In August 1994, S.S. displayed sudden onset of excessive word repetitions. A MRI scan performed in September 1994 was consistent with his MS condition (i.e. plaques were seen in the white matter involving the medulla, cerebellum, basal ganglion, and periventricular white matter). A small, irregular corpus callosum was also noted. Some of S.S.'s dysfluent speech is presented below in orthographic transcription and in Table 8.2 as phonetic transcription:

Well, we-we-we-we-we in-in-in port mo-most of time and-and when-when-when I got-got married, got-got-got-got-got-got an apar-par-partment.

The overriding feature of S.S.'s dysfluent speech is whole-word and part-word repetitions. Sound prolongations or perseverations, which are commonplace in developmental stuttering, were not evident in S.S.'s spoken output. Whole-word repetition occurs only on words of one syllable, a pattern that is similar to the whole-word repetitions observed in relation to developmental stuttering. Part-word repetitions involve consonant–vowel (CV) or consonant–consonant–vowel (CCV) syllables (e.g. [mə] and [krei]). The vowel which is repeated in these syllables is the vowel of the target word. It will be recalled that in developmental stuttering, a schwa vowel was most likely to be repeated and then replaced by the vowel of the target word. In only one instance in the data in Table 8.2 did S.S. repeat and then replace the schwa vowel (see 'with'). In developmental stuttering, part-word repetition led into the fluent production of multisyllabic target words in their entirety (e.g. see how 'January' and

Table 8.2 Repetitions in the speech of an adult with multiple sclerosis and neurogenic stuttering

side	[sai.said]
load	[lo.lo.lod]
crates	[krei.krei.krei.kreits]
with	[wə.wə.wiθ]
most	[mo.most.most]
Monday	[mə.mə.mən.dei]
navy	[nei.nei.nei.vi]
supplies	[sə.sə.sə.plaiz]

Based on: Mower and Younts (2001).

'therapy' were produced by the individuals with developmental stuttering in section 8.2). This does not occur in words of more than one syllable which are produced by S.S. These words are uttered as discrete syllables rather than a fluent whole (e.g. see how S.S. produces 'supplies', 'navy' and 'Monday'). In S.S.'s case, part-word repetitions only lead to the fluent production of the whole target word when that word is a monosyllable. The word 'apartment' is one of several unusual repetition sequences produced by S.S. In these repetitions, S.S. appeared to inch forward in the word by attempting each syllable sequence. Other examples were 'hopefully' (hope-hopeful-fully), 'supervisors' (su-su-su-supervi-vi-visors), 'overboard' (overbo-bo-board), 'Mediterranean' (Me-me-medit-ter-ter-ter-anean) and 'appointment' (a-puh-puh-pointment). A feature of these repetitions is that none of the syllable sequences ever amounted to the full word. The one exception was the word 'parachute' which was uttered as 'par-par-parachute-chute'.

In analysing S.S.'s dysfluencies, comparisons were made with the dysfluencies of developmental stuttering. A question of some interest to investigators is whether the speech features of acquired stuttering are similar to those of developmental stuttering. Helm-Estabrooks (1999: 260) states six features which, she claims, help to distinguish individuals with neurogenic stuttering from developmental stuttering in adults: (1) dysfluencies occur on grammatical words nearly as frequently as on substantive words; (2) the speaker may be annoyed but does not appear anxious; (3) repetitions, prolongations, and blocks do not occur only on initial syllables of words and utterances; (4) secondary symptoms such as facial grimacing, eye blinking, or fist clenching are not associated with moments of dysfluency; (5) there is no adaptation effect whereby there are fewer and fewer dysfluencies on repeated readings of a passage; (6) stuttering occurs relatively consistently across various types of speech tasks. In a review of 25 articles describing cases of individuals with neurogenic stuttering, Ringo and Dietrich (1995) found broad support for these features. Dysfluencies were observed on grammatical words nearly as frequently as on substantive words in 90 per cent of cases of individuals with neurogenic stuttering. Some 80 per cent of individuals with neurogenic stuttering were reported to be annoyed but not anxious about their stuttering. A majority of individuals with neurogenic stuttering (75 per cent) displayed dysfluencies that were not restricted to initial syllables. Secondary symptoms were not observed in 70 per cent of individuals with neurogenic stuttering. Some 60 per cent of individuals with neurogenic stuttering in this review did not exhibit the adaptation effect. The majority of individuals with neurogenic stuttering also displayed dysfluency across speech tasks. In this way, singing and chorus speaking were dysfluent in 8 of 13 and 3 of 8 individuals with neurogenic stuttering, respectively.

Other investigations have tended to indicate that speech features cannot be reliably used to distinguish developmental and acquired (neurogenic) forms of stuttering. A study by Van Borsel and Taillieu (2001) suggests that there is little in the way of speech features to distinguish these two forms of stuttering. These investigators asked a panel of professionals to classify speech samples from four individuals with developmental stuttering and four individuals with neurogenic stuttering which were presented to them at random. Results showed that 24 per cent of the observers' judgements placed patients in the wrong diagnostic group. Also, observers indicated that they were 'not sure' of the classification of a patient in 42 per cent of their judgements. Furthermore, in 18 per cent of the judgements where observers indicated that they were 'rather sure' or 'very sure' of a patient's classification, the patient was erroneously classified. These results, Van Borsel and Taillieu (2001: 392) contend, 'indicate that the demarcation between neurogenic stuttering and developmental stuttering, as far as symptomatology is concerned, is not always very clear'.

KEY POINTS: Acquired stuttering

- The onset of speech dysfluency in adulthood in individuals with previously normal fluency
- Most often related to neurological disease or injury (hence, use of term 'neurogenic stuttering' to describe this type of dysfluency)
- Mainly caused by strokes (CVAs), but also seen in patients with traumatic brain injury and neurodegenerative diseases
- As in developmental stuttering, speakers with acquired stuttering produce iterations or repetitions and perseverations and display secondary features
- There is considerable debate amongst researchers whether the speech and accessory features of acquired stuttering are similar to those found in developmental stuttering

---

8.4 Cluttering

Daly and Burnett (1996: 239) define cluttering as 'a disorder of speech and language processing, resulting in rapid, dysrhythmic, sporadic, unorganized, and frequently unintelligible speech. Accelerated speech is not always present, but an impairment in formulating language almost always is'. This definition captures what Ward (2006: 141) has described as the 'two basic strands to the disorder', that cluttering has both 'a language component and a motor one'. Although cluttering is increasingly the focus of clinical studies, as yet relatively little is known about the epidemiology and aetiology of this fluency disorder. From a survey of speech–language pathologists (SLPs) and educators, St. Louis and Hinzman (1986) obtained sex ratios of 75.1 per cent male versus 24.9 per cent female (for SLPs) and 75.4 per cent male versus 24.6 per cent female (for educators). Genetic and neurological factors have been implicated in the aetiology of cluttering. Many people who clutter have relatives who also have this fluency disorder. Myers and St. Louis (1996) reported the case of a 12-year-old boy with cluttering who had a family history of stuttering and cluttering. Cluttering has been reported to occur in several syndromes including Tourette's syndrome, Down syndrome and fragile X syndrome (Hanson et al., 1986; Van Borsel and Vandermeulen, 2008; Van Borsel and Vanryckeghem, 2000). Cluttering has also been linked to brain damage in adults. Lebrun (1996) described cluttering in two adult patients with idiopathic parkinsonism. Thacker and De Nil (1996) reported the case of a 61-year-old woman with cortical, subcortical, cerebellar and medulla lesions who acquired cluttering. Hashimoto et al. (1999)

described the case of a 57-year-old woman with dementia related to frontal pathology who developed cluttering-like speech.

The features of cluttering have been the focus of numerous clinical studies. In a survey of 29 people who clutter in 12 articles, St. Louis (1996) identified 53 symptoms that were used by the authors of these articles to characterise cluttering. The three most commonly reported symptoms were excessive dysfluencies, rate of speech too fast and rate of speech too irregular. Myers and St. Louis (1996) studied two youths who clutter. These subjects shared the traits of rate anomalies, dysfluencies, poor speech intelligibility and linguistic maze behaviours. Daly and Cantrell (2006) administered a 50-item questionnaire describing characteristics of cluttering to 60 fluency experts from around the world. These experts identified 33 items that they considered to be the most critical diagnostic signs of cluttering in children and adults. The item 'telescopes or condenses words' (omits/transposes sounds/syllables) was ranked by 93 per cent of the experts as the most important characteristic of cluttering. The item 'lack of effective self-monitoring skills' was ranked as the second most important characteristic of cluttering by 90 per cent of experts. A further six items were rated by 80 per cent or more of the experts as significant features of cluttering. These items included lack of pauses between words and sentences, lack of awareness of own communication errors or problems (but see Scaler Scott (2014) for discussion), imprecise articulation, irregular speech rate (speaks in spurts or bursts), the use of revisions, interjections and filler words and compulsive, verbose talker with circumlocutions common. The complete 33 items identified by the experts in this study are the basis of Daly's Predictive Cluttering Inventory.

People who clutter attest to these features of cluttering. Here are some comments about the characteristics of their fluency disorder. These extracts are taken from Scaler Scott and St. Louis (2011: 218–20):

Rate and syllable changes:
My cluttering characteristics (I do not like referring to it as symptoms, as cluttering to me is not a disease) are mostly speech related. If I do not pay attention I tend to eat my letters and speak very fast ... (HBK, adult)

Excessively fast rate of speech, especially when excited, caught off-guard, or unsure of how to explain something ... Condensing of syllables, e.g., 'therapy' might become 'terpy'. (AER, adult)

Dysfluency:
Irregular repetitions of syllables, partial words, and phrases. Repetitions are not consistent with particular sounds/words or circumstances, as you might expect from someone who stutters ... If I'm caught in the moment of a major dysfluency, I have a hard time getting it out right despite multiple attempts/ strategies. It makes me wonder if that's what it feels like to someone who stutters. It's quite frustrating! (AER, adult)

Disorganised thought and language:
[I have] disorganized thoughts. [My cluttering] improves with familiarity (hence I can hide it well professionally!) [I am/tend to be??] rambling [and]

talkative. [I have] difficulty maintaining a topic; ... [I find myself] jumping back and forth between topics over the course of the conversation. Close friends can follow my thinking on this, but people who don't know me well are left confounded at the whole bit. [I have] difficulty 'getting to the point'. (AER, adult)

Lack of awareness:
Poor awareness of dysfluency and rate of speech (lifelong), but this is better now. It's still not great, though ... (AER, adult)

Cluttering often coexists with stuttering in affected individuals. Less often, it exists in a pure form. Of the fluency clients seen by Daly (1986) since the mid-1970s, less than 5 per cent were pure clutterers, while a further 40 per cent were combined clutterers and stutterers. There is also evidence that clinicians frequently disagree in their diagnoses of these two fluency disorders. Van Zaalen-op't Hof et al. (2009a) found that two speech–language pathologists, who were specialised in fluency disorders, agreed upon the fluency diagnosis in only 27 of 54 (50 per cent) dysfluent speakers in their study. The co-existence of cluttering and stuttering in individual speakers, combined with the fact that these disorders are inconsistently diagnosed by therapists, have led some researchers to investigate criteria which may be used in a differential diagnosis of these disorders. An early study by Rieber et al. (1972) found that people who stutter have greater mean pause times and lower mean phonation times than people who clutter. These investigators concluded that automated analysis of on–off speech patterns provides some basis for the differential diagnosis of these fluency disorders. In a study of 15 clients with fluency disorders, Georgieva and Miliev (1996) observed the following characteristics exclusively or predominantly in people who clutter: multiple repetitions of words and phrases, misarticulations of /r/,/s/, /l/,/z/,/ʃ/,/d/, lexical errors, writing problems and poor handwriting, and reduced motor coordination. More recently, Van Zaalen-op't Hof et al. (2009b) examined speech motor control on word level productions in an effort to develop criteria for the differential diagnosis of cluttering and stuttering. Among the speech production criteria examined by these investigators, speech flow and sequencing were found to differentiate people who clutter (PWC) from people who stutter (PWS) (PWC produced significantly more flow and sequencing errors than PWS).

WEBSITE: Cluttering

Visit the website to listen to two speakers who clutter. One speaker exhibits pure cluttering and one displays combined stuttering/cluttering. The former speaker appears in a video file that is hosted on the website of the International Cluttering Association. The latter speaker produces stuttering blocks alongside the inappropriate pauses which are typical of cluttering.

KEY POINTS: Cluttering

- Fluency disorder characterised by rapid speaking rate and disorganised language; people who clutter lack awareness of their communication difficulties
- Prevalence of the disorder is unknown; some evidence that males are affected more than females
- Aetiology is also unknown but association with syndromes and acquired brain damage suggests the involvement of genetic and neurological factors
- Cluttering most often exists alongside stuttering; less often, it occurs in a pure form
- Researchers in fluency disorders are attempting to establish criteria which can be used in the differential diagnosis of cluttering and stuttering

---

8.5   Assessment and treatment

An assessment of stuttering involves more than an examination of the nature and distribution of speech dysfluencies in a client. Ward (2006) describes 'two basic strands' of stuttering that are normally examined during assessment: motor speech activity and the cognitive component of the disorder. The former strand, Ward argues, is assessed by means of speech rate data and fluency counts. The latter strand is assessed using attitudinal questionnaires. The most commonly used method of assessing stuttering severity is the stuttering frequency count. This measure is expressed as a percentage of stuttered syllables or words and is calculated by dividing the total number of stuttered syllables (words) in a speech sample by the total number of syllables (words) spoken. Alongside the stuttering frequency count, clinicians often report various measures of speech rate. Expressed as either the number of syllables or the number of words spoken per minute, these measures are calculated by dividing the total number of all syllables spoken (speaking rate) or the total number of non-stuttered syllables spoken (articulatory rate) by the total length of time taken (in seconds), which is then multiplied by 60. Calculations of this type are only useful to the extent that they can be compared with normative data (see Andrews and Ingham (1971), for normative data on speaking rate). Fluency researchers have used stuttering frequency counts to develop criteria that are indicative of stuttering. Ambrose and Yairi (1999) state that a child who produces three or more stuttering-like dysfluencies per 100 syllables should be suspected of exhibiting stuttering. Conture (1997) claims that if a child exhibits three or more within-word (stuttered) speech dysfluencies per 100 words of conversational speech, then he or she is at risk for continuing to stutter.

Assessments which examine the client's attitude to stuttering began to emerge in the late 1960s. These so-called 'cognitive assessments' go beyond the overt stuttering behaviours that are assessed by means of fluency and rate measures to consider cognitive and affective aspects of the disorder. One of the first cognitive assessments, which is still in use today, is the Perceptions of Stuttering Inventory (PSI) (Woolf, 1967). The PSI contains a list of 60 questions, 20 of which address issues of struggle, avoidance and expectancy in stuttering. A recent cognitive assessment that is based on the World Health Organization's International Classification of Functioning, Disability and Health is the Overall Assessment of the Speaker's Experience of Stuttering (OASES) (Yaruss and Quesal, 2004). This assessment examines all aspects of the stuttering disorder under four headings: (1) general perspectives about stuttering, (2) affective, behavioural and cognitive reactions to stuttering, (3) functional communication difficulties, and (4) impact of stuttering on the speaker's quality of life. The OASES questionnaire probes these areas by having respondents circle a number on a five-point scale. While most cognitive assessments are devised for use with adolescents and adults, a growing number are being used with child clients. Vanryckeghem et al. (2005) used a self-report measure called the KiddyCAT to compare the speech-associated attitude of 45 children aged between 3 and 6 years who stutter with that of 63 non-stuttering children. These investigators found that the children who stutter had a significantly more negative attitude towards their speech than did their non-stuttering peers. Vanryckeghem et al. (2005: 307) state that this finding 'suggests the need to measure, by standardized means, the speech-associated attitude of incipient stutterers'. For further discussion of instruments that are used to measure cognitive and affective aspects of stuttering, see Susca (2006).

Speech fluency measures are also included in the assessment of cluttering. However, a range of other areas must also be comprehensively evaluated in the client who is believed to be a clutterer. St. Louis and Myers (1995) argue that an evaluation protocol for cluttering should contain measures of fluency, rate (average and peak values), articulation, language, psychoeducational and academic skills (e.g. reading and spelling), hearing, auditory and visual perception, fine motor coordination (including handwriting) and cognitive/intellectual function. Daly and Burnett (1996: 240) emphasise seven behaviours that should alert clinicians to the need for further evaluation of a client for cluttering: (1) low awareness level or denial of any difficulty speaking, (2) rapid or fluctuating speech rate, (3) disorganised language, (4) initially loud voice trailing off to a murmur, (5) misarticulations, (6) frequent word or phrase repetitions, (7) improved speaking skills when attention to speech and language production is heightened. Cluttering checklists have proven to be a popular method of assessment amongst clinicians. Ward (2006) uses a checklist of cluttering behaviour that is based on several sources and his own clinical experience. The checklist contains 43 criteria that are arranged according to seven categories – speech rate and speech fluency; articulation; language and linguistic fluency; disorganised thinking; writing; attention; and other non-verbal attributes. Daly's Predictive Cluttering Inventory (PCI) examines 33 cluttering behaviours under the headings of pragmatics, speech–motor features, language–cognition features and motor coordination–writing problems. The comprehensive coverage made possible through checklists may simultaneously reduce their relevance to specific clinical populations. There is some evidence, for example, that the PCI is not suitable for the assessment of cluttering in clients with Down syndrome (Van Borsel and Vandermeulen, 2008).

Numerous treatment programmes are now in use with preschool, school-age and adult clients who stutter. Treatment approaches variously aim to modify the client's speaking environment (in the case of the preschool and school-age child), address attitudes related to speaking and stuttering (cognitive approach), train clients in the use of techniques designed to enhance fluency (fluency shaping approach) or encourage clients to produce less effortful stuttering (stuttering modification approach). The fluency shaping approach makes use of techniques that are designed to control respiration, phonation and articulation. These techniques are implemented initially on stretched syllables which are spoken at a very slow speech rate. Ward (2006) outlines the main features of these so-called 'slow speech' or 'prolonged speech' programmes as applied to stuttering adults: (1) speech segments are stretched by extending vowels and, to varying extents, consonants; (2) a reduction in speech rate, which used to be achieved through delayed auditory feedback, is now mostly modelled by the clinician as a prolonged speech pattern; (3) prolonged speech programmes are administered through intensive group therapy; (4) a highly-structured rate hierarchy is worked through by clients. A speech rate of 60 syllables per minute, or slower, is used initially. Through successive rate increments clients end up with a speaking rate that is normal or near normal; (5) clients are taught a range of fluency skills which are then used alongside the modifications in speech rate. These skills include soft onset of vocal fold vibration, soft articulatory contact, continuous voicing and continuous airflow; (6) clients must be able to use fluency skills within a stipulated range for a certain period of speaking time at each rate level before being allowed to progress to the next rate; (7) the clinician's role is to monitor speech criteria and provide feedback to clients throughout the programme.

Manning (1999: 171) states that the goal of stuttering modification techniques 'is to change the form of a person's stuttering to an open, flowing, and easy, but not necessarily normally fluent form of speaking'. Initially, there can be an increase in stuttering frequency on this approach. This is because clients are encouraged to confront, rather than avoid, those situations which are likely to cause them to stutter. Clients are encouraged to seek out and modify their stuttering behaviour and to become desensitised to their own fluency breaks. Easier and smoother forms of stuttering are achieved through techniques such as cancellations and pull-outs, both devised by Van Riper (1973). Cancellations (or post-block modifications) involve repeating a stuttered word using controlling strategies and then resuming speech. Clients perform this technique incorrectly if they say the stuttered word again, but they do so fluently. Instead, they should repeat the stuttered word using a form of smooth or easy stuttering. Pull-outs (or within-block modifications) involve a smooth withdrawal from an ongoing stuttering moment. Stuttering modification proceeds first with post-block modification, through within-block modification to finally pre-block modification. Of course, pre-block modification is preferred. However, if clients do not achieve this, they may still modify stuttering by using the pull-out technique. If clients fail to modify stuttering using pull-outs, the cancellation technique represents their final attempt to take charge of the stuttering moment.

As well as fluency shaping and stuttering modification approaches, cognitive approaches may be used to treat stuttering. An approach that is strongly cognitive in orientation is Sheehan's approach–avoidance conflict therapy. Sheehan's model is used extensively to treat a subgroup of people who stutter for whom covert or interiorised stuttering is a significant problem. In essence, Sheehan argues that the ability of some people who stutter to suppress their outward stuttering behaviour through the use of avoidance techniques serves only to maintain stuttering: 'With some individual variability, stutterers appear to have the capacity to suppress the outward appearance of their stuttering, thus producing an apparent reduction in frequency. We assume that response suppression is a central continuing cause in maintaining stuttering behavior. This suppression of outward stuttering may temporarily "make stutterers seem better"; actually, it moves them into a retreat position that makes ultimate recovery enormously more difficult' (Sheehan and Sheehan, 1984: 147). Counselling approaches are increasingly being used to treat adults who stutter, particularly in the UK. One such approach is George Kelly's (1955) personal construct psychology, which has been adapted for use in stuttering treatment by Fay Fransella (1972). In this approach, people who stutter are believed to be operating with personal constructs of themselves which serve to reinforce stuttering behaviour. In therapy, clients and therapists jointly work on examining clients' perceptions of themselves. By uncovering clients' personal constructs, and instituting new constructs, specifically those in which the individual is a fluent speaker, progress can be made in therapy.

SUGGESTIONS FOR FURTHER READING

Howell, P. (2011) *Recovery from Stuttering* (Hove, East Sussex: Psychology Press).

Ward, D. (2006) *Stuttering and Cluttering: Frameworks for Understanding and Treatment* (Hove, East Sussex: Psychology Press).

Ward, D. and Scaler Scott, K. (eds) (2011) *Cluttering: A Handbook of Research, Intervention and Education* (Hove, East Sussex: Psychology Press).

EXERCISES

Exercise 8.1 Wingate (2002: 41) uses 16 examples 'to illustrate a representative variety of fluency departures that may be evident at the locus of a stutter event'. The examples take the form of International Phonetic Alphabet (IPA) transcriptions of spoken utterances of 'He said he would take it back'. Some of the examples are typical of normal non-fluency; other examples are characteristic of stuttering. For each example (a) describe the 'fluency departure' that has occurred, and (b) indicate whether this departure is a normal non-fluency or a form of stuttering:

(1) hi sɛd wi kæn t t t tek ɪt bæk
(2) hi sɛd wi kæn ə ə ə tek ɪt bæk
(3) hi sɛd wi kæn rilɪtek ɪt bæk

(4) hi sɛd wi kæn tə::::::ek ɪt bæk
(5) hi sɛd wi kæn wi kæn tə tek ɪt bæk
(6) hi sɛd wi kæn kæn ətek ɪt bæk
(7) hi sɛd wi kæn:: tek ɪt bæk
(8) hi sɛd wi kæn t::::::ek ɪt bæk
(9) hi sɛd wi kæn wi kæn t::ek ɪt bæk
(10) hi sɛd wi kæn tə tə tə tek ɪt bæk
(11) hi sɛd wi kæn ə tek ɪt bæk
(12) hi sɛd wi kæn ə ə ətek ɪt bæk
(13) hi sɛd wi kæn wi kæn tek ɪt bæk
(14) hi sɛd wi kæn kæn t:ek ɪt bæk
(15) hi sɛd wi kænə tek ɪt bæk
(16) hi sɛd wi kæn kæn tek ɪt bæk

Exercise 8.2 Horner and Massey (1983) describe the case of a 62-year-old man who developed a late onset progressive dysfluency following a right-hemisphere stroke. This client displayed extensive word and phrase repetitions and, to a lesser degree, sound and syllable repetitions. Repetitions occurred in all positions (initial, medial, final) of sentences. Secondary features such as facial grimacing were absent. Dysfluencies were more evident in spontaneous speech than oral reading and repetition. Recitation and singing were minimally dysfluent. An extract of conversation between this man (A) and an interlocutor (B) is shown below. Examine the exchange between these speakers. Then (a) characterise the dysfluencies exhibited by A, and (b) list three features that distinguish this man's stuttering behaviour from that seen in developmental stuttering. The extract begins with A being asked to recall a memorable experience:

A: Having having a stroke, h-having a stroke, haven't been able to walk, haven't been able to walk, I get get frustrated, b-b-b-been active a-a-all-all, all my life.

B: Do you remember your stay on the rehabilitation unit?

A: mhmm…stayed over there about two months, I came, to s-see-see you, about everyde-everyde-everyday, t-t-t-took physical therapy, and, speech therapy and, and that's about it, wu-w-w-wor-worked on, re-reading from, left to right, go all the way to the left, I-I had problems go-go-going to my left.

B: Do you repeat yourself?

A: What, repeatin' repeatin' myself? I-I-I just, can't seem to get the words out sometimes. They can't understand me, they can't understand me, I have to repe-repeat it, repeat it for 'em.

Exercise 8.3 Reflecting the fact that cluttering has both motoric and linguistic components, Ward (2006: 144) distinguishes between motoric and linguistic cluttering. Examples of the speech produced in each type of cluttering are shown below. The speaker in (A) is an 18-year-old male. His verbal output is characterised by fast rushes of speech (the symbol (:) represents short pauses). The speaker in (B) is a 25-year-old male. His speech rate is mostly within normal limits. Using these examples, describe two features of motoric cluttering and linguistic cluttering which are not related to speech rate.

(A) Motoric cluttering

Normally I c c come by car, but t t t today I (:) took the bus. My car (:) had to go for a (:) service.

(B) Linguistic cluttering

My, favourite – well, the best, best place for my, for a holiday is um, um, is, er, Australia. The heat, well, the er, the er, climate really is…. It's it's really great.

ANSWERS TO EXERCISES

Exercise 8.1

Examples (7), (11), (13) and (15) are most typical of normal non-fluencies. The other examples are characteristic of stuttering.

 (1) phoneme repetition
 (2) schwa repetition (adjustment aborted)
 (3) word insertion ('pet starter')
 (4) schwa prolongation
 (5) phrase repetition + element insertion (phrase repetition failed to avert stutter)
 (6) word repetition + schwa ('starter')
 (7) final phoneme prolongation
 (8) phoneme prolongation
 (9) phrase repetition + prolongation (phrase repetition failed to avert stutter)
(10) phoneme + schwa repetition
(11) schwa insertion
(12) schwa repetition (final schwa is 'starter')
(13) phrase repetition
(14) word repetition + prolongation ('delay')
(15) schwa addition
(16) word repetition (normal non-fluency)

Exercise 8.2

(a) Characteristics of dysfluencies:
   (i) sound repetitions (e.g. b-b-b-been)
  (ii) syllable repetitions (e.g. go-go-going)
 (iii) word repetitions involving monosyllabic words (e.g. I-I-I just) and multisyllabic words (e.g. repeatin' repeatin' myself)
 (iv) phrase repetitions (e.g. haven't been able to walk, haven't been able to walk)
  (v) combined repetitions involving single sounds and words (e.g. a-a-all-all, all my life) and single sounds and syllables (e.g. wu-w-w-wor-worked on)
 (vi) vowels involved in repetitions can be the same as the target vowel (e.g. wor-worked) or different from the target vowel (e.g. everyde-everyde-everyday)

(b) Features distinguishing A's stuttering behaviour from developmental stuttering:
   (i) there are no sound perseverations or prolongations
  (ii) word and phrase repetitions are more common than sound and syllable repetitions
 (iii) there are no secondary features such as facial grimacing

Exercise 8.3

(A) Motoric cluttering: (i) fast phoneme repetitions (e.g. t t t today); (ii) short pauses at inappropriate junctures; these pauses split subjects from their verbs (e.g. I (:) took the bus) and articles from their nouns (e.g. a (:) service) and are unlike the pauses taken by speakers during normal speech

(B) Linguistic cluttering: language is generally disorganised and confused as evidenced by (i) a preponderance of fillers (e.g. well, er, um), and (ii) excessive phrase and sentence revision (e.g. the heat, well, the er, the er, climate really...).

Glossary

accessory feature: also known as 'secondary behaviours'; describes an extensive range of verbal and non-verbal behaviours which occur alongside stuttering (e.g. eye blinking).

agnosia: a disorder of perception or recognition which can affect visual stimuli (visual agnosia), auditory stimuli (auditory agnosia), etc.; an auditory agnosia is one of the first presenting signs of Landau–Kleffner syndrome.

agrammatism: a feature of non-fluent aphasia (hence, term 'agrammatic' aphasia) in which the speaker retains content words but omits function words and inflectional morphemes from his or her speech; verbal output has the appearance of a telegram, e.g. 'Man … walk … dog' for *The man is walking the dog.*

Alzheimer's disease: a neurodegenerative disease that is the most frequent cause of dementia; amyloid plaques and neurofibrillary tangles develop in the brains of AD sufferers.

anomia: a word-finding difficulty in which speakers are unable to utter a target word; commonly seen in patients with aphasia and semantic dementia.

aphasia (dysphasia): a language disorder that is typically found in adults and which can be broadly classified as fluent and non-fluent types; the expression and/or reception of spoken, written and signed language is variously compromised in speakers with aphasia.

apraxia (dyspraxia): a motor disorder which can affect speech production (verbal dyspraxia), the movement of limbs (limb dyspraxia), the movement of oral structures (oral dyspraxia), etc.; the dominant terms to describe the speech disorder in children and adults are childhood apraxia of speech and apraxia of speech, respectively.

attention deficit hyperactivity disorder: a disorder that is diagnosed on the basis of symptoms of inattention and hyperactivity-impulsivity; there are three main subtypes of ADHD: a combined type; a predominantly inattentive type; a predominantly hyperactive-impulsive type.

autism spectrum disorder: a neurodevelopmental disorder in which there are impairments of social communication and interaction as well as restricted, repetitive patterns of behaviour, interests or activities. The disorder is diagnosed on the basis of criteria contained in the fifth edition of the *Diagnostic and Statistical Manual of Mental Disorders* (American Psychiatric Association, 2013).

cerebral palsy: a neurodevelopmental disorder that results in impairment of gross and fine motor skills, speech production included; cerebral palsy is caused by a range of factors in the pre-, peri- and post-natal periods which cause damage to the brain's motor centres.

cerebrovascular accident: the medical term for a stroke; CVAs may be caused by a blood clot (embolus) in one of the blood vessels in the brain or leading to the brain (embolic stroke) or by a haemorrhage (haemorrhagic stroke) in one of these vessels.

circumlocution: means literally to talk ('locution') around ('circum') a word; circumlocutions are used by speakers with aphasia when they cannot retrieve a target word and people who stutter who are trying to avoid words that will cause them to block.

cleft lip and palate: a disorder of embryological development that results in a cleft of the upper lip, alveolus, hard and soft palates; clefts may be unilateral or bilateral and can affect the primary palate only, the secondary palate only or both primary and secondary palates.

cluttering: a fluency disorder which is characterised by increased rate of speech, disorganised language and lack of awareness of communication difficulties on the part of the speaker; most often found alongside stuttering but sometimes occurs in a pure form.

conversion aphonia: loss of voice, most commonly in females, in response to a traumatic event or some other psychological stressor; vocal folds can still adduct sufficiently to perform vegetative functions (e.g. coughing) but not for the purpose of voicing.

dementia: a deterioration in higher cortical functions (e.g. language, memory) that can be caused by a range of diseases (e.g. vascular disease, Alzheimer's disease), infections (e.g. HIV infection) and lifestyle (e.g. alcohol-related dementia).

diadochokinesis: rapid syllable repetitions, e.g. /pə, tə, kə/, can be used to examine alternating articulatory movements and are a test of oral diadochokinesis; DDK rates are a routine part of the assessment of many speech disorders, e.g. apraxia of speech.

Down syndrome: a chromosomal disorder that results from an extra chromosome 21; this additional chromosome may be found in all cells (trisomy 21), in some cells (mosaic) or attached to another chromosome (translocation); results in physical problems (e.g. heart defects) and cognitive difficulties (learning disability).

dysarthria: a speech disorder that is caused by damage to the central and peripheral nervous systems; can be developmental or acquired in nature and affects articulation, resonation, respiration, phonation and prosody.

dysfluency: any disruption in the flow of speech; most commonly used of the iterations and perseverations of stuttered speech.

dysgraphia: the name of a disorder of written language that is typically found in adults as part of an aphasia; the disorder is linguistic in nature rather than the result of motor difficulties which preclude the use of a pen to form letters.

dyslexia: a reading impairment which can be found in children (developmental dyslexia) and in adults (acquired dyslexia), the latter as part of an aphasia; there are different types of dyslexia (e.g. the individual with deep dyslexia can read words with concrete meanings more easily than words with abstract meanings).

dysphonia: another term for a voice disorder; dysphonias may be caused by structural and/or neurological problems and can manifest as a hoarse, breathy, strain-strangled, etc. voice.

echolalia: the repetition of another speaker's utterance either immediately (immediate echolalia) or after several conversational turns (delayed echolalia); found in children and adults with autism and in some individuals with aphasia.

electropalatography: an instrumental technique that provides a visual display of tongue–palate contacts; used in the assessment and treatment of a range of individuals including children with cleft palate, although not all subjects can tolerate the artificial palate that must be worn in this technique.

fragile X syndrome: the most common inherited form of learning disability; caused by the fragile X mental retardation 1 (FMR1) gene on the X chromosome and more commonly seen in males.

gender dysphoria: a condition in which a person experiences his or her phenotypic sex as incongruous with his or her sense of gender identity; can be treated through surgery (gender reassignment surgery), hormone treatment and voice therapy.

glossectomy: surgical removal of the tongue, either in whole (total glossectomy) or in part (partial glossectomy), due to the presence of tongue cancer (primarily squamous cell carcinoma).

hypernasality: excessive nasal resonance in speech which may be caused by velopharyngeal incompetence; a feature of cleft palate speech and dysarthric speech.

hyponasality: insufficient nasal resonance in speech which may be caused by enlarged adenoids and the presence of nasal polyps, amongst other things.

jargon: a feature of fluent aphasia; can consist of English words linked together to produce meaningless utterances or the extensive use of neologisms in verbal output.

Landau–Kleffner syndrome: also known as 'acquired epileptic aphasia' or 'aphasia with convulsive disorder'; a rare disorder in which a child's language skills regress, either suddenly or gradually, in the presence of seizures.

laryngectomy: surgical removal of the larynx, either in whole (total laryngectomy) or in part (partial laryngectomy), due to the presence of laryngeal cancer; the person who undergoes this procedure is called a laryngectomee.

learning disability: the preferred term in the UK to refer to intellectual disability; children and adults with learning disability have an intelligence quotient (IQ) of 70 or under; present in many syndromes (e.g. Down syndrome) and other disorders (e.g. cerebral palsy).

motor neurone disease: a progressive neurodegenerative disease in which there is a widespread and often rapid deterioration in upper and lower motor neurones; affects all aspects of speech production and, eventually, swallowing and feeding.

multiple sclerosis: a neurodegenerative disease in which the myelin sheath which envelopes the axons of neurones is destroyed (a process known as demyelination); can cause dysarthria and swallowing problems.

neologism: means literally new ('neo') word ('logism'); neologisms are found in aphasia and schizophrenia (e.g. a speaker with schizophrenia who utters 'geshinker').

oesophageal voice: a means of communication after laryngectomy in which the speaker swallows air into the oesophagus which is then vibrated in the oesophageal sphincter to produce voice.

otitis media: an infection of the middle ear that is commonly known as 'glue ear'; otitis media can cause conductive hearing loss and repeated episodes can compromise speech development in children.

Parkinson's disease: a neurodegenerative disease which is caused by the loss of cells that produce dopamine (a neurotransmitter substance) in the substantia nigra of the brain; dysarthria is commonly seen in PD.

phonological disorder: a delay or deviance in the acquisition of the sound system of a child's native language; speech can be severely unintelligible as the child engages in phonological processes such as stopping, fronting, cluster reduction, etc.

poverty of speech: also known as alogia; describes the substantially reduced verbal output that is a negative symptom of schizophrenia.

pragmatic language impairment: a successor to the term 'semantic-pragmatic disorder'; describes a subgroup of children with SLI in which there are marked difficulties with the pragmatics of language.

puberphonia: also known as 'mutational falsetto'; typically seen in adolescent males who continue to speak with a pre-pubescent voice beyond the point at which voice mutation occurs.

schizophrenia: a serious mental illness which is diagnosed on the basis of positive and negative symptoms; positive symptoms include thought disorder, delusions and hallucinations (mostly auditory); negative symptoms include affective flattening, poverty of speech, apathy, avolition and social withdrawal.

specific language impairment: a severe developmental language disorder in children; SLI has been described as a diagnosis by exclusion as language impairment occurs in the absence of hearing loss, craniofacial anomaly, intellectual disability (i.e. a range of factors known to cause language disorder).

stuttering: a fluency disorder which is characterised by word- and syllable-initial iterations (repetitions) and perseverations (prolongations); also known as 'stammering'.

traumatic brain injury: there are two forms of traumatic brain injury: in an open or penetrating head injury, the skull is fractured or otherwise breached by a missile; in a closed head injury, the brain is damaged while the skull remains intact.

velopharyngeal incompetence: the failure of the velopharyngeal port to close adequately during speech production; VPI can be caused by structural anomalies (e.g. a short velum or excessively capacious pharynx) or by neurological impairment (e.g. an immobile velum after a stroke).

vocal abuse and misuse: describes the many ways in which voice users can engage in phonatory behaviours (e.g. hyperadduction of vocal folds) and other practices (e.g. excessive occupational voice use) that put them at risk of developing a voice disorder.

vocal fold abduction: the opening of the vocal folds or cords.

vocal fold adduction: the closure of the vocal folds or cords.

Bibliography

Abitbol, J., Abitbol, P. and Abitbol, B. (1999) 'Sex hormones and the female voice', *Journal of Voice*, 13 (3): 424–46.

Abusamra, V., Côté, H., Joanette, Y. and Ferreres, A. (2009) 'Communication impairments in patients with right hemisphere damage', *Life Span and Disability*, 12 (1): 67–82.

Adams, S.G. and Dykstra, A. (2009) 'Hypokinetic dysarthria', in M.R. McNeil (ed.) *Clinical Management of Sensorimotor Speech Disorders* (New York: Thieme Medical Publishers, 2nd edn), pp. 166–86.

Aguilar-Mediavilla, E.M., Sanz-Torrent, M. and Serra-Raventos, M. (2002) 'A comparative study of the phonology of pre-school children with specific language impairment (SLI), language delay (LD) and normal acquisition', *Clinical Linguistics and Phonetics*, 16 (8): 573–96.

Akif Kiliç, M., Okur, E., Yildirim, I. and Güzelsoy, S. (2004) 'The prevalence of vocal fold nodules in school age children', *International Journal of Pediatric Otorhinolaryngology*, 68 (4): 409–12.

Albery, E. (1991) 'Consonant articulation in the different types of cleft lip and palate', unpublished M. Phil thesis. Leicester: Leicester Polytechnic.

Alcock, K.J., Passingham, R.E., Watkins, K.E. and Vargha-Khadem, F. (2000) 'Oral dyspraxia in inherited speech and language impairment and acquired dysphasia', *Brain and Language*, 75 (1): 17–33.

Altekruse, S.F., Kosary, C.L., Krapcho, M., Neyman, N., Aminou, R., Waldron, W., Ruhl, J., Howlader, N., Tatalovich, Z., Cho, H., Mariotto, A., Eisner, M.P., Lewis, D.R., Cronin, K., Chen, H.S., Feuer, E.J., Stinchcomb, D.G. and Edwards, B.K. (eds) (2010) *SEER Cancer Statistics Review, 1975–2007*, Bethesda, MD: National Cancer Institute.

Altman, K.W., Atkinson, C. and Lazarus, C. (2005) 'Current and emerging concepts in muscle tension dysphonia: A 30-month review', *Journal of Voice*, 19 (2): 261–7.

Altman, K.W., Haines, G.K., Vakkalanka, S.K., Keni, S.P., Kopp, P.A. and Radosevich, J.A. (2003) 'Identification of thyroid hormone receptors in the human larynx', *Laryngoscope*, 113 (11): 1931–4.

Ambrose, N.G. and Yairi, E. (1999) 'Normative disfluency data for early childhood stuttering', *Journal of Speech, Language, and Hearing Research*, 42 (4): 895–909.

American Cleft Palate-Craniofacial Association (2000) Parameters for Evaluation and Treatment of Patients with Cleft Lip/Palate or Other Craniofacial Anomalies (Chapel Hill, NC: American Cleft Palate-Craniofacial Association).

American Psychiatric Association (2013) *Diagnostic and Statistical Manual of Mental Disorders*, 5th edition (Washington: American Psychiatric Association).

American Psychiatric Association (2000) *Diagnostic and Statistical Manual of Mental Disorders (DSM-IV-TR)* (Washington: American Psychiatric Association).

Andersson, K. and Schalén, L. (1998) 'Etiology and treatment of psychogenic voice disorder: Results of a follow-up study of thirty patients', *Journal of Voice*, 12 (1): 96–106.

Andratschke, M., Betz, C. and Leunig, A. (2008) 'Laryngeal papillomatosis: Etiology, diagnostics and therapy', *HNO*, 56 (12): 1190–6.

Andrews, G. and Ingham, R.J. (1971) 'Stuttering: Considerations in the evaluation of treatment', *British Journal of Disorders of Communication*, 6 (2): 129–38.

Angelillo, N., Di Costanzo, B., Angelillo, M., Costa, G., Barillari, M.R. and Barillari, U. (2008) 'Epidemiological study on vocal disorders in paediatric age', *Journal of Preventive Medicine and Hygiene*, 49 (1): 1–5.

Angelillo, N., Di Costanzo, B. and Barillari, U. (2010) 'Speech-language evaluation and rehabilitation treatment in Floating-Harbor syndrome: A case study', *Journal of Communication Disorders*, 43 (3): 252–60.

Annaz, D., Van Herwegen, J., Thomas, M., Fishman, R., Karmiloff-Smith, A. and Rundblad, G. (2009) 'Comprehension of metaphor and metonymy in children with Willliams syndrome', *International Journal of Language and Communication Disorders*, 44 (6): 962–78.

Ardila, A., Bateman, J.R., Nino, C.R., Pulido, E., Rivera, D.B. and Vanegas, C.J. (1994) 'An epidemiologic study of stuttering', *Journal of Communication Disorders*, 27 (1): 37–48.

Aronson, A.E. and Bless, D.M. (2009) *Clinical Voice Disorders* (New York: Thieme Medical Publishers).

Axelrad, M.E., Nicholson, L., Stabley, D.L., Sol-Church, K. and Gripp, K.W. (2007) 'Longitudinal assessment of cognitive characteristics in Costello syndrome', *American Journal of Medical Genetics*, 143A (24): 3185–93.

Aziz, A.A., Shohdi, S., Osman, D.M. and Habib, E.I. (2010) 'Childhood apraxia of speech and multiple phonological disorders in Cairo-Egyptian Arabic speaking children: Language, speech, and oro-motor differences', *International Journal of Pediatric Otorhinolaryngology*, 74 (6): 578–85.

Baker, J. (2003) 'Psychogenic voice disorders and traumatic stress experience: A discussion paper with two case reports', *Journal of Voice*, 17 (3): 308–18.

Baker, J. (1999) 'A report on alterations to the speaking and singing voices of four women following hormonal therapy with virilizing agents', *Journal of Voice*, 13 (4): 496–507.

Baker, J. (1998) 'Psychogenic dysphonia: Peeling back the layers', *Journal of Voice*, 12 (4): 527–35.

Baker, L. and Cantwell, D.P. (1982) 'Psychiatric disorder in children with different types of communication disorders', *Journal of Communication Disorders*, 15 (2): 113–26.

Bakker, A., van Kesteren, P.J., Gooren, L.J. and Bezemer, P.D. (1993) 'The prevalence of transsexualism in The Netherlands', *Acta Psychiatrica Scandinavica*, 87 (4): 237–8.

Balasubramanian, V. and Max, L. (2004) 'Crossed apraxia of speech: A case report', *Brain and Cognition*, 55 (2): 240–6.

Balasubramanian, V., Max, L., Van Borsel, J., Rayca, K.O. and Richardson, D. (2003) 'Acquired stuttering following right frontal and bilateral pontine lesion: A case study', *Brain and Cognition*, 53 (2): 185–9.

Barreto, V.M., D'Avila, J.S., Sales, N.J., Gonçalves, M.I., Seabra, J.D., Salvatori, R. and Aguiar-Oliveira, M.H. (2009) 'Laryngeal and vocal evaluation in untreated growth hormone deficient adults', *Otolaryngology-Head and Neck Surgery*, 140 (1): 37–42.

Barry, W.J. and Timmermann, G. (1985) 'Mispronunciations and compensatory movements of tongue-operated patients', *British Journal of Disorders of Communication*, 20 (1): 81–90.

Bartolucci, G. and Fine, J. (1987) 'The frequency of cohesion weakness in psychiatric syndromes', *Applied Psycholinguistics*, 8 (1): 67–74.

Bayles, K.A., Tomoeda, C.K. and Trosset, M.W. (1992) 'Relation of linguistic communication abilities of Alzheimer's patients to stage of disease', *Brain and Language*, 42 (4): 454–72.

Belafsky, P.C., Rees, C.J., Rodriguez, K., Pryor, J.S. and Katz, P.O. (2008) 'Esophagopharyngeal reflux', *Otolaryngology-Head and Neck Surgery*, 138 (1): 57–61.

Bellugi, U., Reilly, J., Krieter, J., Doyle, T. and Jones, W. (2003) 'Language and non-linguistic cognition in children with Williams syndrome: A complex interaction', *Enfance*, 55: 237–49.

Bennett, K.J., Brown, K.S., Boyle, M., Racine, Y. and Offord, D. (2003) 'Does low reading achievement at school entry cause conduct problems?', *Social Science & Medicine*, 56 (12): 2443–8.

Biddle, K.R., McCabe, A. and Bliss, L.S. (1996) 'Narrative skills following traumatic brain injury in children and adults', *Journal of Communication Disorders*, 29 (6): 447–69.

Biederman, J., Wilens, T.E., Spencer, T.J. and Adler, L.A. (2007) 'Diagnosis and treatment of adults with attention-deficit/hyperactivity disorder', *CNS Spectrums*, 12 (4), Supplement 6: 1–15.

Bihari, A., Meszaros, K., Remenyi, A. and Lichtenberger, G. (2006) 'Voice quality improvement after management of unilateral vocal cord paralysis with different techniques', *European Archives of Oto-Rhino-Laryngology*, 263 (12): 1115–20.

Bishop, D.V.M. (2000) 'What's so special about Asperger syndrome? The need for further exploration of the borderlands of autism', in A. Klin, F.R. Volkmar and S.S. Sparrow (eds) *Asperger Syndrome* (New York: The Guilford Press), pp. 254–77.

Bishop, D.V.M. (1998) 'Development of the Children's Communication Checklist (CCC): A method for assessing qualitative aspects of communicative impairment in children', *Journal of Child Psychology and Psychiatry*, 39 (6): 879–91.

Bishop, D.V.M., Chan, J., Adams, C., Hartley, J. and Weir, F. (2000) 'Conversational responsiveness in specific language impairment: Evidence of disproportionate pragmatic difficulties in a subset of children', *Development and Psychopathology*, 12 (2): 177–99.

Blitzer, A. (2010) 'Spasmodic dysphonia and botulin toxin: Experience from the largest treatment series', *European Journal of Neurology*, 17 (S1): 28–30.

Blumgart, E., Tran, Y. and Craig, A. (2010) 'Social anxiety disorder in adults who stutter', *Depression and Anxiety*, 27 (7): 687–92.

Bonita, R., Solomon, N. and Broad, J.B. (1997) 'Prevalence of stroke and stroke-related disability: Estimates from the Auckland Stroke Studies', *Stroke*, 28 (10): 1898–902.

Bressman, T., Jacobs, H., Quintero, J. and Irish, J.C. (2009) 'Speech outcomes for partial glossectomy surgery: Measures of speech articulation and listener perception', *Canadian Journal of Speech-Language Pathology and Audiology*, 33 (4): 204–10.

Brew, B.J. (2007) 'AIDS dementia complex', in P. Portegies and J.R. Berger (eds) *Handbook of Clinical Neurology: HIV/AIDS and the Nervous System* (Amsterdam: Elsevier), pp. 79–91.

Brown, M., Perry, A., Cheesman, A.D. and Pring, T. (2000) 'Pitch change in male-to-female transsexuals: Has phonosurgery a role to play?', *International Journal of Language & Communication Disorders*, 35 (1): 129–36.

Brundage, S.B. (1996) 'Comparison of proverb interpretations provided by right-hemisphere-damaged adults and adults with probable dementia of the Alzheimer type', *Clinical Aphasiology*, 24: 215–31.

Cakir, Z.A., Yigit, O., Kocak, I., Sunter, A.V. and Dogan, M. (2010) 'Sulcus vocalis in monozygotic twins', *Auris Nasus Larynx*, 37 (2): 255–7.

Campbell, T.F. (1999) 'Functional treatment outcomes in young children with motor speech disorders', in A.J. Caruso and E.A. Strand (eds) *Clinical Management of Motor Speech Disorders in Children*, New York: Thieme Medical Publishers Inc., pp. 385–96.

Campisi, P., Hawkes, M., Simpson, K. and the Canadian Juvenile Onset Recurrent Respiratory Papillomatosis Working Group (2010) 'The epidemiology of juvenile onset recurrent respiratory papillomatosis derived from a population level national database', *Laryngoscope*, 120 (6): 1233–45.

Cantwell, D.P. and Baker, L. (1980) 'Psychiatric and behavioral characteristics of children with communication disorders', *Journal of Pediatric Psychology*, 5 (2): 161–78.

Capps, L., Losh, M. and Thurber, C. (2000) '"The frog ate the bug and made his mouth sad": Narrative competence in children with autism', *Journal of Abnormal Child Psychology*, 28 (2): 193–204.

Carding, P.N., Roulstone, S., Northstone, K. and the ALSPAC Study Team (2006) 'The prevalence of childhood dysphonia: A cross-sectional study', *Journal of Voice*, 20 (4): 623–30.

Carney, L.J. and Chermak, G.D. (1991) 'Performance of American Indian children with fetal alcohol syndrome on the test of language development', *Journal of Communication Disorders*, 24 (2): 123–34.

Carroll, T.L., Gartner-Schmidt, J., Statham, M.M. and Rosen, C.A. (2010) 'Vocal process granuloma and glottal insufficiency: An overlooked etiology?', *Laryngoscope*, 120 (1): 114–20.

Caruso, A.J. and Strand, E.A. (1999) 'Motor speech disorders in children: Definitions, background, and a theoretical framework', in A.J. Caruso and E.A. Strand (eds) *Clinical Management of Motor Speech Disorders in Children* (New York: Thieme Medical Publishers Inc.), pp. 1–27.

Chaika, E. (1990) *Understanding Psychotic Speech: Beyond Freud and Chomsky* (Springfield, IL: Charles C. Thomas).

Chaika, E. (1982) 'A unified explanation for the diverse structural deviations reported for adult schizophrenics with disrupted speech', *Journal of Communication Disorders*, 15 (3): 167–89.

Chaika, E. (1974) 'A linguist looks at "schizophrenic" language', *Brain and Language*, 1 (3): 257–76.

Chaika, E. and Lambe, R.A. (1989) 'Cohesion in schizophrenic narratives, revisited', *Journal of Communication Disorders*, 22 (6): 407–21.

Champagne-Lavau, M. and Joanette, Y. (2009) 'Pragmatics, theory of mind and executive functions after a right-hemisphere lesion: Different patterns of deficits', *Journal of Neurolinguistics*, 22 (5): 413–26.

Cheang, H.S. and Pell, M.D. (2006) 'A study of humour and communicative intention following right hemisphere stroke', *Clinical Linguistics & Phonetics*, 20 (6): 447–62.

Chung, J.H., Tae, K., Lee, Y.S., Jeong, J.H., Cho, S.H., Kim, K.R., Park, C.W. and Han, D.S. (2009) 'The significance of laryngopharyngeal reflux in benign vocal mucosal lesions', *Otolaryngology-Head and Neck Surgery*, 141 (3): 369–73.

Clare, A. (1993) 'Communication in medicine', *European Journal of Disorders of Communication*, 28: 1–12.

Clegg, J., Hollis, C. and Rutter, M. (1999) 'Life sentence', *RCSLT Bulletin*, 571: 16–18.

Cleland, J., Wood, S., Hardcastle, W., Wishart, J. and Timmins, C. (2010) 'Relationship between speech, oromotor, language and cognitive abilities in children with Down's syndrome', *International Journal of Language & Communication Disorders*, 45 (1): 83–95.

Coelho, C.A. (2007) 'Management of discourse deficits following traumatic brain injury: Progress, caveats, and needs', *Seminars in Speech and Language*, 8 (2): 122–35.

Coelho, C.A., Youse, K. and Le, K. (2002) 'Conversational discourse in closed-head-injured and non-brain-injured adults', *Aphasiology*, 16 (4–6): 659–72.

Cohen, B.D. (1978) 'Referent communication disturbances in schizophrenia', in S. Schwartz (ed.) *Language and Cognition in Schizophrenia* (Hillsdale, NJ: Lawrence Erlbaum Associates), pp. 1–34.

Cohen, N.J., Barwick, M.A., Horodezky, M., Vallance, D.D. and Im, N. (1998) 'Language, achievement, and cognitive processing in psychiatrically disturbed children with previously identified and unsuspected language impairments', *Journal of Child Psychology and Psychiatry*, 39 (6): 865–77.

Cohen, S.M. and Garrett, C.G. (2008) 'Hoarseness: Is it really laryngopharyngeal reflux', *Laryngoscope*, 118 (2): 363–6.

Conti-Ramsden, G. and Botting, N. (2008) 'Emotional health in adolescents with and without a history of specific language impairment', *Journal of Child Psychology and Psychiatry*, 49 (5): 516–25.

Conture, E.G. (1997) 'Evaluating childhood stuttering', in R.F. Curlee and G.M. Siegal (eds) *Nature and Treatment of Stuttering: New Directions* (Boston: Allyn & Bacon), pp. 239–56.

Coppens, P., Hungerford, S., Yamaguchi, S. and Yamadori, A. (2002) 'Crossed aphasia: An analysis of the symptoms, their frequency, and a comparison with left-hemisphere aphasia symptomatology', *Brain and Language*, 83 (3): 425–63.

Corcoran, R. and Frith, C.D. (1996) 'Conversational conduct and the symptoms of schizophrenia', *Cognitive Neuropsychiatry*, 1 (4): 305–18.

Covington, M.A., He, C., Brown, C., Naçi, L., McClain, J.T., Fjordbak, B.S., Semple, J. and Brown, J. (2005) 'Schizophrenia and the structure of language: The linguist's view', *Schizophrenia Research*, 77 (1): 85–98.

Craig, A., Hancock, K., Tran, Y., Craig, M. and Peters, K. (2002) 'Epidemiology of stuttering in the community across the entire life span', *Journal of Speech, Language, and Hearing Research*, 45 (6): 1097–105.

Craig, H.K. (1991) 'Pragmatic characteristics of the child with specific language impairment: An interactionist perspective', in T.M. Gallagher (ed.) *Pragmatics of Language: Clinical Practice Issues* (San Diego, CA: Singular Publishing Group), pp. 163–98.

Crary, M.A. (1983) 'Phonological process analysis from spontaneous speech: The influence of sample size', *Journal of Communication Disorders*, 16 (2): 133–41.

Crystal, D. (1997) *The Cambridge Encyclopedia of Language* (Cambridge: Cambridge University Press, 2nd edn).

Crystal, D. and Varley, R. (1998) *Introduction to Language Pathology* (London: Whurr Publishers, 4th edn).

Cummings, L. (2014a) 'Clinical pragmatics and theory of mind', in A. Capone, F. Lo Piparo and M. Carapezza (eds) *Perspectives on Linguistic Pragmatics* (Dordrecht: Springer).

Cummings, L. (2014b) 'Clinical pragmatics', in Y. Huang (ed.) *Oxford Handbook of Pragmatics* (Oxford: Oxford University Press).

Cummings, L. (2014c) 'Pragmatic disorders and theory of mind', in L. Cummings (ed.) *Cambridge Handbook of Communication Disorders* (Cambridge: Cambridge University Press), pp. 559–77.

Cummings, L. (2013a) 'Clinical linguistics: A primer', *International Journal of Language Studies*, 7 (2): 1–30.

Cummings, L. (2013b) 'Clinical linguistics: State of the art', *International Journal of Language Studies*, 7 (3): 1–32.

Cummings, L. (2012a) 'Pragmatic disorders', in H.-J. Schmid (ed.) *Handbook of Pragmatics: Cognitive Pragmatics* (Berlin and Boston: De Gruyter Mouton), pp. 291–315.

Cummings, L. (2012b) 'Theorising context: The case of clinical pragmatics', in R. Finkbeiner, J. Meibauer and P.B. Schumacher (eds) *What is a Context? Linguistic Approaches and Challenges* (Amsterdam and Philadelphia: John Benjamins), pp. 55–80.

Cummings, L. (2011) 'Pragmatic disorders and their social impact', *Pragmatics and Society*, 2 (1): 17–36.

Cummings, L. (2009) *Clinical Pragmatics* (Cambridge: Cambridge University Press).

Cummings, L. (2008) *Clinical Linguistics* (Edinburgh: Edinburgh University Press).

Cummings, L. (2007a) 'Pragmatics and adult language disorders: Past achievements and future directions', *Seminars in Speech and Language*, 28 (2): 98–112.

Cummings, L. (2007b) 'Clinical pragmatics: A field in search of phenomena?', *Language & Communication*, 27 (4): 396–432.

Cummings, L. (2005) *Pragmatics: A Multidisciplinary Perspective* (Edinburgh: Edinburgh University Press).

Dabul, B.L. (2000) *Apraxia Battery for Adults-2* (Austin, TX: Pro-Ed, 2nd edn).

Dacakis, G. (2000) 'Long-term maintenance of fundamental frequency increases in male-to-female transsexuals', *Journal of Voice*, 14 (4): 549–56.

Daly, D.A. (1986) 'The clutterer', in K.O. St. Louis (ed.) *The Atypical Stutterer: Principles and Practices of Rehabilitation* (Orlando, FL: Academic Press, Inc.), pp. 155–92.

Daly, D.A. and Burnett, M.L. (1996) 'Cluttering: Assessment, treatment planning, and case study illustration', *Journal of Fluency Disorders*, 21 (3–4): 239–48.

Daly, D.A. and Cantrell, R.P. (2006) 'Cluttering: Characteristics identified as diagnostically significant by 60 fluency experts', paper presented at the International Fluency Congress, Dublin, Ireland, July 27, 2006.

Davis, B.L., Jacks, A. and Marquardt, T.P. (2005) 'Vowel patterns in developmental apraxia of speech: Three longitudinal case studies', *Clinical Linguistics & Phonetics*, 19 (4): 249–74.

Davis, B.L., Jakielski, K.J. and Marquardt, T.P. (1998) 'Developmental apraxia of speech: Determiners of differential diagnosis', *Clinical Linguistics & Phonetics*, 12 (1): 25–45.

De Letter, M., Santens, P., De Bodt, M., Van Maele, G., Van Borsel, J. and Boon, P. (2007) 'The effect of levodopa on respiration and word intelligibility in people with advanced Parkinson's disease', *Clinical Neurology and Neurosurgery*, 109 (6): 495–500.

Department of Health (2001) *Valuing People: A New Strategy for Learning Disability for the 21st Century* (London: Department of Health).

Devenny, D.A. and Silverman, W.P. (1990) 'Speech dysfluency and manual specialization in Down's syndrome', *Journal of Mental Deficiency Research*, 34 (3): 253–60.

Dewarrat, G.M., Annoni, J.-M., Fornari, E., Carota, A., Bogousslavsky, J. and Maeder, P. (2009) 'Acute aphasia after right hemisphere stroke', *Journal of Neurology*, 256 (9): 1461–7.

Diehl, J.J., Bennetto, L. and Young, E.C. (2006) 'Story recall and narrative coherence of high-functioning children with autism spectrum disorders', *Journal of Abnormal Child Psychology*, 34 (1): 87–102.

Dobbinson, S., Perkins, M.R. and Boucher, J. (1998) 'Structural patterns in conversations with a woman who has autism', *Journal of Communication Disorders*, 31 (2): 113–34.

Dogan, M., Midi, I., Yazici, M.A., Kocak, I., Gunal, D. and Sehitoglu, M.A. (2007) 'Objective and subjective evaluation of voice quality in multiple sclerosis', *Journal of Voice*, 21 (6): 735–40.

Doi, M., Nakayasu, H., Soda, T., Shimoda, K., Ito, A. and Nakashima, K. (2003) 'Brainstem infarction presenting with neurogenic stuttering', *Internal Medicine*, 42 (9): 884–7.

Douglas, J.M. and Bracy, C.A. (2006) 'The nature of impaired conversational skill following severe traumatic brain injury', International Aphasia Rehabilitation Conference, Sheffield, UK, 4–6 June 2006.

Douglas, J.M., O'Flaherty, C.A. and Snow, P.C. (2000) 'Measuring perception of communicative ability: The development and evaluation of the La Trobe communication questionnaire', *Aphasiology*, 14 (3): 251–68.

Drew, R.L. and Thompson, C.K. (1999) 'Model-based semantic treatment for naming deficits in aphasia', *Journal of Speech, Language, and Hearing Research*, 42 (4): 972–89.

Duff, M.C., Proctor, A. and Yairi, E. (2004) 'Prevalence of voice disorders in African American and European American preschoolers', *Journal of Voice*, 18 (3): 348–53.

Duffy, J.R. (1995) *Motor Speech Disorders: Substrates, Diagnosis and Management* (St. Louis, MO: Mosby).

Durbin, M. and Martin, R.L. (1977) 'Speech in mania: Syntactic aspects', *Brain and Language*, 4 (2): 208–18.

Dyrborg, J. and Goldschmidt, V.V. (1996) 'Language disorders in a child psychiatric center: Demographic characteristics and comorbidity', *Nordic Journal of Psychiatry*, 50 (4): 317–24.

Echternach, M., Maurer, C., Mencke, T., Schilling, M., Verse, T. and Richter, B. (2009) 'Laryngeal complications after thyroidectomy: Is it always the surgeon?', *Archives of Surgery*, 144 (2): 149–52.

Elizur, Y. and Perednik, R. (2003) 'Prevalence and description of selective mutism in immigrant and native families: A controlled study', *Journal of the American Academy of Child and Adolescent Psychiatry*, 42 (12): 1451–9.

Eme, R.F. (2007) 'Sex differences in child-onset, life-course-persistent conduct disorder. A review of biological influences', *Clinical Psychology Review*, 27 (5): 607–27.

Emerich, D.M., Creaghead, N.A., Grether, S.M., Murray, D. and Grasha, C. (2003) 'The comprehension of humorous materials by adolescents with high-functioning autism and Asperger's syndrome', *Journal of Autism and Developmental Disorders*, 33 (3): 253–7.

Emerson, J. and Enderby, P. (1996) 'Prevalence of speech and language disorders in a mental illness unit', *European Journal of Disorders of Communication*, 31: 221–36.

Enderby, P. (1983) *Frenchay Dysarthria Assessment* (San Diego: College-Hill Press).

Enderby, P. and Palmer, R. (2008) *Frenchay Dysarthria Assessment-2* (Austin, TX: Pro-Ed, 2nd edn).

Enderby, P. and Philipp, R. (1986) 'Speech and language handicap: Towards knowing the size of the problem', *British Journal of Disorders of Communication*, 21 (2): 151–65.

Eurocleft Speech Group: Brondsted, K., Grunwell, P., Henningsson, G., Jansonius, K., Karling, J., Meijer, M., Ording, U., Sell, D., Wyatt, R. and Verneij-Zieverink, E. (1993) 'A six-center international study of speech outcome in patients with clefts of the lip and palate: results and conclusions', Paper presented at the Seventh International Congress on Cleft Palate and Craniofacial Anomalies. Broadbeach, Queensland, Australia.

Fairley, J.W. and Hughes, M. (1992) 'Acute stridor due to bilateral vocal fold paralysis as a presenting sign of myasthenia gravis', *Journal of Laryngology & Otology*, 106 (8): 737–8.

Felsenfeld, S., Kirk, K.M., Zhu, G., Statham, D.J., Neale, M.C. and Martin, N.G. (2000) 'A study of the genetic and environmental etiology of stuttering in a selected twin sample', *Behavior Genetics*, 30 (5): 359–66.

Felsenfeld, S., McGue, M. and Broen, P.A. (1995) 'Familial aggregation of phonological disorders: Results from a 28-year follow-up', *Journal of Speech and Hearing Research*, 38 (5): 1091–107.

Feyereisen, P., Berrewaerts, J. and Hupet, M. (2007) 'Pragmatic skills in the early stages of Alzheimer's disease: An analysis by means of a referential communication task', *International Journal of Language & Communication Disorders*, 42 (1): 1–17.

Fine, J. (2006) *Language in Psychiatry: A Handbook of Clinical Practice* (London: Equinox).

First, M.B., Frances, A. and Pincus, H.A. (2002) *DSM-IV-TR Handbook of Differential Diagnosis* (Washington, DC: American Psychiatric Publishing).

Fontes Rezende, R.E., Lescano, M.A., Zambelli Ramalho, L.N., de Castro Fiqueiredo, J.F., Oliveira Dantas, R., Garzella Meneghelli, U. and Pimenta Modena, J.L. (2006) 'Reactivation of Chagas' disease in a patient with non-Hodgkin's lymphoma: Gastric, oesophageal and laryngeal involvement', *Transactions of the Royal Society of Tropical Medicine and Hygiene*, 100 (1): 74–8.

Forbes-McKay, K.E. and Venneri, A. (2005) 'Detecting subtle spontaneous language decline in early Alzheimer's disease with a picture description task', *Neurological Sciences*, 26 (4): 243–54.

Fransella, F. (1972) *Personal Change and Reconstruction* (New York: Academic Press).

Freed, D.B., Marshall, R.C. and Frazier, K.E. (1997) 'Long-term effectiveness of PROMPT treatment in a severely apractic-aphasic Speaker', *Aphasiology*, 11 (4–5): 365–72.

Freeman, M. and Fawcus, M. (2000) *Voice Disorders and Their Management* (London: Whurr Publishers).

Freidenberg, C.B. (2002) 'Working with male-to-female transgendered clients: Clinical considerations', *Contemporary Issues in Communication Science and Disorders*, 29: 43–58.

Gallena, S.K. (2007) *Voice and Laryngeal Disorders: A Problem-Based Clinical Guide with Voice Samples* (St. Louis, MO: Mosby Elsevier).

Gallivan, G.J., Gallivan, K.H. and Gallivan, H.K. (2007) 'Inhaled corticosteroids: Hazardous effects on voice – an update', *Journal of Voice*, 21 (1): 101–11.

Garcia, A.M., Freeman, J.B., Francis, G., Miller, L.M. and Leonard, H.L. (2004) 'Selective mutism', in T.H. Ollendick and J.S. March (eds) *Phobic and Anxiety Disorders in Children and Adolescents: A Clinician's Guide to Effective Psychosocial and Pharmacological Interventions* (New York: Oxford University Press), pp. 433–55.

Georgieva, D. and Miliev, D. (1996) 'Differential diagnosis of cluttering and stuttering in Bulgaria', *Journal of Fluency Disorders*, 21 (3–4): 249–60.

Gibbon, F.E. (2004) 'Abnormal patterns of tongue-palate contact in the speech of individuals with cleft palate', *Clinical Linguistics & Phonetics*, 18 (4–5): 285–311.

Gibbon, F.E. and Wood, S.E. (2003) 'Using electropalatography (EPG) to diagnose and treat articulation disorders associated with mild cerebral palsy: A case study', *Clinical Linguistics & Phonetics*, 17 (4–5): 365–74.

Gil, M., Cohen, M., Korn, C. and Groswasser, Z. (1996) 'Vocational outcome of aphasic patients following severe traumatic brain injury', *Brain Injury*, 10 (1): 39–45.

Gilmour, J., Hill, B., Place, M. and Skuse, D.H. (2004) 'Social communication deficits in conduct disorder: A clinical and community survey', *Journal of Child Psychology and Psychiatry*, 45 (5): 967–78.

Giovanni, A., Chanteret, C. and Lagier, A. (2007) 'Sulcus vocalis: A review', *European Archives of Oto-Rhino-Laryngology*, 264 (4): 337–44.

Glaze, L.E. (1996) 'Treatment of voice hyperfunction in the pre-adolescent', *Language, Speech, and Hearing Services in Schools*, 27 (3): 244–50.

Goldman, R. and Fristoe, M. (2000) *Goldman-Fristoe Test of Articulation 2* (San Antonio, TX: Pearson, 2nd edn).

Goodglass, H., Kaplan, E. and Barresi, B. (2001) *Boston Diagnostic Aphasia Examination* (Baltimore, MD: Lippincott Williams & Wilkins, 3rd edn).

Goozée, J.V., Murdoch, B.E., Theodoros, D.G. and Stokes, P.D. (2000) 'Kinematic analysis of tongue movements in dysarthria following traumatic brain injury using electromagnetic articulography', *Brain Injury*, 14 (2): 153–74.

Gorwood, P., Leboyer, M., Jay, M., Payan, C. and Feingold, J. (1995) 'Gender and age at onset in schizophrenia: Impact of family history', *American Journal of Psychiatry*, 152 (2): 208–12.

Goswami, S. and Patra, T.K. (2003) 'A clinicopathological study of Reinke's oedema', *Indian Journal of Otolaryngology and Head & Neck Surgery*, 55 (3): 160–5.

Grant, B.F. and Weissman, M.M. (2007) 'Gender and the prevalence of psychiatric disorders', in W.E. Narrow, M.B. First, P.J. Sirovatka and D.A. Regier (eds) *Age and Gender Considerations in Psychiatric Diagnosis: A Research Agenda for DSM-IV* (Arlington, VA: American Psychiatric Association), pp. 31–46.

Grigos, M.I. and Kolenda, N. (2010) 'The relationship between articulatory control and improved phonemic accuracy in childhood apraxia of speech: A longitudinal case study', *Clinical Linguistics & Phonetics*, 24 (1): 17–40.

Gross, M. (1999) 'Pitch-raising surgery in male-to-female transsexuals', *Journal of Voice*, 13 (2): 246–50.

Grossman, L.S. and Harrow, M. (1996) 'Interactive behavior in bipolar manic and schizophrenic patients and its link to thought disorder', *Comprehensive Psychiatry*, 37 (4): 245–52.

Grunwell, P. (1981) *The Nature of Phonological Disability in Children* (New York: Academic Press).

Hale, C.M. and Tager-Flusberg, H. (2005) 'Social communication in children with autism: The relationship between theory of mind and discourse development', *Autism*, 9 (2): 157–78.

Haley, K.L., Wertz, R.T. and Ohde, R.N. (1998) 'Single word intelligibility in aphasia and apraxia of speech', *Aphasiology*, 12 (7–8): 715–30.

Hall, P.K., Jordan, L.S. and Robin, D.A. (1993) *Developmental Apraxia of Speech: Theory and Clinical Practice* (Austin, TX: Pro-ed).

Hanson, D.M., Jackson, A.W. and Hagerman, R.J. (1986) 'Speech disturbances (cluttering) in mildly impaired males with the Martin-Bell/fragile X syndrome', *American Journal of Medical Genetics*, 23 (1–2): 195–206.

Harasty, J. and McCooey, R. (1994) 'The prevalence of communication impairment in adults: A summary and critical evaluation of the literature', *Australian Journal of Human Communication Disorders*, 21 (1): 81–95.

Harding, A. and Grunwell, P. (1993) 'The relationship between speech and timing of hard palate repair', in P. Grunwell (ed.) *Analysing Cleft Palate Speech*, London: Whurr, 48–82.

Harding, A. and Grunwell, P. (1996) 'Characteristics of cleft palate speech', *European Journal of Disorders of Communication*, 31 (4): 331–57.

Harding, A. and Grunwell, P. (1998) 'Active versus passive cleft-type speech characteristics', *International Journal of Language and Communication Disorders*, 33 (3): 329–52.

Harris, J. and Cottam, P. (1985) 'Phonetic features and phonological features in speech assessment', *British Journal of Disorders of Communication*, 20 (1): 61–74.

Hartelius, L., Runmarker, B. and Andersen, O. (2000) 'Prevalence and characteristics of dysarthria in a multiple-sclerosis incidence cohort: Relation to neurological data', *Folia Phoniatrica et Logopaedica*, 52 (4): 160–77.

Hashimoto, R., Taguchi, T., Kano, M., Hanyu, S., Tanaka, Y., Nishizawa, M. and Nakano, I. (1999) 'A case report of dementia with cluttering-like speech disorder and apraxia of gait', *Rinsho Shinkeigaku*, 39 (5): 520–6.

Hebert, L.E., Scherr, P.A., Bienias, J.L., Bennett, D.A. and Evans, D.A. (2003) 'Alzheimer disease in the US population: Prevalence estimates using the 2000 census', *Archives of Neurology*, 60 (8): 1119–22.

Heck, J.E., Berthiller, J., Vaccarella, S., Winn, D.M., Smith, E.M., Shan'gina, O., Schwartz, S.M., Purdue, M.P., Pilarska, A., Eluf-Neto, J., Menezes, A., McClean, M.D., Matos, E., Koifman, S., Kelsey, K.T., Herrero, R., Hayes, R.B., Franceschi, S., Wünsch-Filho, V., Fernández, L., Daudt, A.W., Curado, M.P., Chen, C., Castellsaqué, X., Ferro, G., Brennan, P., Boffetta, P. and Hashibe, M. (2010) 'Sexual behaviours and the risk of head and neck cancers: A pooled analysis in the International Head and Neck Cancer Epidemiology (INHANCE) consortium', *International Journal of Epidemiology*, 39 (1): 166–81.

Helm-Estabrooks, N. (1999) 'Stuttering associated with acquired neurological disorders', in R.F. Curlee (ed.) *Stuttering and Related Disorders of Fluency* (New York: Thieme), pp. 255–68.

Helm-Estabrooks, N. and Hotz, G. (1998) 'Sudden onset of "stuttering" in an adult: Neurogenic or psychogenic?', *Seminars in Speech and Language*, 19 (1): 23–9.

Hilari, K., Northcott, S., Roy, P., Marshall, J., Wiggins, R.D., Chataway, J. and Ames, D. (2010) 'Psychological distress after stroke and aphasia: The first six months', *Clinical Rehabilitation*, 24 (2): 181–90.

Hillis, A.E., Oh, S. and Ken, L. (2004) 'Deterioration of naming nouns versus verbs in primary progressive aphasia', *Annals of Neurology*, 55 (2): 268–75.

Hirano, M. (1981) *Clinical Examination of Voice* (New York: Springer Verlag).

Hirano, Y.M., Yamazaki, Y., Shimizu, J., Togari, T. and Bryce, T.J. (2006) 'Ventilator dependence and expressions of need: A study of patients with amyotrophic lateral sclerosis in Japan', *Social Science & Medicine*, 62 (6): 1403–13.

Hird, K. and Kirsner, K. (2003) 'The effect of right hemisphere damage on collaborative planning in conversation: An analysis of intentional structure', *Clinical Linguistics & Phonetics*, 17 (4–5): 309–15.

Hirdes, J.P., Ellis-Hale, K. and Pearson Hirdes, B. (1993) 'Prevalence and policy implications of communication disabilities among adults', *Augmentative and Alternative Communication*, 9 (4): 273–80.

Hocevar-Boltezar, I., Janko, M. and Zargi, M. (1998) 'Role of surface EMG in diagnostics and treatment of muscle tension dysphonia', *Acta Oto-laryngologica*, 118 (5): 739–43.

Hochman, I., Sataloff, R.T., Hillman, R.E. and Zeitels, S.M. (1999) 'Ectasias and varices of the vocal fold: Clearing the striking zone', *Annals of Otology, Rhinology, and Laryngology*, 108 (1): 10–16.

Hodge, M.M. and Wellman, L. (1999) 'Management of children with dysarthria', in A.J. Caruso and E.A. Strand (eds) *Clinical Management of Motor Speech Disorders in Children* (New York: Thieme Medical Publishers Inc.), pp. 209–80.

Hoffman, R.E., Kirstein, L., Stopek, S. and Cicchetti, D.V. (1982) 'Apprehending schizophrenic discourse: A structural analysis of the listener's task', *Brain and Language*, 15 (2): 207–33.

Holmberg, E., Nordqvist, K. and Ahlström, G. (1996) 'Prevalence of dysarthria in adult myotonic dystrophy (M. Steinert) patients: Speech characteristics and intelligibility', *Logopedics Phoniatrics Vocology*, 21 (1): 21–7.

Honbolygó, F., Csépe, V., Fekésházy, A., Emri, M., Márián, T., Sárközy, G. and Kálmánchey, R. (2006) 'Converging evidences on language impairment in Landau–Kleffner syndrome revealed by behavioral and brain activity measures: A case study', *Clinical Neurophysiology*, 117 (2): 295–305.

Horner, J. and Heyman, A. (1981) 'Language changes associated with Alzheimer's dementia: A discussion session', in R.H. Brookshire (ed.) *Clinical Aphasiology Conference Proceedings* (Minneapolis: BRK Publishers), pp. 330–8.

Horner, J. and Massey, E.W. (1983) 'Progressive dysfluency associated with right hemisphere disease', *Brain and Language*, 18 (1): 71–85.

Hough, M.S. (1993) 'Treatment of Wernicke's aphasia with jargon: A case study', *Journal of Communication Disorders*, 26 (2): 101–11.

Houtz, D.R., Roy, N., Merrill, R.M. and Smith, M.E. (2010) 'Differential diagnosis of muscle tension dysphonia and adductor spasmodic dysphonia using spectral moments of the long-term average spectrum', *Laryngoscope*, 120 (4): 749–57.

Huff, F.J., Corkin, S. and Growdon, J.H. (1986) 'Semantic impairment and anomia in Alzheimer's disease', *Brain and Language*, 28 (2): 235–49.

Hunter, L., Pring, T. and Martin, S. (1991) 'The use of strategies to increase speech intelligibility in cerebral palsy: An experimental evaluation', *British Journal of Disorders of Communication*, 26 (2): 163–74.

Issing, W.J., Karkos, P.D., Perreas, K., Folwaczny, C. and Reichel, O. (2004) 'Dual-probe 24-hour ambulatory pH monitoring for diagnosis of laryngopharyngeal reflux', *Journal of Laryngology & Otology*, 118 (11): 845–8.

Jacks, A., Marquardt, T.P. and Davis, B.L. (2006) 'Consonant and syllable structure patterns in childhood apraxia of speech: Developmental change in three children', *Journal of Communication Disorders*, 39 (6): 424–41.

Joanette, Y., Ska, B. and Côté, H. (2004) *Protocole Montréal d'Evaluation de la Communication (MEC)* (Isbergues, France: Ortho-Edition).

Johnson, M. and Wintgens, A. (2001) *The Selective Mutism Resource Manual* (Bicester, Oxon: Speechmark).

Jones, S.M., Carding, P.N. and Drinnan, M.J. (2006) 'Exploring the relationship between severity of dysphonia and voice-related quality of life', *Clinical Otolaryngology*, 31 (5): 411–17.

Jorgensen, M. and Togher, L. (2009) 'Narrative after traumatic brain injury: A comparison of monologic and jointly-produced discourse', *Brain Injury*, 23 (9): 727–40.

Kagan, A., Black, S.E., Duchan, F.J., Simmons-Mackie, N. and Square, P. (2001) 'Training volunteers as conversation partners using "Supported Conversation for Adults With Aphasia" (SCA): A controlled trial', *Journal of Speech, Language, and Hearing Research*, 44 (3): 624–38.

Karnell, M.P., Melton, S.D., Childes, J.M., Coleman, T.C., Dailey, S.A. and Hoffman, H.T. (2007) 'Reliability of clinician-based (GRBAS and CAPE-V) and patient-based (V-RQOL and IPVI) documentation of voice disorders', *Journal of Voice*, 21 (5): 576–90.

Kauhanen, M.L., Korpelainen, J.T., Hiltunen, P., Määttä, R., Mononen, H., Brusin, E., Sotaniemi, K.A. and Myllylä, V.V. (2000) 'Aphasia, depression, and non-verbal cognitive impairment in ischaemic stroke', *Cerebrovascular Diseases*, 10 (6): 455–61.

Kay Elemetrics (1993) *Multi-Dimensional Voice Program (MDVP) – Computer Program* (Pine Brook, NJ: Author).

Kazi, R., Prasad, V.M.N., Kanagalingam, J., Georgalas, C., Venkitaraman, R., Nutting, C.M., Clarke, P., Rhys-Evans, P. and Harrington, K.J. (2007) 'Analysis of formant frequencies in patients with oral or oropharyngeal cancers treated by glossectomy', *International Journal of Language & Communication Disorders*, 42 (5): 521–32.

Kelly, G. (1955) *The Psychology of Personal Constructs* (New York: Norton).

Kendall, K.A. and Leonard, R.J. (2011) 'Interarytenoid muscle Botox injection for treatment of adductor spasmodic dysphonia with vocal tremor', *Journal of Voice*, 25 (1): 114–19.

Kertesz, A. (2006) *Western Aphasia Battery-Revised* (San Antonio, TX: Harcourt Assessment).

Khan, L. and Lewis, N. (2002) *Khan-Lewis Phonological Analysis 2*, (San Antonio, TX: Pearson, 2nd edn).

Khan, O.A. and Ramsay, A. (2006) 'Herpes encephalitis presenting as mild aphasia: Case report', *BMC Family Practice*, 7: 22.

Kim, Y.T. and Lombardino, L.J. (1991) 'The efficacy of script contexts in language comprehension intervention with children who have mental retardation', *Journal of Speech and Hearing Research*, 34 (4): 845–57.

Kjelgaard, M.M. and Tager-Flusberg, H. (2001) 'An investigation of language impairment in autism: Implications for genetic subgroups', *Language and Cognitive Processes*, 16 (2–3): 287–308.

Knott, P.D., Milstein, C.F., Hicks, D.M., Abelson, T.I., Byrd, M.C. and Strome, M. (2006) 'Vocal outcomes after laser resection of early-stage glottic cancer with adjuvant cryotherapy', *Archives of Otolaryngology–Head & Neck Surgery*, 132 (11): 1226–30.

Kotsopoulos, A. and Boodoosingh, L. (1987) 'Language and speech disorders in children attending a day psychiatric programme', *International Journal of Language and Communication Disorders*, 22 (3): 227–36

Kozloff, N., Cheung, A.H., Schaffer, A., Cairney, J., Dewa, C.S., Veldhuizen, S., Kurdyak, P. and Levitt, A.J. (2010) 'Bipolar disorder among adolescents and young adults: Results from an epidemiological sample', *Journal of Affective Disorders*, 125 (1–3): 350–4.

Kumin, L., Councill, C. and Goodman, M. (1994) 'A longitudinal study of the emergence of phonemes in children with Down syndrome', *Journal of Communication Disorders*, 27 (4): 293–303.

La Pointe, L.L. and Johns, D.F. (1975) 'Some phonemic characteristics in apraxia of speech', *Journal of Communication Disorders*, 8 (3): 259–69.

Lacy, P.D., Alderson, D.J. and Parker, A.J. (1994) 'Late congenital syphilis of the larynx and pharynx presenting at endotracheal intubation', *Journal of Laryngology & Otology*, 108 (8): 688–9.

Lahey, M. and Edwards, J. (1999) 'Naming errors of children with specific language impairment', *Journal of Speech, Language, and Hearing Research*, 42 (1): 195–205.

Laver, J.D., Wirz, S.L., Mackenzie, J. and Miller, S. (1981) 'A perceptual protocol for the analysis of vocal profiles', *Edinburgh University Department of Linguistics Work in Progress*, 14: 139–55.

Law, J., Lindsay, G., Peacey, N., Gascoigne, M., Soloff, N., Radford, J., Band, S. and Fitzgerald, L. (2000) *Provision for Children with Speech and Language Needs in England and Wales: Facilitating Communication between Education and Health Services* (London: Department for Education and Employment).

Laws, G. and Bishop, D.V.M. (2004) 'Pragmatic language impairment and social deficits in Williams syndrome: A comparison with Down's syndrome and specific language impairment', *International Journal of Language and Communication Disorders*, 39 (1): 45–64.

Leblebicioglu, H., Turan, D., Eroglu, C., Esen, S., Sunbul, M. and Bostanci, F. (2006) 'A cluster of anthrax cases including meningitis', *Tropical Doctor*, 36 (1): 51–3.

Lebrun, Y. (1996) 'Cluttering after brain damage', *Journal of Fluency Disorders*, 21 (3–4): 289–95.

Lee, A.S. and Rosen, C.A. (2004) 'Efficacy of cidofovir injection for the treatment of recurrent respiratory papillomatosis', *Journal of Voice*, 18 (4): 551–6.

Lee, E.K. and Son, Y.I. (2005) 'Muscle tension dysphonia in children: Voice characteristics and outcome of voice therapy', *International Journal of Pediatric Otorhinolaryngology*, 69 (7): 911–17.

Lehman, B. (2006) 'Clinical relevance of discourse characteristics after right hemisphere brain damage', *American Journal of Speech-Language Pathology*, 15 (3): 255–67.

Leonard, L.B. (1998) *Children with Specific Language Impairment* (Cambridge, MA: MIT Press).

Leong, S.C.L., Pinder, E., Sasae, R. and Mortimore, R. (2007) 'Mucoepidermoid carcinoma of the tongue', *Singapore Medical Journal*, 48 (10): e272–e274.

Levy, J.A. and Chelune, G.J. (2007) 'Cognitive-behavioral profiles of neurodegenerative dementias: Beyond Alzheimer's disease', *Journal of Geriatric Psychiatry and Neurology*, 20 (4): 227–38.

Lewis, B.A., Freebairn, L.A., Hansen, A.J., Iyengar, S.K. and Taylor, H.G. (2004) 'School-age follow-up of children with childhood apraxia of speech', *Language, Speech and Hearing Services in Schools*, 35 (2): 122–40.

Lim, J.Y., Kim, J., Hee Choi, S., Kim, K.M., Ho Kim, Y., Su Kim, H. and Choi, H.S. (2009) 'Sulcus configurations of vocal folds during phonation', *Acta Oto-Laryngologica*, 129 (10): 1127–35.

Liu, H.-M., Tsao, F.-M. and Kuhl, P.K. (2005) 'The effect of reduced vowel working space on speech intelligibility in Mandarin-speaking young adults with cerebral palsy', *Journal of the Acoustical Society of America*, 117 (6): 3879–89.

Lott, P.R., Guggenbühl, S., Schneeberger, A., Pulver, A.E. and Stassen, H.H. (2002) 'Linguistic analysis of the speech output of schizophrenic, bipolar, and depressive patients', *Psychopathology*, 35 (4): 220–7.

Loukusa, S., Leinonen, E., Jussila, K., Mattila, M.-L., Ryder, N., Ebeling, H. and Moilanen, I. (2007) 'Answering contextually demanding questions: Pragmatic errors produced by children with Asperger syndrome or high-functioning autism', *Journal of Communication Disorders*, 40 (5): 357–81.

Luna-Ortiz, K., Carmona-Luna, T., Cano-Valdez, A.M., Mosqueda-Taylor, A., Herrera-Gómez, A. and Villavicencio-Valencia, V. (2009) 'Adenoid cystic carcinoma of the tongue – a clinicopathological study and survival analysis', *Head & Neck Oncology*, 1: 15.

Lyons, K., Kemper, S., Labarge, E., Ferraro, F.R., Balota, D. and Storandt, M. (1994) 'Oral language and Alzheimer's disease: A reduction in syntactic complexity', *Aging, Neuropsychology, and Cognition*, 1 (4): 271–81.

MacLennan, D.L., Cornis-Pop, M., Picon-Nieto, L. and Sigford, B. (2002) 'The prevalence of pragmatic communication impairments in traumatic brain injury', *Premier Outlook*, 3 (4): 38–45.

Makhadoom, N., Abouloyoun, A., Bokhary, H.A., Dhafar, K.O., Gazzaz, Z.J. and Azab, B.A. (2007) 'Prevalence of gastroesophageal reflux disease in patients with laryngeal and voice disorders', *Saudi Medical Journal*, 28 (7): 1068–71.

Manders, E., Dammekens, E., Leemans, I. and Michiels, K. (2010) 'Evaluation of quality of life in people with aphasia using a Dutch version of the SAQOL-39', *Disability & Rehabilitation*, 32 (3): 173–82.

Manning, W.H. (1999) 'Management of adult stuttering', in R.F. Curlee (ed.) *Stuttering and Related Disorders of Fluency*, 2nd edn, New York: Thieme, pp. 160–80.

Månsson, H. (2000) 'Childhood stuttering: Incidence and development', *Journal of Fluency Disorders*, 25 (1): 47–57.

Marelli, R.A., Biddinger, P.W. and Gluckman, J.L. (1992) 'Cytomegalovirus infection of the larynx in the acquired immunodeficiency syndrome', *Otolaryngology–Head and Neck Surgery*, 106 (3): 296–301.

Marini, A., Carlomagno, S., Caltagirone, C. and Nocentini, U. (2005) 'The role played by the right hemisphere in the organization of complex textual structures', *Brain and Language*, 93 (1): 46–54.

Marshall, J., Pring, T., Chiat, S. and Robson, J. (2001) 'When ottoman is easier than chair: An inverse frequency effect in jargon aphasia', *Cortex*, 37 (1): 33–53.

Martin, I. and McDonald, S. (2004) 'An exploration of causes of non-literal language problems in individuals with Asperger syndrome', *Journal of Autism and Developmental Disorders*, 34 (3): 311–28.

Martins, R.H.G., Dias, N.H., dos Santos, D.C., Fabro, A.T. and Braz, J.R.C. (2009) 'Clinical, histological and electron microscopic aspects of vocal fold granulomas', *Brazilian Journal of Otorhinolaryngology*, 75 (1): 116–22.

Martins, R.H.G., Santana, M.F. and Tavares, E.L.M. (2011) 'Vocal cysts: Clinical, endoscopic, and surgical aspects', *Journal of Voice*, 25 (1): 107–10.

Martins, R.H.G., Silva, R., Ferreira, D.M. and Dias, N.H. (2007) 'Sulcus vocalis: Probable genetic etiology. Report of four cases in close relatives', *Brazilian Journal of Otorhinolaryngology*, 73 (4): 573.

Mathieson, L. (2001) *Greene and Mathieson's The Voice and Its Disorders* (London: Whurr) Publishers.

Mayer, M. (1969) *Frog, Where Are You?* (New York: Dial Press).

McAuliffe, M.J., Ward, E.C. and Murdoch, B.E. (2006) 'Speech production in Parkinson's disease: II. Acoustic and electropalatographic investigation of sentence, word and segment durations', *Clinical Linguistics & Phonetics*, 20 (1): 19–33.

McCabe, P.J., Sheard, C. and Code, C. (2008) 'Communication impairment in the AIDS dementia complex (ADC): A case report', *Journal of Communication Disorders*, 41 (3): 203–22.

McCardle, P. and Wilson, B. (1993) 'Language and development in FG syndrome with callosal agenesis', *Journal of Communication Disorders*, 26 (2): 83–100.

McClure, E.B., Treland, J.E., Snow, J., Schmajuk, M., Dickstein, D.P., Towbin, K.E., Charney, D.S., Pine, D.S. and Leibenluft, E. (2005) 'Deficits in social cognition and response flexibility in pediatric bipolar disorder', *American Journal of Psychiatry*, 162 (9): 1644–51.

McDonald, S. (2000) 'Neuropsychological studies of sarcasm', *Metaphor and Symbol*, 15 (1–2): 85–98.

McDonald, S. (1992) 'Communication disorders following closed head injury: New approaches to assessment and rehabilitation', *Brain Injury*, 6 (3): 293–8.

McDonald, S. and Flanagan, S. (2004) 'Social perception deficits after traumatic brain injury: Interaction between emotion recognition, mentalizing ability, and social communication', *Neuropsychology*, 18 (3): 572–9.

McGrath, J.J. (2006) 'Variations in the incidence of schizophrenia: data versus dogma', *Schizophrenia Bulletin*, 32 (1): 195–7.

McGregor, D.K., Citron, D. and Shahab, I. (2003) 'Cryptococcal infection of the larynx simulating laryngeal carcinoma', *Southern Medical Journal*, 96 (1): 74–7.

McGregor, K.K., Newman, R.M., Reilly, R.M. and Capone, N.C. (2002) 'Semantic representation and naming in children with specific language impairment', *Journal of Speech, Language, and Hearing Research*, 45 (5): 998–1014.

McNeil, E.J. (2006) 'Management of the transgender voice', *Journal of Laryngology & Otology*, 120 (7): 521–3.

Medical Research Council (2001) *MRC Review of Autism Research: Epidemiology and Causes* (London: Medical Research Council).

Melo, T.P., Bogousslavsky, J., van Melle, G. and Regli, F. (1992) 'Pure motor stroke: A reappraisal', *Neurology*, 42 (4): 789–95.

Merati, A.L., Heman-Ackah, Y.D., Abaza, M., Altman, K.W., Sulica, L. and Belamowicz, S. (2005) 'Common movement disorders affecting the larynx: A report from the Neurolaryngology Committee of the AAO-HNS', *Otolaryngology–Head and Neck Surgery*, 133 (5): 654–5.

Milutinović, Z. and Vasiljević, J. (1992) 'Contribution to the understanding of the etiology of vocal fold cysts: A functional and histologic study', *Laryngoscope*, 102 (5): 568–71.

Montero-Odasso, M. (2006) 'Dysphonia as first symptom of late-onset myasthenia gravis', *Journal of General Internal Medicine*, 21 (6): C4–6.

Moore, M.E. (2001) 'Third person pronoun errors by children with and without language impairment', *Journal of Communication Disorders*, 34 (3): 207–28.

Moreira, L.M., de Carvalho, A.F., Borja, A.L., Pinto, P.S., Silveira, A., de Freitas, L.M. and Falcão, M. de L.L. (2008) 'Mosaic cri-du-chat syndrome in a girl with a mild phenotype', *Journal of Applied Genetics*, 49 (4): 415–20.

Morgan, A.T., Mageandran, S.-D. and Mei, C. (2009) 'Incidence and clinical presentation of dysarthria and dysphagia in the acute setting following paediatric traumatic brain injury', *Child: Care, Health and Development*, 36 (1): 44–53.

Morgan Barry, R.A. (1995a) 'EPG treatment of a child with the Worster-Drought syndrome', *European Journal of Disorders of Communication*, 30 (2): 256–63.

Morgan Barry, R.A. (1995b) 'The relationship between dysarthria and verbal dyspraxia in children: A comparative study using profiling and instrumental analyses', *Clinical Linguistics & Phonetics*, 9 (4): 277–309.

Morgan Barry, R.A. (1995c) 'A comparative study of the relationship between dysarthria and verbal dyspraxia in adults and children', *Clinical Linguistics & Phonetics*, 9 (4): 311–32.

Moriarty, B.C. and Gillon, G.T. (2006) 'Phonological awareness intervention for children with childhood apraxia of speech', *International Journal of Language & Communication Disorders*, 41 (6): 713–34.

Morley, M.E. (1970) *Cleft Palate and Speech*, 7th edition, Edinburgh: Churchill Livingstone.

Morris, H. and Ozanne, A. (2003) 'Phonetic, phonological, and language skills of children with a cleft palate', *Cleft Palate-Craniofacial Journal*, 40 (5): 460–70.

Morris, R.J., Gorham-Rowan, M.M. and Harman, A.B. (2011) 'The effect of initiating oral contraceptive use on voice: A case study', *Journal of Voice*, 25 (2): 223–9.

Morrish, E.C.E. (1988) 'Compensatory articulation in a subject with total glossectomy', *British Journal of Disorders of Communication*, 23 (1): 13–22.

Morrish, E.C.E. (1984) 'Compensatory vowel articulation of the glossectomee: Acoustic and videofluoroscopic evidence', *British Journal of Disorders of Communication*, 19 (2): 125–34.

Mount, K.H. and Salmon, S.J. (1988) 'Changing the vocal characteristics of a postoperative transsexual patient: A longitudinal study', *Journal of Communication Disorders*, 21 (3): 229–38.

Mower, D.E. and Younts, J. (2001) 'Sudden onset of excessive repetitions in the speech of a patient with multiple sclerosis: A case report', *Journal of Fluency Disorders*, 26 (4): 269–309.

Muir, N.J. (1996) 'The role of the speech and language therapist in psychiatry', *Psychiatric Bulletin*, 20: 524–6.

Murdoch, B.E. and Chenery, H.J. (1990) 'Latent aphasia and flaccid dysarthria associated with subcortical and brainstem calcification 20 years post-radiotherapy', *Journal of Neurolinguistics*, 5 (1): 55–73.

Murdoch, B.E. and Horton, S.K. (1998) 'Acquired and developmental dysarthria in childhood', in B.E. Murdoch (ed.) *Dysarthria: A Physiological Approach to Assessment and Treatment* (Cheltenham: Stanley Thornes), pp. 373–427.

Murdoch, B.E. and Hudson-Tennent, L.J. (1994) 'Speech disorders in children treated for posterior fossa tumours: Ataxic and developmental features', *European Journal of Disorders of Communication*, 29 (4): 379–97.

Murdoch, B.E. and Theodoros, D.G. (1998) 'Ataxic dysarthria', in B.E. Murdoch (ed.) *Dysarthria: A Physiological Approach to Assessment and Treatment* (Cheltenham, Stanley Thornes), pp. 242–65.

Murdoch, B.E., Ward, E.C. and Theodoros, D.G. (2000) 'Dysarthria: Clinical features, neuroanatomical framework and assessment', in I. Papathanasiou (ed.) *Acquired Neurogenic Communication Disorders: A Clinical Perspective* (London: Whurr Publishers), pp. 103–48.

Myers, F.L. and St. Louis, K.O. (1996) 'Two youths who clutter, but is that the only similarity?', *Journal of Fluency Disorders*, 21 (3–4): 297–304.

Myers, P.S. (1979) 'Profiles of communication deficits in patients with right cerebral hemisphere damage: Implications for diagnosis and treatment', Clinical Aphasiology Conference, Phoenix: BRK Publishers, pp. 38–46.

Nachtegaal, J., Smit, J.H., Smits, C., Bezemer, P.D., van Beek, J.H., Festen, J.M. and Kramer, S.E. (2009) 'The association between hearing status and psychosocial health before the age of 70 years: Results from an internet-based national survey on hearing', *Ear and Hearing*, 30 (3): 302–12.

Nalini, B. and Vinayak, S. (2006) 'Tuberculosis in ear, nose, and throat practice: Its presentation and diagnosis', *American Journal of Otolaryngology*, 27 (1): 39–45.

Natke, U., Sandrieser, P., Pietrowsky, R. and Kalveram, K.T. (2006) 'Disfluency data of German preschool children who stutter and comparison children', *Journal of Fluency Disorders*, 31 (3): 165–76.

Neely, J.L. and Rosen, C. (2000) 'Vocal fold hemorrhage associated with coumadin therapy in an opera singer', *Journal of Voice*, 14 (2): 272–7.

Nguyen, D.D., Kenny, D.T., Tran, N.D. and Livesey, J.R. (2009) 'Muscle tension dysphonia in Vietnamese female teachers', *Journal of Voice*, 23 (2): 195–208.

O'Brien, G. and Pearson, J. (2004) 'Autism and learning disability', *Autism*, 8 (2): 125–40.

Odell, K., McNeil, M.R. and Rosenbek, J.C. (1991) 'Perceptual characteristics of vowel and prosody production in apraxic, aphasic and dysarthric speakers', *Journal of Speech and Hearing Research*, 34 (1): 67–80.

Odell, K.H. and Shriberg, L.D. (2001) 'Prosody-voice characteristics of children and adults with apraxia of speech', *Clinical Linguistics & Phonetics*, 15 (4): 275–307.

Oestreicher-Kedem, Y., DeRowe, A., Nagar, H., Fishman, G. and Ben-Ari, J. (2008) 'Vocal fold paralysis in infants with tracheoesophageal fistula', *Annals of Otology, Rhinology, and Laryngology*, 117 (12): 896–901.

Ogar, J., Willock, S., Baldo, J., Wilkins, D., Ludy, C. and Dronkers, N. (2006) 'Clinical and anatomical correlates of apraxia of speech', *Brain and Language*, 97 (3): 343–50.

Oliver, B. and Buckley, S. (1994) 'The language development of children with Down's syndrome: First words to two-word phrases', *Down Syndrome Research and Practice*, 2 (2): 71–5.

Olvera, R.L., Semrud-Clikeman, M., Pliszka, S.R. and O'Donnell, L. (2005) 'Neuropsychological deficits in adolescents with conduct disorder and comorbid bipolar disorder: A pilot study', *Bipolar Disorders*, 7 (1): 57–67.

Ono, T., Hamamura, M., Honda, K. and Nokubi, T. (2005) 'Collaboration of a dentist and speech-language pathologist in the rehabilitation of a stroke patient with dysarthria: A case study', *Gerodontology*, 22 (2): 116–19.

Ozudogru, E., Cakli, H., Altuntas, E.E. and Gurbuz, M.K. (2005) 'Effects of laryngeal tuberculosis on vocal fold functions: Case report', *ACTA Otorhinolaryngologica Italica*, 25 (6): 374–7.

Paniello, R.C., Martin-Bredahl, K.J., Henkener, L.J. and Riew, K.D. (2008) 'Preoperative laryngeal nerve screening for revision anterior cervical spine procedures', *Annals of Otology, Rhinology, and Laryngology*, 117 (8): 594–7.

Papagno, C., Curti, R., Rizzo, S., Crippa, F. and Colombo, M.R. (2006) 'Is the right hemisphere involved in idiom comprehension? A neuropsychological study', *Neuropsychology*, 20 (5): 598–606.

Paul, R., Augustyn, A., Klin, A. and Volkmar, F.R. (2005) 'Perception and production of prosody by speakers with autism spectrum disorders', *Journal of Autism and Developmental Disorders*, 35 (2): 205–20.

Paydarfar, J.A. and Birkmeyer, N.J. (2006) 'Complications in head and neck surgery: A meta-analysis of postlaryngectomy pharyngocutaneous fistula', *Archives of Otolaryngology–Head & Neck Surgery*, 132 (1): 67–72.

Peach, R.K. (2004) 'Acquired apraxia of speech: Features, accounts, and treatment', *Topics in Stroke Rehabilitation*, 11 (1): 49–58.

Peach, R.K. and Tonkovich, J.D. (2004) 'Phonemic characteristics of apraxia of speech resulting from subcortical hemorrhage', *Journal of Communication Disorders*, 37 (1): 77–90.

Pedersen, P.M., Jorgensen, H.S., Kammersgaard, L.P., Nakayama, H., Raaschou, H.O. and Olsen, T.S. (2001) 'Manual and oral apraxia in acute stroke, frequency and influence on functional outcome: The Copenhagen Stroke Study', *American Journal of Physical Medicine & Rehabilitation*, 80 (9): 685–92.

Peelle, J.E., Cooke, A., Moore, P., Vesely, L. and Grossman, M. (2007) 'Syntactic and thematic components of sentence processing in progressive nonfluent aphasia and non-aphasic frontotemporal dementia', *Journal of Neurolinguistics*, 20 (6): 482–94.

Perkins, L., Whitworth, A. and Lesser, R. (1997) *Conversation Analysis Profile for People with Cognitive Impairment* (London: Whurr Publishers).

Pickuth, D., Brandt, S., Neumann, K., Berghaus, A., Spielmann, R.P. and Heywang-Köbrunner, S.H. (2000) 'Value of spiral CT in patients with cricothyroid approximation', *British Journal of Radiology*, 73 (872): 840–2.

Pinborough-Zimmerman, J., Satterfield, R., Miller, J., Bilder, D., Hossain, S. and McMahon, W. (2007) 'Communication disorders: Prevalence and comorbid intellectual disability, autism, and emotional/behavioral disorders', *American Journal of Speech-Language Pathology*, 16, 359–67.

Plank, C., Schneider, S., Eysholdt, U., Schützenberger, A. and Rosanowski, F. (2011) 'Voice- and health-related quality of life in the elderly', *Journal of Voice*, 25 (3): 265–8.

Pollock, K.E. and Hall, P.K. (1991) 'An analysis of the vowel misarticulations of five children with developmental apraxia of speech', *Clinical Linguistics & Phonetics*, 5 (3): 207–24.

Pontes, P., Brasolotto, A. and Behlau, M. (2005) 'Glottic characteristics and voice complaint in the elderly', *Journal of Voice*, 19 (1): 84–94.

Pontes, P., Yamasaki, R. and Behlau, M. (2006) 'Morphological and functional aspects of the senile larynx', *Folia Phoniatrica et Logopaedica*, 58 (3): 151–8.

Portegies, P. and Rosenberg, N.R. (1998) 'AIDS dementia complex: Diagnosis and drug treatment options', *CNS Drugs*, 9 (1): 31–40.

Postma, G.N., Courey, M.S. and Ossoff, R.H. (1998) 'Microvascular lesions of the true vocal fold', *Annals of Otology, Rhinology, and Laryngology*, 107 (6): 472–6.

Powell, J.E., Edwards, A., Edwards, M., Pandit, B.S., Sungum-Paliwal, S.R. and Whitehouse, W. (2000) 'Changes in the incidence of childhood autism and other autistic spectrum disorders in preschool children from two areas of the West Midlands, UK', *Developmental Medicine & Child Neurology*, 42 (9): 624–8.

Powell, T.W., Miccio, A.W., Elbert, M., Brasseur, J.A. and Strike-Roussos, C. (1999) 'Patterns of sound change in children with phonological disorders', *Clinical Linguistics & Phonetics*, 13 (3): 163–82.

Pryce, M. (1994) 'The voice of people with Down's syndrome: An EMG biofeedback study', *Down Syndrome Research and Practice*, 2 (3): 106–11.

Radanovic, M., Villela Nunes, P., Farid Gattaz, W. and Vicente Forlenza, O. (2008) 'Language impairment in euthymic, elderly patients with bipolar disorder but no dementia', *International Psychogeriatrics*, 20 (4): 687–96.

Rammage, L., Morrison, M. and Nichol, H. (2001) *Management of the Voice and its Disorders* (San Diego, CA: Singular, 2nd edn).

Ray, S., Masood, A., Pickles, J. and Moumoulidis, I. (2008) 'Severe laryngitis following chronic anabolic steroid abuse', *Journal of Laryngology & Otology*, 122 (3): 230–2.

Redmond, S.M. and Rice, M.L. (2001) 'Detection of irregular verb violations by children with and without SLI', *Journal of Speech, Language, and Hearing Research*, 44 (3): 655–69.

Reilly, J., Losh, M., Bellugi, U. and Wulfeck, B. (2004) ' "Frog, where are you?" Narratives in children with specific language impairment, early focal brain injury, and Williams syndrome', *Brain and Language*, 88 (2): 229–47.

Reilly, J., Rodriguez, A.D., Lamy, M. and Neils-Strunjas, J. (2010) 'Cognition, language, and clinical pathological features of non-Alzheimer's dementias: An overview', *Journal of Communication Disorders*, 43 (5): 438–52.

Reilly, S., Onslow, M., Packman, A., Wake, M., Bavin, E.L., Prior, M., Eadie, P., Cini, E., Bolzonello, C. and Ukoumunne, O.C. (2009) 'Predicting stuttering onset by the age of 3 years: A prospective, community cohort study', *Pediatrics*, 123 (1): 270–7.

Ribeiro, B.T. (1994) *Coherence in Psychotic Discourse* (New York: Oxford University Press).

Rice, M.L., Wexler, K. and Cleave, P.L. (1995) 'Specific language impairment as a period of extended optional infinitive', *Journal of Speech and Hearing Research*, 38 (4): 850–63.

Rice, M.L., Wexler, K. and Hershberger, S. (1998) 'Tense over time: The longitudinal course of tense acquisition in children with specific language impairment', *Journal of Speech, Language, and Hearing Research*, 41 (6): 1412–31.

Richards, R.G., Sampson, F.C., Beard, S.M. and Tappenden, P. (2002) 'A review of the natural history and epidemiology of multiple sclerosis: Implications for resource allocation and health economic models', *Health Technology Assessment*, 6: 10.

Rieber, R.W., Breskin, S. and Jaffe, J. (1972) 'Pause time and phonation time in stuttering and cluttering', *Journal of Psycholinguistic Research*, 1 (2): 149–54.

Ringo, C.C. and Dietrich, S. (1995) 'Neurogenic stuttering: An analysis and critique', *Journal of Medical Speech-Language Pathology*, 3 (2): 111–22.

Robson, J., Pring, T., Marshall, J. and Chiat, S. (2003) 'Phoneme frequency effects in jargon aphasia: A phonological investigation of nonword errors', *Brain and Language*, 85 (1): 109–24.

Rohrer, J.D., Rossor, M.N. and Warren, J.D. (2010) 'Apraxia in progressive nonfluent aphasia', *Journal of Neurology*, 257 (4): 569–74.

Rosanowski, F. and Eysholdt, U. (1999) 'Expert phoniatric assessment of voice adaptation in male to female transsexualism', *HNO*, 47 (6): 556–62.

Rosen, C.A. and Simpson, C.B. (2008) *Operative Techniques in Laryngology* (Berlin, Heidelberg: Springer-Verlag).

Rosen, K.M., Kent, R.D., Delaney, A.L. and Duffy, J.R. (2006) 'Parametric quantitative acoustic analysis of conversation produced by speakers with dysarthria and healthy speakers', *Journal of Speech, Language and Hearing Research*, 49 (2): 395–411.

Roy, N., Merrill, R.M., Gray, S.D. and Smith, E.M. (2005) 'Voice disorders in the general population: Prevalence, risk factors, and occupational impact', *Laryngoscope*, 115 (11): 1988–95.

Roy, N., Merrill, R.M., Thibeault, S., Parsa, R.A., Gray, S.D. and Smith, E.M. (2004) 'Prevalence of voice disorders in teachers and the general population', *Journal of Speech, Language, and Hearing Research*, 47 (2): 281–93.

Royal College of Speech and Language Therapists (2010) *Call to Action: Communication Disability Services* (London: RCSLT).

Rubin, A.D. and Sataloff, R.T. (2007) 'Vocal fold paresis and paralysis', *Otolaryngologic Clinics of North America*, 40 (5): 1109–31.

Saha, S., Chant, D., Welham, J. and McGrath, J. (2005) 'A systematic review of the prevalence of schizophrenia', *PLoS Medicine*, 2 (5): e141.

Sakai, K., Furui, E., Komai, K., Notoya, M. and Yamada, M. (2002) 'Acquired stuttering as an early symptom in a patient with progressive supranuclear palsy', *Rinsho Shinkeigaku*, 42 (2): 178–80.

Sancho, J.J., Pascual-Damieta, M., Pereira, J.A., Carrera, M.J., Fontané, J. and Sitges-Serra, A. (2008) 'Risk factors for transient vocal cord palsy after thyroidectomy', *British Journal of Surgery*, 95 (8): 961–7.

Santos, V.J.B., Mattioli, F.M., Mattioli, W.M., Daniel, R.J. and Cruz, V.P.M. (2006) 'Laryngeal dystonia: Case report and treatment with botulinum toxin', *Brazilian Journal of Otorhinolaryngology*, 72 (3): 425–7.

Sargent, L.A. (1999) *The Craniofacial Surgery Book* (Chattanooga, TN: Williams).

Scaler Scott, K. (2014) 'Stuttering and cluttering', in L. Cummings (ed.) *Cambridge Handbook of Communication Disorders* (Cambridge University Press), pp. 341–58.

Scaler Scott, K. and St. Louis, K.O. (2011) 'Self-help and support groups for people with cluttering', in D. Ward and K. Scaler Scott (eds) *Cluttering: A Handbook of Research, Intervention and Education* (Hove, East Sussex: Psychology Press), pp. 211–29.

Schalén, L. and Andersson, K. (1992) 'Differential diagnosis and treatment of psychogenic voice disorder', *Clinical Otolaryngology & Allied Sciences*, 17 (3): 225–30.

Schindler, A., Bottero, A., Capaccio, P., Ginocchio, D., Adorni, F. and Ottaviani, F. (2008) 'Vocal improvement after voice therapy in unilateral vocal fold paralysis', *Journal of Voice*, 22 (1): 113–18.

Seddoh, S.A.K., Robin, D.A., Sim, H.S., Hageman, C. and Moon, J.B. (1996) 'Speech timing in apraxia of speech versus conduction aphasia', *Journal of Speech and Hearing Research*, 39 (3): 590–603.

Sellars, C., Hughes, T. and Langhorne, P. (2005) 'Speech and language therapy for dysarthria due to non-progressive brain damage', *The Cochrane Database of Systematic Reviews*, Issue 3. Art. No.: CD002088.DOI: 10.1002/14651858. CD002088. pub 2.

Semel, E., Wiig, E.H. and Secord, W.A. (2003) *Clinical Evaluation of Language Fundamentals* (Australia: Psychological Corporation, 4th edn).

Sewall, G.K., Jiang, J. and Ford, C.N. (2006) 'Clinical evaluation of Parkinson's-related dysphonia', *Laryngoscope*, 116 (10): 1740–4.

Shames, G.H. and Anderson, N.B. (2002) *Human Communication Disorders: An Introduction* (Boston: Allyn & Bacon).

Sharp, W.G., Sherman, C. and Gross, A.M. (2007) 'Selective mutism and anxiety: A review of the current conceptualization of the disorder', *Journal of Anxiety Disorders*, 21 (4): 568–79.

Sheehan, J.G. (1974) 'Stuttering behavior: A phonetic analysis', *Journal of Communication Disorders*, 7 (3): 193–212.

Sheehan, J.G. and Sheehan, V.M. (1984) 'Avoidance-reduction therapy: A response-suppression hypothesis', in W.H. Perkins (ed.) *Stuttering Disorders* (New York, Thieme-Stratton), pp. 147–51.

Shewan, C.M. (1980) 'Verbal dyspraxia and its treatment', *Human Communication*, 5 (1): 3–12.

Shewell, C. (1998) 'The effect of perceptual training on ability to use the Vocal Profile Analysis Scheme', *International Journal of Language & Communication Disorders*, 33 (Supplement): 322–6.

Shriberg, L.D. (1994) 'Developmental phonological disorders: Moving toward the 21st century – forwards, backwards, or endlessly sideways?', *American Journal of Speech-Language Pathology*, 3 (3): 26–8.

Shriberg, L.D., Aram, D.M. and Kwiatkowski, J. (1997a) 'Developmental apraxia of speech: I. Descriptive and theoretical perspectives', *Journal of Speech, Language, and Hearing Research*, 40 (2): 273–85.

Shriberg, L.D., Aram, D.M. and Kwiatkowski, J. (1997b) 'Developmental apraxia of speech: II. Toward a diagnostic marker', *Journal of Speech, Language and Hearing Research*, 40 (2): 286–312.

Shriberg, L.D., Lewis, B.A., Tomblin, J.B., McSweeny, J.L., Karlsson, H.B. and Scheer, A.R. (2005) 'Toward diagnostic and phenotype markers for genetically transmitted speech delay', *Journal of Speech, Language, and Hearing Research*, 48 (4): 834–52.

Shuster, L.I. and Wambaugh, J.L. (2000) 'Perceptual and acoustic analyses of speech sound errors in apraxia of speech accompanied by aphasia', *Aphasiology*, 14 (5–6): 635–51.

Siemons-Lühring, D.I., Moerman, M., Martens, J.-P., Deuster, D., Müller, F. and Dejonckere, P. (2009) 'Spasmodic dysphonia, perceptual and acoustic analysis: Presenting new diagnostic tools', *European Archives of Oto-Rhino-Laryngology*, 266 (12): 1915–22.

Sigurdsson, E., Fombonne, E., Sayal, K. and Checkley, S. (1999) 'Neurodevelopmental antecedents of early-onset bipolar affective disorder', *British Journal of Psychiatry*, 174 (2): 121–7.

Simpson, C.B., Cheung, E.J. and Jackson, C.J. (2009) 'Vocal fold paresis: Clinical and electrophysiologic features in a tertiary laryngology practice', *Journal of Voice*, 23 (3): 396–8.

Singer Harris, N.G., Bellugi, U., Bates, E., Jones, W. and Rossen, M. (1997) 'Contrasting profiles of language development in children with Williams and Down syndromes', *Developmental Neuropsychology*, 13 (3): 345–70.

Skuse, D.H. (2000) 'Imprinting, the X-chromosome, and the male brain: Explaining sex differences in the liability to autism', *Pediatric Research*, 47 (1): 9–16.

Sliwinska-Kowalska, M., Niebudek-Bogusz, E., Fiszer, M., Los-Spychalska, T., Kotylo, P., Sznurowska-Przygocka, B. and Modrzewska, M. (2006) 'The prevalence and risk factors for occupational voice disorders in teachers', *Folia Phoniatrica et Logopaedica*, 58 (2): 85–101.

Snaith, P. (1998) 'Gender dysphoria', *Advances in Psychiatric Treatment*, 4 (6): 356–9.

Speyer, R., Speyer, I. and Heijnen, M.A. (2008) 'Prevalence and relative risk of dysphonia in rheumatoid arthritis', *Journal of Voice*, 22 (2): 232–7.

St. Louis, K.O. (1996) 'A tabular summary of cluttering subjects in the special edition', *Journal of Fluency Disorders*, 21 (3–4): 337–43.

St. Louis, K.O. and Hinzman, A.R. (1986) 'Studies of cluttering: Perceptions of cluttering by speech-language pathologists and educators', *Journal of Fluency Disorders*, 11 (2): 131–49.

St. Louis, K.O. and Myers, F.L. (1995) 'Clinical management of cluttering', *Language, Speech, and Hearing Services in Schools*, 26 (2): 187–95.

Stackhouse, J. (1992) 'Developmental verbal dyspraxia I: A review and critique', *European Journal of Disorders of Communication*, 27 (1): 19–34.

Stackhouse, J. and Snowling, M. (1992) 'Developmental verbal dyspraxia II: A developmental perspective on two case studies', *European Journal of Disorders of Communication*, 27 (1): 35–54.

Stansfield, J. (1990) 'Prevalence of stuttering and cluttering in adults with mental handicaps', *Journal of Mental Deficiency Research*, 34 (4): 287–307.

Stemple, J.C., Glaze, L.E. and Klaben, B.G. (2009) *Clinical Voice Pathology: Theory and Management* (San Diego, CA: Plural Publishing, 4th edn).

Stengelhofen, J. (1993) 'The nature and causes of communication problems in cleft palate', in J. Stengelhofen (ed.) *Cleft Palate: The Nature and Remediation of Communication Problems* (London: Whurr Publishers), pp. 1–30.

Stich, H.F., Parida, B.B. and Brunnemann, K.D. (1992) 'Localized formation of micronuclei in the oral mucosa and tobacco-specific nitrosamines in the saliva of "reverse" smokers, Khaini-tobacco chewers and gudakhu users', *International Journal of Cancer*, 50 (2): 172–6.

Stoel-Gammon, C. and Dunn, C. (1985) *Normal and Disordered Phonology in Children* (Baltimore: University Park Press).

Stoel-Gammon, C., Stone-Goldman, J. and Glaspey, A. (2002) 'Pattern-based approaches to phonological therapy', *Seminars in Speech and Language*, 23 (1): 3–13.

Storck, C., Brockmann, M., Zimmerman, E., Nekahm-Heis, D. and Zorowka, P.G. (2009) 'Laryngeal granuloma. Aetiology, clinical signs, diagnostic procedures, and treatment', *HNO*, 57 (10): 1075–80.

Strand, E.A. (1995) 'Treatment of motor speech disorders in children', *Seminars in Speech and Language*, 16 (2): 126–39.

Strand, E.A. and McNeil, M.R. (1996) 'Effects of length and linguistic complexity on temporal acoustic measures in apraxia of speech', *Journal of Speech and Hearing Research*, 39 (5): 1018–33.

Strauss, M. and Klich, R.J. (2001) 'Word length effects on EMG/vowel duration relationships in apraxic speakers', *Folia Phoniatrica et Logopaedica*, 53 (1): 58–65.

Subramaniam, S., Abdullah, A.H. and Hairuzah, I. (2005) 'Histoplasmosis of the larynx', *Medical Journal of Malaysia*, 60 (3): 386–8.

Subtelny, J.D. and Subtelny, J.T. (1959) 'Intelligibility and associated physiological factors of cleft palate speakers', *Journal of Speech and Hearing Research*, 2 (4): 353–60.

Sugishita, M., Konno, K., Kabe, S., Yunoki, K., Togashi, O. and Kawamura, M. (1987) 'Electropalatographic analysis of apraxia of speech in a left hander and in a right hander', *Brain*, 110 (5): 1393–417.

Sulica, L. (2008) 'The natural history of idiopathic unilateral vocal fold paralysis: Evidence and problems', *Laryngoscope*, 118 (7): 1303–7.

Sulica, L. and Blitzer, A. (2007) 'Vocal fold paresis: Evidence and controversies', *Current Opinion in Otolaryngology & Head and Neck Surgery*, 15 (3): 159–62.

Surian, L. (1996) 'Are children with autism deaf to Gricean maxims?', *Cognitive Neuropsychiatry*, 1 (1): 55–72.

Susca, M. (2006) 'Connecting stuttering measurement and management: II. Measures of cognition and affect', *International Journal of Language & Communication Disorders*, 41 (4): 365–77.

Takano, S., Kimura, M., Nito, T., Imagawa, H., Sakakibara, K. and Tayama, N. (2010) 'Clinical analysis of presbylarynx: Vocal fold atrophy in elderly individuals', *Auris Nasus Larynx*, 37 (4): 461–4.

Tani, T. and Sakai, Y. (2010) 'Stuttering after right cerebellar infarction: A case study', *Journal of Fluency Disorders*, 35 (2): 141–5.

Tannock, R. (2005) 'Language and mental health disorders: The case of ADHD', in W. Østreng (ed.) *Convergence: Interdisciplinary Communications 2004/2005* (Oslo: Centre for Advanced Study), pp. 45–53.

Temple, C. (1997) *Developmental Cognitive Neuropsychology* (Hove: Psychology Press).

Thacker, R.C. and De Nil, L.F. (1996) 'Neurogenic cluttering', *Journal of Fluency Disorders*, 21 (3–4): 227–38.

Theys, C., van Wieringen, A. and De Nil, L.F. (2008) 'A clinician survey of speech and non-speech characteristics of neurogenic stuttering', *Journal of Fluency Disorders*, 33 (1): 1–23.

Thomas, P. (1997) 'What can linguistics tell us about thought disorder?', in J. France and N. Muir (eds) *Communication and the Mentally Ill Patient: Developmental and Linguistic Approaches to Schizophrenia* (London: Jessica Kingsley Publishers), pp. 30–42.

Tjaden, K., Rivera, D., Wilding, G. and Turner, G.S. (2005) 'Characteristics of the lax vowel space in dysarthria', *Journal of Speech, Language and Hearing Research*, 48 (3): 554–66.

Togher, L. and Hand, L. (1998) 'Use of politeness markers with different communication partners: An investigation of five subjects with traumatic brain injury', *Aphasiology*, 12 (7–8): 755–70.

Tsunoda, K., Kondou, K., Kaga, K., Niimi, S., Baer, T., Nishiyama, K. and Hirose, H. (2005) 'Autologous transplantation of fascia into the vocal fold: Long-term result of type-1 transplantation and the future', *Laryngoscope*, 115 (12): 1–10.

Turkstra, L.S., McDonald, S. and Kaufmann, P.M. (1995) 'Assessment of pragmatic communication skills in adolescents after traumatic brain injury', *Brain Injury*, 10 (5): 329–45.

US Department of Education (2007) *27th Annual Report to Congress on the Implementation of the Individuals with Disabilities Education Act, 2005* (Washington, DC: Westat).

Van Beijsterveldt, C.E., Felsenfeld, S. and Boomsma, D.I. (2010) 'Bivariate genetic analyses of stuttering and nonfluency in a large sample of 5-year-old twins', *Journal of Speech, Language, and Hearing Research*, 53 (3): 609–19.

Van Borsel, J., De Cuypere, G., Rubens, R. and Destaerke, B. (2000) 'Voice problems in female-to-male transsexuals', *International Journal of Language & Communication Disorders*, 35 (3): 427–42.

Van Borsel, J., De Grande, S., Van Buggenhout, G. and Fryns, J.P. (2004) 'Speech and language in Wolf-Hirschhorn syndrome: A case-study', *Journal of Communication Disorders*, 37 (1): 21–33.

Van Borsel, J., Moeyaert, J., Mostaert, C., Rosseel, R., Van Loo, E. and Van Renterghem, T. (2006) 'Prevalence of stuttering in regular and special school populations in Belgium based on teacher perceptions', *Folia Phoniatrica et Logopaedica*, 58 (4): 289–302.

Van Borsel, J. and Taillieu, C. (2001) 'Neurogenic stuttering versus developmental stuttering: An observer judgement study', *Journal of Communication Disorders*, 34 (5): 385–95.

Van Borsel, J., van der Made, S. and Santens, P. (2003) 'Thalamic stuttering: A distinct clinical entity?', *Brain and Language*, 85 (2): 185–9.

Van Borsel, J. and Vandermeulen, A. (2008) 'Cluttering in Down syndrome', *Folia Phoniatrica et Logopaedica*, 60 (6): 312–17.

Van Borsel, J. and Vanryckeghem, M. (2000) 'Dysfluency and phonic tics in Tourette syndrome: A case report', *Journal of Communication Disorders*, 33 (3): 227–39.

Van de Beek, D., De Gans, J., Spanjaard, L., Weisfelt, M., Reitsma, J.B. and Vermeulen, M. (2004) 'Clinical features and prognostic factors in adults with bacterial meningitis', *New England Journal of Medicine*, 351 (18): 1849–59.

Van Demark, D.R., Morris, H.L. and Vandehaar, C. (1979) 'Patterns of articulation abilities in speakers with cleft palate', *Cleft Palate Journal*, 16 (3): 230–9.

Van Gogh, C.D., Verdonck-de Leeuw, I.M., Boon-Kamma, B.A., Langendijk, J.A., Kuik, D.J. and Mahieu, H.F. (2005) 'A screening questionnaire for voice problems after treatment of early glottic cancer', *International Journal of Radiation Oncology, Biology, Physics*, 62 (3): 700–5.

Van Houtte, E., Van Lierde, K. and Claeys, S. (2011) 'Pathophysiology and treatment of muscle tension dysphonia: A review of the current knowledge', *Journal of Voice*, 25 (2): 202–7.

Van Houtte, E., Van Lierde, K., D'Haeseleer, E. and Claeys, S. (2010) 'The prevalence of laryngeal pathology in a treatment-seeking population with dysphonia', *Laryngoscope*, 120 (2): 306–12.

Van Nieuwenhuizen, A.J., Rinkel, R.N., de Bree, R., Leemans, C.R. and Verdonck-de Leeuw, I.M. (2010) 'Patient reported voice outcome in recurrent respiratory papillomatosis', *Laryngoscope*, 120 (1): 188–92.

Van Riper, C. (1973) *The Treatment of Stuttering* (Englewood Cliffs, NJ: Prentice-Hall).

Van Zaalen-op't Hof, Y., Wijnen, F. and De Jonckere, P.H. (2009a) 'Differential diagnostic characteristics between cluttering and stuttering – Part one', *Journal of Fluency Disorders*, 34 (3): 137–54.

Van Zaalen-op't Hof, Y., Wijnen, F. and De Jonckere, P.H. (2009b) 'A test of speech motor control on word level productions: The SPA test', *International Journal of Speech-Language Pathology*, 11 (1): 26–33.

Vance, J.E. (1994) 'Prosodic deviation in dysarthria: A case study', *European Journal of Disorders of Communication*, 29 (1): 61–76.

Vanryckeghem, M., Brutten, G.J. and Hernandez, L.M. (2005) 'A comparative investigation of the speech-associated attitude of preschool and kindergarten children who do and do not stutter', *Journal of Fluency Disorders*, 30 (4): 307–18.

Vanryckeghem, M., Brutten, G.J., Uddin, N. and Van Borsel, J. (2004) 'A comparative investigation of the speech-associated coping responses reported by adults who do and do not stutter', *Journal of Fluency Disorders*, 29 (3): 237–50.

Verdolini, K., Rosen, C.A. and Branski, R.C. (eds) (2006) *Classification Manual for Voice Disorders-I* (Mahwah, NJ: Lawrence Erlbaum Associates).

Viswanath, N.S., Rosenfield, D.B., Alexander, J.P., Lee, H.S. and Chakraborty, R. (2000) 'Genetic basis of developmental stuttering: Preliminary observations', in H.-G. Bosshardt, J.S. Yaruss and H.F.M. Peters (eds) *Fluency Disorders: Theory, Research, Treatment and Self-Help. Proceedings of the Third World Congress on Fluency Disorders* (Nijmegen: Nijmegen University Press), pp. 102–8.

Volden, J. (2004) 'Conversational repair in speakers with autism spectrum disorder', *International Journal of Language & Communication Disorders*, 39 (2): 171–89.

von Tetzchner, S. and Martinsen, H. (2000) *Introduction to Augmentative and Alternative Communication* (London: Whurr Publishers).

Wacker, A., Holder, M., Will, B.E., Winkler, P.A. and Ilmberger, J. (2002) 'Comparison of the Aachen Aphasia Test, clinical study and Aachen Aphasia Bedside Test in brain tumor patients', *Der Nervenarzt*, 73 (8): 765–9.

Wallis, L., Jackson-Menaldi, C., Holland, W. and Giraldo, A. (2004) 'Vocal fold nodule vs. vocal fold polyp: Answer from surgical pathologist and voice pathologist point of view', *Journal of Voice*, 18 (1): 125–9.

Walsh, I., Regan, J., Sowman, R., Parsons, B. and McKay, A.P. (2007) 'A needs analysis for the provision of a speech and language therapy service to adults with mental health disorders', *Irish Journal of Psychological Medicine*, 24 (3): 89–93.

Wambaugh, J.L., Kalinyak-Fliszar, M.M., West, J.E. and Doyle, P.J. (1998) 'Effects of treatment for sound errors in apraxia of speech and aphasia', *Journal of Speech, Language, and Hearing Research*, 41 (4): 725–43.

Wambaugh, J.L. and Martinez, A.L. (2000) 'Effects of rate and rhythm control treatment on consonant production accuracy in apraxia of speech', *Aphasiology*, 14 (8): 851–71.

Wang, C.-P., Ko, J.-Y., Wang, Y.-H., Hu, Y.-L. and Hsiao, T.-Y. (2009) 'Vocal process granuloma: A result of long-term observation in 53 patients', *Oral Oncology*, 45 (9): 821–5.

Wang, Y.-T., Kent, R.D., Duffy, J.R. and Thomas, J.E. (2005) 'Dysarthria associated with traumatic brain injury: Speaking rate and emphatic stress', *Journal of Communication Disorders*, 38 (3): 231–60.

Ward, D. (2006) *Stuttering and Cluttering: Frameworks for Understanding and Treatment* (Hove, East Sussex: Psychology Press).

Warrington, E.K. (1981a) 'Neuropsychological studies of verbal semantic systems', *Philosophical Transactions of the Royal Society London, Series B*, 295: 411–23.

Warrington, E.K. (1981b) 'Concrete word dyslexia', *British Journal of Psychology*, 72 (2): 175–96.

Wells, J.E., McGee, M.A., Scott, K.M. and Oakley Browne, M.A. (2010) 'Bipolar disorder with frequent mood episodes in the New Zealand Mental Health Survey', *Journal of Affective Disorders*, 126 (1–2): 65–74.

Wenke, R.J., Cornwell, P. and Theodoros, D.G. (2010) 'Changes to articulation following LSVT(R) and traditional dysarthria therapy in non-progressive dysarthria', *International Journal of Speech-Language Pathology*, 12 (3): 203–20.

Whitehouse, A.J.O., Watt, H.J., Line, E.A. and Bishop, D.V.M. (2009) 'Adult psychosocial outcomes of children with specific language impairment, pragmatic language impairment and autism', *International Journal of Language & Communication Disorders*, 44 (4): 511–28.

Whitworth, A., Perkins, L. and Lesser, R. (1997) *Conversation Analysis Profile for People with Aphasia* (London: Whurr Publishers).

Wilson, P., Sharp, C. and Carr, S. (1999) 'The prevalence of gender dysphoria in Scotland: A primary care study', *British Journal of General Practice*, 49 (449): 991–2.

Wingate, M.E. (2002) *Foundations of Stuttering* (San Diego, CA: Academic Press).

Wolk, L. and Edwards, M.L. (1993) 'The emerging phonological system of an autistic child', *Journal of Communication Disorders*, 26 (3): 161–77.

Woodson, G., Hochstetler, H. and Murry, T. (2006) 'Botulinum toxin therapy for abductor spasmodic dysphonia', *Journal of Voice*, 20 (1): 137–43.

Woolf, G. (1967) 'The assessment of stuttering as struggle, avoidance, and expectancy', *British Journal of Disorders of Communication*, 2 (2): 158–71.

Wu, X., Su, Z.Z., Jiang, A.Y., Lin, A.H., Chai, L.P., Wen, W.P. and Lei, W.B. (2005) 'Analysis of relevant factors causing laryngeal stenosis after partial laryngectomy', *Chinese Journal of Otorhinolaryngology, Head and Neck Surgery*, 40 (12): 929–32.

Yairi, E. and Ambrose, N.G. (1999) 'Early childhood stuttering I: Persistency and recovery rates', *Journal of Speech, Language, and Hearing Research*, 42 (5): 1097–112.

Yairi, E., Ambrose, N.G., Paden, E.P. and Throneburg, R.N. (1996) 'Predictive factors of persistence and recovery: Pathways of childhood stuttering', *Journal of Communication Disorders*, 29 (1): 51–77.

Yamout, B., Fuleihan, N., Hajj, T., Sibai, A., Sabra, O., Rifai, H. and Hamdan, A.L. (2009) 'Vocal symptoms and acoustic changes in relation to the expanded disability status scale, duration and stage of disease in patients with multiple sclerosis', *European Archives of Oto-Rhino-Laryngology*, 266 (11): 1759–65.

Yaruss, J.S. and Quesal, R.W. (2004) 'Overall Assessment of the Speaker's Experience of Stuttering (OASES)', in A. Packman, A. Meltzer and H.F.M. Peters (eds) *Theory, Research and Therapy in Fluency Disorders. Proceedings of the Fourth World Congress on Fluency Disorders* (Nijmegen: Nijmegen University Press), pp. 237–40.

Yavaş, M. (1998) *Phonology Development and Disorders* (San Diego, CA: Singular Publishing Group, Inc.).

Yavuzer, G., Güzelküçük, S., Küçükdeveci, A., Gök, H. and Ergin, S. (2001) 'Aphasia rehabilitation in patients with stroke', *International Journal of Rehabilitation Research*, 24 (3): 241–4.

Yorkston, K.M. and Beukelman, D.R. (2000) 'Dysarthria: An overview of treatment', in I. Papathanasiou (ed.) *Acquired Neurogenic Communication Disorders: A Clinical Perspective* (London: Whurr Publishers), pp. 149–72.

Yorkston, K.M., Beukelman, D.R., Strand, E.A. and Bell, K.R. (1999) *Management of Motor Speech Disorders in Children and Adults* (Austin, TX: Pro-Ed).

Zebrowski, P.M. (1991) 'Duration of the speech disfluencies of beginning stutterers', *Journal of Speech and Hearing Research*, 34 (3): 483–91.

Zeitels, S.M., Akst, L.M., Bums, J.A., Hillman, R.E., Broadhurst, M.S. and Anderson, R.R. (2006) 'Pulsed angiolytic laser treatment of ectasias and varices in singers', *Annals of Otology, Rhinology, and Laryngology*, 115 (8): 571–80.

Zheng, Y., Xia, P., Zheng, H.C., Takahashi, H., Masuda, S. and Takano, Y. (2010) 'The screening of viral risk factors in tongue and pharyngolaryngeal squamous carcinoma', *Anticancer Research*, 30 (4): 1233–8.

Ziatas, K., Durkin, K. and Pratt, C. (2003) 'Differences in assertive speech acts produced by children with autism, Asperger syndrome, specific language impairment, and normal development', *Development and Psychopathology*, 15 (1): 73–94.

Zraick, R.J. and LaPointe, L.L. (2009) 'Hyperkinetic dysarthria', in M.R. McNeil (ed.) *Clinical Management of Sensorimotor Speech Disorders* (New York: Thieme Medical Publishers, 2nd edn), pp. 152–65.

Index

Printed and bound by CPI Group (UK) Ltd, Croydon, CR0 4YY